TACOMA
CONFIDENTIAL

TACOMA CONFIDENTIAL

Paul LaRosa

A SIGNET BOOK

SIGNET
Published by New American Library, a division of
Penguin Group (USA) Inc., 375 Hudson Street,
New York, New York 10014, USA
Penguin Group (Canada), 90 Eglinton Avenue East, Suite 700, Toronto,
Ontario M4P 2Y3, Canada (a division of Pearson Penguin Canada Inc.)
Penguin Books Ltd., 80 Strand, London WC2R 0RL, England
Penguin Ireland, 25 St. Stephen's Green, Dublin 2,
Ireland (a division of Penguin Books Ltd.)
Penguin Group (Australia), 250 Camberwell Road, Camberwell, Victoria 3124,
Australia (a division of Pearson Australia Group Pty. Ltd.)
Penguin Books India Pvt. Ltd., 11 Community Centre, Panchsheel Park,
New Delhi - 110 017, India
Penguin Group (NZ), cnr Airborne and Rosedale Roads, Albany,
Auckland 1310, New Zealand (a division of Pearson New Zealand Ltd.)
Penguin Books (South Africa) (Pty.) Ltd., 24 Sturdee Avenue,
Rosebank, Johannesburg 2196, South Africa

Penguin Books Ltd., Registered Offices:
80 Strand, London WC2R 0RL, England

First published by Signet, an imprint of New American Library,
a division of Penguin Group (USA) Inc.

First Printing, January 2006
10 9 8 7 6 5 4 3

Copyright © Paul LaRosa, 2006
All rights reserved

 REGISTERED TRADEMARK—MARCA REGISTRADA

Printed in the United States of America

PUBLISHER'S NOTE

For Susan . . .

ACKNOWLEDGMENTS

This book is an offshoot of an hour I produced for the CBS newsmagazine *48 Hours,* where I'm still employed as a producer. I must thank the following people for their ideas and encouragement and general help along the way: Susan Zirinsky, Katie Boyle, Bill Lagattuta, Shoshanah Wolfson, Fred Hawthorne, Gregory McLaughlin, Bill Hitchcock, Larry Warner and Glenn Aust. In Tacoma, I received invaluable help from the Judson family (and their spokesman Mark Firmani), the Brame family, Sylvia Boskovich, and John Hathaway. Kudos also to my agent, Scott Miller of the Trident Media Group, and my editor at NAL, Martha Bushko. Finally, all the time on the road and working on this book would not have been possible without the enduring support of my wife, Susan, and my children, Alexandra and Peter.

BOOK I

MARRIED LIFE

"I Love Me"

It was the night of February 15, 2003, and David Brame and Crystal, his wife of eleven years, were fighting again. Their house on Eagle Creek Lane in Gig Harbor, Washington, sits in a cul-de-sac, and because Gig Harbor is so quiet, it was easy for the neighbors to hear what was going on. But not one of them called the police. There were a couple of reasons for that: they'd heard the ugly words a hundred times before and they knew who lived in the house. David Brame *was* the police, the chief of police in Tacoma, the city that sits just north of Gig Harbor. Calling the cops, well, what good would that do?

"I told you before and I'm going to tell you again. I'm not going with you," Crystal told her husband, David.

Brame sat on the bed, barely looking up. He was putting on his best dress shoes and he was concentrating on them, having noticed a small spot. "Yes, you are."

"No, David, I'm not."

The couple's children, Haley, eight, and David Jr., five, were just a few feet away, over in the living room watching television, but it hardly mattered to either parent. There had been years of fighting and yelling and screaming. It was normal to them. The kids couldn't help

but notice and it certainly upset them but there was little
they could do. They processed what was happening and
put it away for another time. David and Crystal Brame
argued so often that they didn't try to hide it anymore.
It had become a way of life, Crystal later said when she
retold the story of this night. A neighbor disagreed; he
said he once saw little Haley after one such fight and
could see that she was not used to the fighting, not at
all. After one such fight, he said, he noticed that Haley
"had the saddest eyes I've ever seen."

As for David Brame, well, everyone agreed that he
loved his kids but he was nothing if not self-absorbed. His
administrative assistant recalled a time when he called her
at nearly eleven p.m. and asked what she was doing. "I'm
driving my daughter to the emergency room," she told
Brame. Without hesitation, he said, "Well, let me tell you
what's going on with me." She couldn't believe it, but that
was David Brame. He was Number One and the rest of
the human race was a distant second.

David Brame wiped the spot on his shoe to his satis-
faction and stood up. He walked over to the mirror
above the sink and brushed his hair. Standing straight,
he smoothed his good pants and smiled at his reflection.
As he often did, he folded his arms across his chest,
admired his reflection and whispered, "I love me." It
was a weird little habit but Crystal had seen it before.
She was shocked the first time but now it was just another strange little thing that David did, and he did
plenty of them. At least this one was harmless. He was
a narcissist, handsome and proud of it. For a person who
liked to keep secrets, he had a remarkably open and
friendly face; a small lock of hair that fell onto his fore-
head only accentuated his boyish charm. David Brame
had charisma; he was a born leader. *That,* there was
no denying.

He smiled at his reflection a second time. He had
come a long way from his upbringing in East Tacoma,

the perennial poor side of town. And now here he was: he'd achieved his lifelong dream, becoming chief in his hometown of Tacoma, Washington. And it felt good. He was forty-four years old and looked like a man in his prime, a powerful man. He was just over six feet tall and had put on a few pounds, but so what? He had power and he looked great when he wore that police uniform. If you were making a movie and looking to cast someone in the role of David Brame, police chief, you would pick someone imposing but with all-American good looks, perhaps Kevin Costner in his prime. That's how handsome David Brame was. And he knew that plenty of women would do whatever he wanted.

Plenty of women, but not Crystal. And that's what galled him more than anything. For the first time, he let sink in what she'd been telling him for the better part of an hour: she didn't feel well and wasn't going to accompany him and his cop buddies over to Anthony's, a terrific seafood restaurant that sits on the Gig Harbor waterfront. It has views to die for; there are no bad tables at Anthony's. Brame enjoyed going there and this was a special night. They were celebrating the appointments of Brame's new assistant chiefs. He looked over at Crystal. She was just barely five feet tall and he towered over her. And he knew for a fact that she didn't weigh more than 105 pounds. He saw to that. Each morning after her shower, he made her stand on the scale while he watched. Still, she looked heavier than she used to. Must be gravity, he thought. Happens to every woman and, after all, Crystal had borne him two children. But so what? Was that an excuse? There were plenty of female cops older than Crystal who looked a lot better and, truth be told, he'd already picked out one he especially liked. If only Crystal would do some exercise. He took a step toward her.

"Crystal, you're going to make us late. I'm the chief. I can't be late. Now get dressed."

She bristled: "Get this right. I am not going with you."

Crystal's voice was an octave higher than usual and had a slightly hysterical edge. He wasn't even sure he wanted her to come but he wasn't going to give in that easily. She'd been challenging his authority much too much lately. He had to try to reassert his control over her.

"I think I need to change this shirt. Have you seen my blue turtleneck?"

"It's in the closet."

Brame took a step into the bedroom's walk-in closet but then had a better idea. "Can you at least show me where it is?"

Crystal slithered past him in her usual, scared-shit way. As soon as she did, he took a step and blocked the doorway, the only way out.

Then Brame reached out, clamped one hand hard onto her throat and pushed her to the very back of the closet. He pulled the door closed behind him. "You fucking bitch," he snarled. "You'll do what I tell you to do. Now get dressed before I dress you myself."

"No," she gasped.

Her voice reflected the strain of having Brame's hand around her neck.

"Why do you have to be such a bitch? Do you want to spend another two hours in here?"

Her eyes jumped, registering fear. He'd locked her in here—this six-by-nine-foot closet—once before and, when he went to get her, she was lying on the floor crying like a whipped dog. He'd picked her up that time, thrown her into the bathroom and told her to clean herself up. Brame knew she didn't want to go through that again.

"So are you going to come?"

She said nothing and for a moment, neither did he. Deep inside, Brame knew something had changed in their marriage. He'd even let a couple of associates know he was having trouble. Crystal had been standing up to him more and more in the past year and he didn't like it one bit. She'd always had her moments when she lashed out at him, sometimes physically, but she'd always been under his thumb. Now she was talking back, gaining strength. He thought it had something to do with her dopey family. That pissed him off even more. There was her overweight, pathetic sister, Julie; Julie's blustering husband, Dave Ahrens, who acted like he was better than everyone else; and Crystal's parents, Lane and Patty Judson.

Patty was especially annoying. Crystal had been talking to her, telling her things. Brame could tell by the way Patty had been treating him in the past year. She once even had the gall to tell him, "You'd be nothing without your uniform and your gun." Brame hated her for that. And to make matters worse, she was always around, always underfoot or on the phone. She was irritating him—a human barnacle—so that's just what he'd begun to call her: the Barnacle. And he wished he could crush her like one too.

Patty's entire goal in life seemed to be making sure her kitchen was spotless. Oh, she did have one hobby, Brame thought wearily. She liked to collect stupid figurines of roosters and she treated her hobby like it was fucking brain surgery. He hated it all the more because Crystal had picked up the hobby so that now his kitchen had all these stupid fucking roosters in it. Brame thought of Patty Judson as a sad little woman, who, like Crystal, was standing up to him a little too much lately. He was the chief but she showed no respect, and somewhere down the line, he was going to make her pay.

And then there was Crystal's father, Lane. A former Navy man who had worked for Boeing for decades, Lane was at least a man's man. But his talking—God, he never stopped talking. With his thick white hair and Coke-bottle, oversized glasses, he was a dead ringer for

Phil Donahue. And wouldn't you know it? The guy never stopped chattering on and on about the Navy, telling one boring story after another, popping open cans of beer until he was red in the face. The guy had no restraint. He could never be a cop like Brame. Restraint. Strength. Those were qualities Brame admired. He liked to rule with those in mind, like his hero, Michael Corleone, the Godfather. Brame kept a photo—a signed photo—of Al Pacino as Michael Corleone in his office to remind the cops beneath him that he was the Godfather of the department. They had all seen the movie, of course, and they all knew what happened to those who crossed Michael. Restraint and strength. Just like Michael Corleone. You would never see David Brame drinking beer and retelling the same old war stories. Shit.

Brame looked again into Crystal's eyes. He wanted to just snap her neck right that instant like he'd always promised he would. But he had to act with restraint. And then his eye fell on his service weapon, a Glock .45 caliber, the gun he always kept in the walk-in closet.

Brame let go of Crystal's neck. She started whimpering and rubbing it, complaining that he'd hurt her. He picked up his gun. "Quit crying and look at me, Crystal."

She looked at him and the gun.

He popped out the clip. "Okay, if you really want to stay home by yourself with the kids I'm going to teach you how to protect yourself. Here," he said, holding the gun by the barrel and handing it to her.

She withdrew. "I'm not touching that gun."

"No, really, I want you to learn how to use it. Don't worry, I took the clip out."

Crystal had her back to the closet wall. Her eyes flickered all over the place but she was trapped. He had her.

"No," she told him.

"Take it, you stupid bitch. There's no live ammo in it. Look."

He raised the gun over his head and pulled the trigger. There was a click but that was it. Crystal still wasn't buying it. "I don't know how stupid you think I am but I'm not touching that gun."

"What if there's an intruder? Don't you wanna protect the kids?"

"David, you must think I'm really stupid."

He sneered at her. "I don't *think* you're stupid, Crystal. You *are* stupid."

He shoved the clip back in with a violent thrust and put the gun back down on the shelf. But then he picked it up again and turned back to her. He stuck the barrel in her face. "Remember one thing, Crystal. Accidents happen."

Then Brame grabbed his blue turtleneck, pulled it on, turned and walked out. He passed right by the kids watching television and stormed out of the house without another word. Haley and David both looked up at their father but Brame never even said goodbye.

Crystal lay in the closet for a long time, trying to regain her composure. David had threatened to kill her before but this time, this thing with the gun, this was different. He had crossed a line. She'd majored in criminal justice at the University of Washington in Tacoma and had seen enough television programs about criminals to know that Brame had been trying to get her fingerprints on the weapon. This was more than just a fit of anger. This time, he seemed to have something more in mind. This time, she thought he was *planning* to kill her. He was thinking in advance. Once her fingerprints were on that gun, he could kill her anytime—in her sleep even—and she knew he didn't care much about the kids. He wouldn't care if they were home when he did it. He was sick, a monster. But he was the police chief. No one was going to question him too carefully. He'd already filled the department with his friends and gotten rid of his enemies, just like Michael Corleone, the sicko movie mobster that he admired so much. For years—Crystal knew, because Brame had told her—he had let it slip to his colleagues that his wife was becoming more and more irrational, hyper, excitable. Even the kids had noticed it, he'd say. So if she wound up dead one day from a self-inflicted wound, so what? She must have just snapped. Case closed.

"Accidents happen."

Crystal could not shake those words. It was a threat. He was right. Accidents do happen and there would be no investigation. He's the chief of police, she thought bitterly. She'd be dead and that would be that. She could hear what Brame would tell those who came to her funeral: "Poor Crystal. She was really getting nuts toward the end there. I guess I should have gotten her help. Thank God she didn't hurt the children like that woman in Texas."

Crystal cried softly to herself. Thank God she had her escape already planned. She would get out and then he'd be sorry. But he'd also really be angry. How angry? That was the question. Lying there, Crystal couldn't help but wonder—how had it come to this? How had her life gotten this bad? Not just for her, but for her children too.

In her divorce papers and from what she told to others, this was the picture Crystal painted of her life with David but, when investigators later dug into the details of their lives, a different, fuller picture emerged that was not quite so simple.

2

The Aroma of Tacoma

"**Tacoma's had a lot of hard luck** over the years."

That's John Hathaway talking, and if you want to know about Tacoma—what it's like now, what it's been through, the politics—Hathaway is a good place to start. A fifty-eight-year-old would-be dandy from the dark side of town, Hathaway is more than a little different. He was once a fashion reporter and later a clothing store owner but, these days, he works as a bartender at Lincoln Lanes, a run-down bowling alley at Thirty-eighth Street and Yakima in the heart of Tacoma's Little Saigon. To drink at a place more forlorn, you'd have to excuse yourself to your uncle's wood-paneled basement.

Most nights, the bowling alley is all but empty except for a couple of lanes where Asian Americans pass the time smoking and bowling the odd game. It's a good bet that some wagers are being placed but who would know and really, who would care? Tacoma's got so many problems that a little illegal wagering is the least of it. The rest of the folks there—serious drinkers, political yentas or both—sit clustered around the small bar where Hathaway holds court. He's something to see. He always wears a fedora; in fact, he claims to have a collection of more than 130. He sports a thin mustache and wears a gold bracelet that dangles precariously from his wrist. Dashiell Hammett once spent some time in Tacoma—in 1920, Hammett, weighing a gaunt 132 pounds and suffering from TB, was admitted to the Public Health Service hospital in Tacoma where he was nursed back to health by his future wife, Jose Dolan—and to look at Hathaway, you'd swear the great writer had left behind one of his creations. Hathaway is all but channeling Hammett, with his nonstop smoking (Camels, of course) and affected noir attitude. He clearly loves the 1940s. In fact, you get the sense that Hathaway only comes out after dark or when there's a saxophone somewhere blowing "Harlem Nocturne." He's liable to call women "dolls," phones "blowers" and elevators "freights."

On any given night, Hathaway might start you off with one of his patented lines: "I never make a good drink unless I'm thirsty."

It's an old joke but you've got to laugh, because Hathaway is good-natured and tries so hard to put over the tough-guy act that you know, at heart, he's a softie. And he is. Nothing gets his eyes to tear up faster than talking about his hometown of Tacoma, how much he loves it, and how long the city's been taking it up the butt from Seattle.

In that regard, Tacoma is like a lot of second cities in the United States that exist in the shadow of an overwhelmingly bigger and more powerful sibling. Think Akron and Cleveland, Philadelphia and New York, Fort Worth and Dallas. Tacoma is a perennial also-ran, and that defensiveness now defines it. Most Tacomans know they can't compete with Seattle but what galls them, what has seeped into the city's soul over generations, is the way Seattle has beaten Tacoma at every turn for more than a hundred years.

Not to say that Tacoma hasn't any good points; it

surely does. It is not, after all, Cleveland; Tacoma is located in the Pacific Northwest—"the gateway to the Pacific Rim"—and it's surrounded by natural beauty like stunning, snow-capped Mount Rainier, a national treasure that looms over the city. Tacoma has all that and more *and,* let's not forget, it's only twenty-seven miles south of Seattle, the area's cultural and aesthetic hub.

It looks great on paper and postcards but what outsiders don't know is that Tacoma has something of a black cloud hanging over it, a karmic black cloud from which there seems no escape. Some people think it's no coincidence that it's the hometown of Ted Bundy, one of the nation's most notorious serial killers. Back in the nineteenth century, Tacoma was christened "the City of Destiny" for winning a key railroad terminus and it's been sagging under that moniker ever since. Sad to say, even after all these decades, no one seems to know just what Tacoma's destiny is.

John Hathaway's own life parallels Tacoma a bit—even *he* moved to Seattle at one point. He got married, had kids and opened up a men's clothing store, but all he's got left are his kids and even they are grown and on their own. Seattle whipped him too. But then Hathaway found his way back to Tacoma where he spent many a night at a now-defunct bar called Kelly's. There the late Red Kelly, a former jazz great, took pity on Hathaway and helped him along, sometimes letting him sleep in the bar after hours. It was rough going; Hathaway was nearly homeless until he met Carolyn Cohen, a shy, plump woman who recently had a quadruple bypass that seemed to slow down her smoking, oh, for about a week or so. Hang around Hathaway and Cohen long enough and you get a three-dimensional crash course on the dangers of secondhand smoke. Cohen resurrected Hathaway's life and, more importantly, his spirit.

"Take that Mount Rainier. It was supposed to be

called Mount Tacoma," Hathaway says. "But Seattle got
its way like it always does and it's called Mount Rainier.
Tacoma got the western terminus of the Pacific Northwest Railroad in the nineteenth century. It was supposed
to mean great things for Tacoma but then the Alaska
gold rush hit and everyone took off from Seattle. It was
closer. We lost again. Then we built that damned suspension bridge . . ."

Oh yes, *that* bridge. Even if you didn't know where it
was, you've probably seen old newsreel footage of *that*
bridge swaying in the breeze before it collapses into the
Narrows. It was called the first Tacoma Narrows Bridge
and it was one of the longest suspension bridges in the
country when it was opened in July 1940. It connected
Tacoma and Gig Harbor, but the bridge only lasted four
months before it began to sway crazily in the wind—
hence the nickname "Galloping Gertie"—and finally
collapsed in November 1940. The film of its final moments has been seen all over the world, over and over
again. In the dramatic newsreel of the bridge's ignominious ending, a dog trots along the roadway near a car as
the bridge sways back and forth with increasing ferocity
until finally the whole thing crashes into the water
below.

"Now *that's* Tacoma, that bridge right there."

Well, that's *part* of Tacoma right there. The truth is
that the city has had more than its share of bizarre
events, one of the reasons it gets absolutely no respect
from Seattle. Consider:

  • On July 4, 1900, the city fathers were celebrat-
    ing a new streetcar line with a parade. As the
    train reached its endpoint, the brakes failed
    and the streetcar, overcrowded with par-
    tygoers, plunged off an eighty-foot trestle, kill-
    ing forty-three people.
  • During the thirties, at the same time the kid-

napping of Charles Lindbergh's son was making national headlines, Tacoma became known as the kidnapping capital of the West after two young boys were taken in separate incidents. George Weyerhaeuser, the nine-year-old son of prominent lumberman J. P. Weyerhaeuser, was pulled into a car and later released unharmed. About the same time, Charles Matson, a prominent doctor's son, was kidnapped from his home and murdered.

- In 1951, State Senator Al Rosellini, who later became governor, conducted a series of hearings in Tacoma to investigate charges that Tacoma was an "open city" where a certain amount of vice was tolerated. A bevy of prostitutes testified about paying off the police, and the star witness was none other than a woman who claimed to be the mistress of the city's police commissioner.

Hathaway knows those stories and more, and when he finishes telling them, he pauses to take a long drag on his nonfiltered Camel and to freshen up a few drinks for his regulars, who've heard all of this many, many times before.

"You know what Tacoma's got? It's got pulp and paper mills down at the Tideflats. That's where the aroma of Tacoma comes from. That, and the political corruption. For years, this city really stunk."

It's true. For decades, Tacoma's air was so filled with the foul-smelling, distinctive odor of the local wood pulp mills that some smart aleck (probably a guy from Seattle) came up with a nickname for the smell—the "Aroma of Tacoma." Tacoma eventually lost most but not all of the despised wood pulp business; it makes the city smell better but also makes it less economically viable.

"I don't know why but we can't seem to do anything right."

And so Hathaway begins his nightly rant about political shenanigans, most of which make no sense to an
outsider. But the charm of Hathaway, you see, is that
he's not content to be a bartender—he's also an intrepid
Internet reporter who runs a site called "The New Takhoman." He runs it out of his small apartment on East
Thirty-fourth Street, surrounded by his ever-present
Camels, his collection of fedoras, double-shot cans of
Starbucks and a white cat named Betsy.

And he does have a knack for ferreting out information from his patrons, as even David Zeeck, editor in
chief of the Tacoma *News Tribune*—the city's one major
daily—has acknowledged. Zeeck has even been known
to make the pilgrimage down to Lincoln Lanes to have
a Budweiser now and again, a Budweiser served in a
bottle the shape of a bowling pin. "John is a thorn in
the side of a lot of people but it's probably a healthy
thing to have in a city like Tacoma," Zeeck said. "John
Hathaway listens to gossip and gets it out there before
a lot of people. He'll talk to anybody and I think a lot
of his sources come from the rank and file, people who
come into the bar at the bowling alley, people John
meets all over town. He works and lives in a part of
Tacoma that's always where the great stories come from
in this town. I think he's suspicious of power, as he ought
to be."

His Web site, a mixture of silly cartoons, very broad
humor and stinging commentary, is dedicated to getting
under the skin of Tacoma's elected officials. It is Hathaway's vocation; he's a gadfly in the true sense of the
word. He's paying attention at times when the city fathers think no one is. And Hathaway's wife, Carolyn, as
quiet as Hathaway is noisy, happens to be a crack re-
searcher who's worked years in the city's library system.
She helps Hathaway collect valuable information that

elected officials would rather have ignored by its citizens. It would be easy to dismiss the two of them but, as David Brame ultimately found out, that would be a mistake.

3

"She's Really Something"

Back in 1989, Tacoma, the so-called City of Destiny, was suffering even more than usual. "Back then, this was the Bronx," says one local shopkeeper. This perennial sad sack stepsister to Seattle had a downtown that was littered with roughnecks, drug dealers and prostitutes. It was dangerous for a civilian to walk around, and up in the neighborhood called Hilltop, the gangs had taken over. The night was an open-air marketplace for cheap drugs and even cheaper women.

On this sweltering summer night, the cops were engaged in one of their periodic cleanups that calmed the streets for at least a few hours. Down on Puyallup Avenue, a run-down strip of gas stations and motels not far from the local bus station, Patrol Officer David Brame was assigned a backup role to an undercover bust of johns who were frequenting the prostitutes loitering along the avenue. He was sitting in his patrol car, commenting on the young woman he'd just seen on a street corner. She was wearing tight shorts, high heels and, in the style of girl rocker Pat Benatar, a headband holding back her curly brown hair.

"Wow, she's really something," he told his partner.

"Yeah, you'd hardly know she's a decoy, huh?"

They both laughed. They'd worked Puyallup Avenue long enough to know that the only working girls worth a second look had to be police decoys.

"Wow, she's really good-looking," Brame repeated.

"Yeah, you said that already. Heads up, we've got company."

Brame and his partner watched as a john pulled up in a tan Bonneville sedan. The decoy prostitute gave a sign so the vice cops stationed nearby in a van knew when to move in. Once the john established the price and what he wanted, Brame's radio came to life.

"Let's go," he said.

They rolled in quickly and arrested the john. Brame smiled at the woman posing as a prostitute but said nothing. At this point in his life, he just accepted the fact that he was not good around women. But this was his lucky night, because the woman had noticed him as well. Later, in the police station, she told him she needed a ride home. Could he help her out? Could he ever.

And just like that, David Brame met his future wife, Crystal Judson.

At the time, David Brame was a twenty-nine-year-old divorcée and career cop; Crystal was a thin, pretty twenty-year-old University of Washington coed who had just graduated from the school's Tacoma campus with a degree in criminal justice. Crystal had been interning in the Tacoma police department (TPD) and had been hired part-time to work undercover on prostitution stings. She was asked to dress up as a prostitute decoy to help out the vice squad. It was pretty exciting work for a criminal justice major just out of school and Crystal took to it like she took to everything—with gusto.

In the locker room that night, Brame approached his partner. "I asked her if she wanted to go out and she said yes," Brame said, breathless with excitement.

"Well, go get her, tiger," his friend said.

Brame did, and the relationship blossomed. He was psyched about it but Brame's cop buddy was leery. The more he got to know Crystal, the less he thought she had anything at all in common with David Brame.

"We went out a couple of times with Dave and Crystal, me and my wife. They were in different places in their lives. He was a veteran cop and she was just out of school. She was spontaneous and wanted to go out and have fun and David was like, 'Well, maybe a week from Tuesday we could go to a movie.' They were totally different. So I said to him, 'Is this what you really want?' And he said yes and what could I say? My friend was happy."

They began to date more and more steadily. There's no doubt why she was attracted to him. He was great-looking, an alpha male, strong and silent but also a good provider with a good job. Crystal was beautiful and saw in David the type of man who could give her a family like the one her mom and dad had. She was hooked, much to the chagrin of her sister, Julie.

Julie, two years younger than Crystal, did not like Brame almost from the moment she first met him but gave her sister some slack. "I thought she had to live her own life," she said. "It just seemed that he was making all the decisions for her, instead of her making her own decisions."

It was Julie who first picked up on Brame's controlling nature. Crystal had told Julie that David preferred she look for jobs in offices where only women worked. The request certainly was odd but Julie let it pass. She didn't want to interfere in her sister's life.

"I didn't feel he was quite right but that was her decision. He was having a big say in where she could apply for jobs because he didn't want her working around or with men. That was something that bothered me because, at that point, they weren't married and I felt it was my sister's decision on where to apply for work."

Long before they ever met, Crystal DeEtte Judson and David Allen Brame had something in common: each appeared to be the favored child in their family. Neither of them was an only child but that hardly mattered. Crystal was one of two sisters but she was the beautiful sister, the talker, the ballerina, the ice-skater, the center of attention. David was the youngest of four. He had two older brothers and a sister but David was the brilliant one, the handsome son, the high achiever, the athlete on a state championship high school basketball team. The Brames had their hopes for the future resting on David's broad shoulders; the Judsons had their hopes pinned on Crystal. Over the years, each family developed a fierce pride, a pride that seems to have imbued David and Crystal with a sense of entitlement. They were the center of their parents' universe. No one would ever be good enough for Crystal; no one could ever question David's judgment.

4

"A Little Dresden Doll"

Starting out in life, Crystal Judson had the good fortune to be born into a loving, solidly middle-class family that was successful in every way a family could be.

Lane and Patty Judson raised Crystal and Julie on South Junett Street, not far from the Tacoma Mall. Lane is a former Navy officer and he has the tattoos to prove it. His life is defined by his service to his country. He's liable to let you know he's a Navy man within five minutes of meeting him and pretty much never let you forget it. His first tour was from 1952 until 1957 but he re-upped for the Naval Reserve in 1965, 1982 and even as recently as 1995. In between, he had a fabulously successful career at the Boeing company, starting as a machinist and ending as an engineering supervisor. Meanwhile his wife, Patty, was a stay-at-home mom who tended to the house and family with an intensity matched only by Lane's. It's hard to say who's more obsessive about keeping house but there's no doubt that Lane runs a very tight ship. He obviously learned a lot about discipline from his years in the Navy and has tried to transfer some of that to his home base. He once conducted an exercise with Crystal and Julie where he had

them put away their lunch boxes and hang up their jack-
ets over and over again until it became second nature.
They did it so many times and eventually became so
good at it that even Lane tired of the exercise. But the
girls didn't. They treated it as a game at first, but soon
that orderliness was ingrained in their lives just as Lane
hoped it would be.

Lane is a neat freak and he's proud of it. One time,
he met me at the door of his house wearing a gas-
powered leaf blower that fit like a backpack. But he
wasn't chasing away leaves; he was blowing away the few
caterpillars that dared descend on his driveway. The inside of his new upscale home in a gated community,
where the Judsons moved a few years ago to be closer
to their girls, has the unlived-in look of a model home;
the living room floor is covered in a pure white carpet
that looks untouched by human feet. I was admiring the
décor when I backed up and accidentally knocked over
a small evergreen tree. I doubt a Navy SEAL could
jump into action faster than Lane did; in seconds, he
had the tree upright, looking as though it had never been
moved. But it didn't end there. He refused to pay attention to anything else until every last pine needle was off
that carpet.

The stories about him are legion. One time, a visitor
to Lane's previous home on South Junett Street noticed
that one of his armchairs was covered with a towel.

Lane whipped off the towel like an artist unveiling his
latest masterpiece. "I've had this chair for two years and
there's not a mark on it," he said by way of voilà. Another time, the same visitor saw him explode in anger
at Crystal because the phone wasn't put back in the cra-
dle the way it should have been.

Lane may be the kind of guy who wears out floor
sweepers but what saves him is his charm; he's a friendly
sort and a man who enjoys telling stories, tall and otherwise. He's also something of a cornball, the kind of guy

who registers for supermarket discount cards under pseudonyms like "Russell Upsomegrub." He thinks that's pretty hilarious; in fact, he's got a walletful of cards in similarly ridiculous pseudonyms.

Patty, or P. J., as Lane calls his wife, is a perfect match for her husband. She gives Lane a run for his money when it comes to being neat. I watched with wonderment one day as tiny Patty—who is no more than five feet tall—flitted like a hummingbird between her two grand-children, Haley, then eight, and David Jr., then five, as they ate breakfast. Between bites, she wiped their mouths any time a crumb or smear of jam appeared. Now, there's nothing wrong with being neat; it's not a character flaw after all—it's just who Lane and Patty Judson are. Both are gracious hosts and have an aw-shucks quality about them. What's especially sweet—especially after forty-five years of marriage—is that they seem not to have lost any of their love for each other. Lane's hobby and passion are his antique cars, a 1937 roadster and a 1949 vintage Cadillac, that—no surprise—are in pristine condition. He confided to me one day that a perfect Sunday "for me and P. J. is going to a car show, putting out the lawn chairs, talking to the other folks and having a bottle of pop." Theirs may be an old-fashioned love but there's no doubt it's genuine.

Crystal's early life was very ordered in accordance with her parents' wishes. "There were ballet lessons and ice-skating lessons and school and there didn't seem to be much time for anything else," Patty says.

Indeed, Patty would often drive both Crystal and Julie to the skating rink at five a.m. But it paid off, because Crystal was especially good at ice-skating and, years later, her parents would remember with a chuckle the time Crystal, just nine years old, entered a competition against another highly-thought-of young skater from the Pacific Northwest. Before the event, Crystal's ice-skating coach told Lane and Patty that the competition was going to be rough. "He told us Crystal might finish eighth or ninth," Lane remembers. Well, that didn't happen. Crystal finished first, beating all the other girls, including the favorite. It's become one of those funny little family stories, because Crystal's main competitor that day eventually went on to compete in the Olympic ice-skating competition. You might even have heard of her—Tonya Harding.

Judy Hellstrom, now a matronly saleswoman at the local Bon Marche department store, is Crystal's godmother and a close friend of Patty's. She remembers Crystal from the moment she was born. "She was like a little Dresden doll," Judy said. "Very petite, and she remained petite all her life, but you couldn't miss her. She lit up the room when she walked in."

Just two years apart in age, Crystal and her younger sister, Julie, were joined at the hip growing up, but it was always Crystal who led the way. "I think she was the stronger of our two girls," says Patty, "because when they'd kind of get in a little bit of trouble, she'd fold her arms and say to Julie, 'Don't cry because I'm not gonna cry.' And she would be very firm about it."

In high school, Crystal was one of those students who make you shake your head in wonder at how she accomplished so much at such at early age. She was in many ways the archetype of the firstborn child, a classic over-achiever. She was a cheerleader; she was something called a Daffodil Princess because she won a local competition; she spoke fluent French *and* she was a sign language interpreter. She picked up that skill outside of school so she could communicate with a relative who could not hear. The Judsons like to tell the story of how Crystal stepped in at Sea-Tac Airport one time to assist a hearing-impaired family who were having trouble making their way through the airport's maze.

The two Judson girls were not allowed to run wild; they knew what was expected of them and toed the line.

When they went to college, they chose a local college—
the University of Washington at Tacoma—and the sisters even roomed together. There was no room for rebel-
lion and, with their parents taking them from lesson to
lesson and encouraging an ultra-close relationship between Crystal and Julie, there wasn't a lot of time left
over for anyone outside the Judsons' little nuclear family. You might say the Judsons closed ranks around their
two daughters and kept the outside world at arm's
length—at least until David Allen Brame came along.

5

"He Makes Me Feel Safe"

Unlike Crystal, David Brame was raised in East Tacoma, the working-class side of town. His father, Gene Brame, is a tall, Gary Cooper type of guy; he doesn't say much, just goes about his business quietly. He joined the Tacoma police department in 1951, retiring as a detective back in 1977. He built his no-frills middle-class house back in 1958—the year David was born—and has never found a reason to move. He lives there still, over on East Thirty-fourth Street, even though the neighborhood has lost much of its middle-class veneer and is now the sort of out-of-the-way working-class hamlet shunned by today's "gotta have it bigger and better" yuppies. Gene and his wife, Beverly, who would be better described as a housewife than a stay-at-home mom, had four children: Gene, Dan, David and Jane. All three boys followed their father's footsteps into law enforcement. Only Jane, who bears a striking resemblance to David, went her own way. She is the secretary to the CEO of a children's psychiatric hospital.

His parents describe David as a quiet child who loved sports. He was close to his mother; in fact, Beverly even taught him to play cribbage at the age of five, and he'd often engage her and her friends in a game. He had two passions early on and neither one involved the opposite sex. "All my sons were not allowed to date until they were sixteen," says Beverly. "I told them they could look but they couldn't touch." So David restricted his love life to sports and Bible study. He memorized passages from the Bible and wowed kids of similar bent on his block. He grew to his adult height of six feet in high school and was a standout athlete in basketball and baseball. His basketball team won the state championship.

His sister remembers he had such a serious demeanor as a kid that it was almost comic. A mother at twenty, Jane Brazell remembers David, then fifteen, buying her newborn a car bed. "I remember being touched because he bought it with his own money and he carried it out at this family party, so proud. We got along really well. In fact, we never had a fight—never."

Jane says that she could see early on that David thought differently than the rest of the Brame family, who seem to aspire to nothing more than a good job and a middle-class life. "When he was fourteen, he told me one day that when he grew up he wanted to run a government facility. Can you imagine?" Jane asks.

When David did turn sixteen, he was allowed to date and he quickly made up for lost time. At the age of nineteen, while he was a student at Tacoma Community College, he was married for the first time, to a woman I'll call Betty. It was a classic rebound situation. David never really dated Betty; he just admired her from afar and when her flighty boyfriend dumped her, David was there to lend a shoulder to cry on. Before long, they were married and moved to Spanaway, an ugly little section of town.

David became a cop after graduating from the University of Puget Sound, where one of his teachers was Bill Baarsma, who became Tacoma's mayor. Gene Brame says David wasn't really looking to follow in the family footsteps but the Tacoma police department was hiring and it seemed like a good solid job with which to raise a family. The family part, however, didn't quite work out with Betty.

"Betty was often depressed," says Beverly, "and when she wasn't, watch out." Still, the Brames approved of David's first wife even though there were rough patches. David, however, found too many rough patches for his taste. When Betty wasn't depressed, Brame told others, she was fooling around behind his back. After eight years the marriage collapsed, because, according to Brame, he once followed Betty to the house of another cop and found them in bed together. Not long after, she left that cop as well and took up with a next-door neighbor in Spanaway, a man the Brames claim "had a long criminal record." Even though his ex-wife was living next door with another man, Brame did not move from their house in Spanaway; he continued to live there by himself for another eight years. If it bothered him that his former wife was shacking up next door and having his neighbor's kid, he never mentioned it to anyone.

By then, Brame was a veteran with the Tacoma police department, but he confided to his mother that he wanted to marry again. Brame was remarkably open with his mother about everything, including his love life. Beverly swears that Brame even mentioned a one-night stand that had made *him* uncomfortable. At that point, he was almost thirty years old and newly divorced.

"Mom," David said, "I'm never going to do that again. I only want to sleep with the woman who's going to be my wife."

"David," his mother told him, "that's none of my business. You're a grown man and can do what you want. Don't give it a second thought."

But David told her even more. He told Beverly that

the woman had undressed him and he was embarrassed by it, but he did the right thing and used "a prophylactic, I think you call it," Beverly said.

It was a tough time for Brame. He obviously was lonely and uncomfortable around women despite his good looks and solid job. One time, after a day at the firing range, Brame and a bunch of cops went to a restaurant called the Poodle Dog. The waitress who came over to take their order was the kind of off-the-charts beauty they write songs about. Needless to say, the cops noticed, but Brame more so than anyone. He kept going on and on about how beautiful she was. Finally the other cops, who knew about his sad-sack love life, told him to go over and ask her out.

"So he gets up and goes over to her and we're all sitting there watching," said a cop who was there that day. "Now you've got to understand that David is prudish, almost puritanical. He doesn't know how to pick up girls so he winds up handing her his business card. We're all watching this and she hands him the card back. So then he just walks out. He leaves us there."

The cops hustled outside to find their friend. "He was standing there and his face was beet red."

"What happened?" they asked.

"She's going out with somebody."

"It was no big deal but to David it was. He was just so embarrassed he couldn't even come back to the table. He had to leave. That's the kind of guy he was. He had no dating skills. None."

With Crystal, however, he must have done something right because, after a two-year courtship, she accepted his marriage proposal. When Crystal told her mother, Patty, about the marriage plans, she said the idea that David Brame was a patrol officer appealed to her. "Mom, he makes me feel safe," she said.

Many years later, her mother would still remember that line with a mixture of bitterness and regret.

For his part, David Brame was crazy about Crystal but he did see something in her that gave him pause. Just before the wedding, at the eleventh hour really, Brame went to his parents and told them he was thinking of calling it off. He had seen a side of Crystal that troubled him. He very much wanted to avoid a second marriage like his first. This time, he wanted a woman he could control; he thought he had that in Crystal, but then something happened. He wouldn't go into details except to say that he'd seen a side of Crystal that scared him—she had a ferocious temper. Later, he told his parents that Crystal had apologized for her outburst and had been remorseful. He would go through with the wedding.

And so, on August 3, 1991, Crystal DeEtte Judson and David Allen Brame married in front of 175 family and friends. They moved into the plain two-story house in Spanaway where David had lived with his first wife and where he'd spent the time alone before marrying Crystal. Having been a bachelor pad for a couple of years, the house was a controlled mess. David wasn't a slob but he was a male and, except for throwing in the bare necessities, there was no sense of who lived in the house. The one personal touch was a framed three-by-five-feet framed shadow box made by Brame's parents to spotlight his high school achievements; there were photos of him playing basketball and baseball, and the net from the state basketball championship game. It was something any proud parents might do for their child, but Brame made it the centerpiece of a spare room together with a couple of other trophies and a few commendation certificates he'd received on the job. One woman who was friends with Brame during those years said it looked to her like he'd built a "shrine" to himself.

But there was something else in the house when Crystal moved in, she later told her parents. As she began to clean, Crystal told her parents that she found lists written by Brame's first wife, lists detailing how much she had spent on groceries, gas and other mundane household expenses. Again, there was nothing too odd about it except that every item was recorded down to the last penny.

6

The Controller

After their wedding in 1991, Crystal and David settled into a life together. At first she worked in the court system but after Haley was born in 1994, Crystal became a full-time mother. The couple then had a son—David Jr.—in November 1997, and their lives seemed complete. "Those kids were the love of her life," Judy Hellstrom says. "She would make crafts for them and all the kids in their classes. She loved to bake and would make them little cakes and draw them pictures of Snoopy characters. There was nothing she wouldn't do for those kids."

With their all-American good looks, beautiful kids and new home, Crystal and David Brame appeared happy, but those who knew them well always had the feeling that something was more than a little off. There were just some small things that became larger the more closely you got to know them. For starters, said Julie, "They were total opposites. He was a very very quiet fellow and she was very vibrant. They couldn't have been more different."

One cop who was a close friend of Brame's agrees. "I always thought they were a bad match. She was gregarious, outgoing; he was quiet and more of a stay-at-home type. His first wife was a lot more like him. Crystal was nothing like that. I think she liked that he was a cop, and him, I think he found someone who he thought he could control and he was very much a controller," the friend said.

David Ahrens saw that side of Brame firsthand on Christmas Day, 1994. Crystal loved Christmas; it was her favorite holiday and she always went all out. But this one was extra special. A day before, Crystal, at the age of twenty-six, had become a mother for the first time, to Haley Crystal Brame. Everything was going perfectly in her life. She had convinced David to buy a $200,000 house in the lovely seaside town of Gig Harbor and had just finished decorating it; the house was across the Narrows Bridge but a world away from the run-down streets of Tacoma. The house, her first child and Christmas— everything was perfect and it's no wonder that Crystal was just bursting with joy when her sister, Julie, and brother-in-law, David Ahrens, came to the front door.

David Brame greeted Julie and Dave heartily at the door and ushered them into the living room to see their new niece. Crystal was the picture of the happy new mother, holding her tiny baby girl in her arms. The house was filled with good feeling.

"Say, Dave, can I get you anything? Cup of coffee?" Brame asked.

"Sure, coffee sounds good."

Brame turned to Crystal, who was cradling baby Haley and showing her off to her sister.

"Crystal, get Dave a cup of coffee."

And just like that, Dave Ahrens says, the good feeling oozed out of the room. Everyone shifted uncomfortably but Brame didn't notice.

Dave, however, was "mortified."

"Forget it," he mumbled.

Later, Ahrens remembered the day vividly. "Here's a

brand-new mom with her brand-new daughter in her hands and he's ordering her around when he's doing nothing. I couldn't believe it. He was a textbook example of how not to be a husband."

The family dynamics did not improve when Crystal and David visited her in-laws because, among the Judsons, David was clearly the odd man out. The Judsons are a close-knit bunch, enjoy each other's company and like to have a lot of get-togethers. In some ways, you might say that Crystal and Julie were encouraged never to grow up. They had daily contact with their parents, Lane and Patty, who often referred to Crystal by her childhood nickname, "Chrissy Boo."

Lane especially is a gregarious man who is never without a story or a joke. For her part, Patty is—at least on the surface—demure and supportive of her husband's clownish behavior. But those who know her say there is a steely resolve behind the soft-spoken façade. Normally, Patty brags incessantly about her grandchildren, Haley and David. She repeats conversations she's had with them word for word, conversations where they always say something beyond cute. Make no mistake—Patty Judson speaks fluent grandmother.

Between Patty and Lane and Julie and Dave Ahrens, there is never a lull in the conversation. Their personalities are truly the opposite of David Brame's; work was his thing.

At first, Brame made a bit of an effort to tag along with the nonstop talking but, as the years went by, he obviously grew weary of it. At birthdays, Christmas, whatever the occasion, Brame would say hello to his in-laws and then simply walk into another room to sit quietly by himself, either flipping through a magazine or staring off into space. When they first moved into their new house in Gig Harbor, Julie and Dave Ahrens recalled a time when Brame simply went into an empty spare room and lay down on the floor so he could be alone. It got to the point where the only word he would exchange with his relatives other than "hello" was "goodbye."

Truth be told, the Judsons were happy to leave David to his own devices. He'd given them their grandchildren and he was a good provider but beyond that, they really had no use for him. In fact, they'd been observing a lot of things about the marriage that caused them more than a little concern. David had control issues and, in their opinion, Crystal was becoming David's puppet. It all revolved, they said, around the issue of money.

"Crystal never had any money," her mother said. "One day, when we met her, she was driving David's car instead of her own and when I asked her why, she told me her car had no gas and she had no money to buy any."

"She'd go driving around with fifty cents in her pocket and that's it. This wasn't once. It went on for three, four months at a time," Lane said, shaking his head. "We would say to her, 'You know, Crystal, we're married and we don't live that way' but she'd say, 'We have to save and this is the way David wants it.' "

7

Paradise Found?

David Brame really put the lid on spending, the Judsons say, when the family moved from the dull strip mall universe of Spanaway to the charming little town of Gig Harbor. The best way to envision Gig Harbor is to imagine a New England fishing village with a marina full of boats bobbing in pristine waters; the houses sit on a gentle rise and overlook the peaceful harbor. But it's even prettier than that because the town is full of evergreen trees that give it a look and smell that New England fishing villages wish they had. Gig Harbor's main street runs along the water in an arc and, at certain times of the year, especially on summer and fall evenings when the weather is clear and the late-day sun is bathing Mount Rainier in a golden light, the small town is breathtaking in its beauty. For a lot of people in the Pacific Northwest, Gig Harbor is synonymous with the good life.

David and Crystal loved Gig Harbor but they found it far from the tranquil oasis that other families did. The move was mostly Crystal's idea; she wanted more in life than to be stuck in Spanaway near the gun shops and dry cleaners. Eventually, Crystal's parents, sister and brother-in-law moved close to her in Gig Harbor. David's family, however, was back in East Tacoma. But it was great for Crystal to have her parents and sister very close by. David, meanwhile, began to spend more and more time at work and invested himself in getting ahead.

The Brames' house was in a cul-de-sac on Eagle Creek Lane; it was a nice neighborhood even though theirs was the most modest house on the block. With Brame concentrating on his job, Crystal was often left alone with the kids. "It almost seemed that she was more of a single parent than being married," says Julie. "She did almost everything around the house with the exception of mowing the lawn."

With the new expense of the house, Brame watched every penny. The Judsons say he put Crystal on a strict budget and didn't allow her to have a credit card or a checking account. She was expected to feed and care for a family of four on a budget of $100 every two weeks and not a penny more. Crystal tried her best to live within the confines of an exceedingly tight budget. Her family says she went years without new clothes, yet never asked them to help her out. "David had convinced her that this was the way to live and she went along with it," says Patty. "It broke my heart to see how she scrimped and saved but she did it."

Lane remembers one of David's pet sayings: "He'd say, 'It says David Brame on that check. It doesn't say Crystal. If you don't like it, do something about it.' "

The Judsons weren't the only ones to recognize the control that David was exerting on Crystal. Occasionally, an outsider would get a glimpse of the life Crystal was leading. Linda Lee Clark, a shop owner who runs Seasons on the Bay, a lovely little gift shop in Gig Harbor, got to know Crystal as a customer, although a very frugal one. Clark was a benevolent mother figure in Crystal's life. Clark cherished Crystal and obviously saw her as more than just the run-of-the-mill customer. "She was just a lovely person and a wonderful mother. She always came in with little Haley and David, who were always dressed perfectly, but we all felt so sorry for her. We would literally watch her count out nickels and pennies for any little thing she wanted to buy," Clark said. "It finally got to the point where, if there was something that Crystal wanted, we would suddenly have a sale.

"I was curious about what her husband did for a living because she never had any money, and one day she told me he was a police officer. I thought, 'I can't believe that she has no money.'"

And then, almost as if she were reading Clark's mind, Crystal said, "You wouldn't believe how cheap he is. I only get one hundred dollars every two weeks."

"For a family of four?"

"Yes."

"Well, you have credit cards and checks, right?"

"No. That's it. One hundred dollars every two weeks. Period."

"Crystal, it's none of my business but . . ."

"I know."

"Well, this isn't the way things are these days. You should stand up to him."

"But you don't understand. He controls everything I do. He checks the mileage on the car to see where I've gone, he asks for receipts."

"You don't have to live that way. You have to stand up to him."

"I know, I know."

Things ultimately got so desperate that Crystal began selling any leftover clothing—her own or her children's—at a consignment shop. It brought in a little extra money that she used to supplement what David gave her. Unfortunately for her, one day she accidentally let slip to David what she was up to and Crystal's family claims that he immediately demanded half of the proceeds.

David kept Crystal on a very short leash, according to her family. If she went to the store, she had to tell him which store and what she was going to buy. At the end of the day, when he got home, he demanded receipts to check prices and marched out to the car to check the odometer to make sure she hadn't strayed beyond where she said she was going. And of course, he demanded to see the change from every purchase.

In those years before David was appointed chief, Crystal's world shrunk more and more. By monitoring the odometer and checking the time stamp on the store's receipts, David literally knew where Crystal had been every moment of every day. Occasionally, if it was on the way, Crystal would sneak a quick stop at her parents' home, "but she was always in a hurry," Patty said. "She'd come in and say, 'I can't stay very long, David's expecting me.' And then she'd be gone."

The Judsons did not know what to think; they watched Crystal's life almost as though they were watching a movie. Clearly, they felt helpless and were as confused as anyone by the two David Brames—the controlling husband, but also the upstanding member of the community who was rising fast in the Tacoma police department. He got promotion on top of promotion and was widely admired. Crystal warned her parents many times that they had better not complain publicly, to keep everything inside the family, because she did not want to jeopardize her husband's career. Lane and Patty agreed. They hated to watch Crystal suffer but they honored her wishes.

The Judsons did make one thing perfectly clear: if Crystal ever wanted to leave Brame, they loved her and would be there for her no matter what. "We just told her we were here for her if she wanted to leave David,"

Lane says. "What else could we do? We couldn't interfere with her life but she knew how we felt."

It's not surprising then that, with all the restrictions placed on her, Crystal had few friends. "She was isolated," Julie said. "Mom and I tried to get her to go shopping or meet for lunch but something always came up with David. He wouldn't let her go anywhere and, when she did come along, she had no money."

David Brame socialized with his cop buddies and the people he needed to get ahead but he felt that it was a waste of time for Crystal to have friends. "One day, Crystal was outside the house talking to a neighbor. David called her over, looked at his watch, and said, 'Hey, you spent nineteen minutes talking to that neighbor. Don't talk to her on my time. Do it on your own time,' " Lane recalls.

As the years went by, it was no longer just the money and control that made the Judsons and Ahrenses wonder about Brame. To them, Brame's behavior was well beyond the normal limits of a man who wanted to rein in his wife's spending. Patty just shakes her head now when she recalls things that Crystal told her, like the times Brame insisted on visiting Crystal's gynecologist with her. He wasn't doing it to be a doting husband; he insisted on being in the examination room for routine Pap smears. "She told me, 'Mom, I don't even want to go there. I can't understand why he wants to be there. I don't understand it.' "

And then there was the weight issue. Crystal was a beautiful and vivacious woman before she married Brame. As she aged and had kids, she kept her figure; David wouldn't have it any other way. The Judsons claim that it was all right for him to put on a few pounds over the years but he wanted to make sure Crystal did not. In fact, both of them could not help but notice the way Crystal's sister had turned out. Julie struggled with her weight and David wanted to make sure Crystal never had the same problem. Crystal told her parents that David marched her into the bathroom every morning, made her strip naked and step on the scale so he could check her weight. Anything over 105 pounds on her five-feet-one-inch body was cause for concern.

And, if all of that wasn't bad enough, there was one other thing that bugged Lane and Patty more than almost anything else. It was a very small thing but they saw it as symptomatic of the way Brame treated their daughter. David, they said, would not allow his daughter, Haley, to learn how to count money. "He just would not allow it," Patty said.

8

"I Feel Like I'm Raising Three Kids"

However cheap or insensitive David Brame may have been, his family says it was not all one-sided. In fact, they claim both they and Brame often debated whether Crystal was suffering from a personality disorder or perhaps even mental illness.

David Brame began thinking that way within weeks of Haley's birth. One day, he arrived home much earlier than usual and entered the house. He walked through the quiet house and hesitated before speaking aloud, knowing how much Crystal hated to have baby Haley wake up from her nap. He tiptoed from room to room but couldn't find Crystal anywhere. He looked into Haley's room. The baby was sleeping, but what caught his eye was Crystal down on the floor on all fours. Her back was to him so she didn't notice he was there. As he watched, Crystal crawled around, poking her head up occasionally to look at Haley. Then she'd crawl over to the window to look out. Then back to Haley. Then back to the window. She did this over and over until David couldn't take any more.

"What are you doing?" he asked in a whisper.

Crystal jumped. "Oh, I thought I saw something out the window."

And with that, she got up and walked out of the bedroom.

It was that kind of strange behavior that befuddled David. He had previously noticed her turning lights on and off and checking the gas stove repeatedly; he began to suspect her of having an obsessive-compulsive disorder.

Another woman, who is not a member of the Brame family, recalls helping Crystal change one of Haley's diapers. "She did the whole thing with the powder and everything and we were about to walk out of the bedroom when she felt the elastic band of the diaper and said, 'Oh, I think this is wet.' I felt it myself and said, 'Crystal, it's dry. Don't be silly.' But she wouldn't hear of it. She changed that diaper then and there and then did it again a half hour later."

While Lane and Patty paint a picture of their daughter as the perfect wife and mother controlled by a monstrous husband, the Brame family says nothing was further from the truth. Gene and Beverly Brame are adamant not only that wasn't Crystal afraid of David—they claim she was an abuser who had a volcanic temper and a mouth that could make a sailor like her father blush.

"We used to have a lot of fun with Crystal," says Gene Brame. "We loved her like she was our own daughter but something happened to her after Haley was born."

To the Brame family, Crystal was a neurotic mess with wild mood swings. "During their marriage, David felt like he never knew what he was going to come home to," his sister, Jane, said. After both children were born, Brame often told her, "I feel like I'm raising three kids."

Jane, who was very close to David, says that one time, when she was talking to him on the phone, David broke off the conversation because he saw Crystal pulling into the driveway. "I have to go," he said. "She doesn't like me being on the phone too long."

"How will she even know?"

"Jane, you're not going to believe this but she feels the phone to see if it's warm."

Brame told his sister of Crystal's "crazy" behavior over the years although, in fairness, someone else could have witnessed the same incident and chalked it up to the frustration faced by a stay-at-home mom with two young children. "David came home from work early one day and heard Crystal screaming at the kids," Jane recalls. "Another time he came home and changed David Jr.'s diaper and his bare bottom was beet red with handprints on it. She told David that she had 'almost lost it.' He had real concerns and expressed this to our family and their family physician. David thought maybe it was a hormone imbalance."

Brame also told his sister that Crystal had a "ferocious" temper and would explode over any little thing. There was the time that Haley lost a baby tooth and couldn't find it. "Crystal screamed and yelled at little Haley until she was in tears," Jane says David told her. He also told Jane how David Jr. had picked up his mother's habit of cursing, how he once was putting David Jr. to sleep and he told his father, "Good night, asshole." Another time, at Gene Brame's seventieth birthday party, David Jr. told his cousin, "Come on, you little bastard."

The Judsons deny all of this but others sometimes heard Crystal. One of David's friends once called the house around the children's bedtime and could barely hear David on the phone because there was so much screaming in the background.

"What is that?"

"That's Crystal," David said. "She's putting the kids to sleep."

"Like that?"

"Now you know what I have to go through."

The friend said it sounded like the ravings of a maniac.

One thing is absolutely clear—Crystal detested David's mother, Beverly. The two nearly came to blows in 1999 when Brame was promoted to assistant chief. The day began with Haley running over to "Grandma Brame" during the ceremony, kissing her, hugging her and sitting in her lap. That did not sit well with Crystal who, according to Beverly, ran over and jerked Haley by the arms back to the Judson side of the family. At the end of the ceremony, Beverly thought it would be nice to get a photograph of all the Brame men together who at one time or another worked in law enforcement. Maybe Crystal didn't hear what Beverly had in mind, but Crystal insisted on being in the photograph. When Beverly asked her to step away, the two almost had a fistfight in front of a group of other officers until the embarrassed Brame boys stepped in to separate them.

In later years, there was a lot of friction over babysitting. Gene and Beverly Brame sometimes watched the kids when Crystal and David had a function to attend. One time, little David hit Beverly in the chest, causing her a great deal of pain; she'd had a number of operations on her breasts due to cancer and they were very sensitive. Beverly Brame reacted instinctively and gave David Jr. a swat on his bottom. As soon as Crystal and David arrived to pick up the kids, Haley told Crystal that Beverly had spanked David Jr. Crystal flew into a rage, screaming at her mother-in-law and David.

But it wasn't only Beverly who felt Crystal's sharp tongue. At one point, Gene Brame says that Crystal got it into her head that he had been talking about her at a local restaurant, a charge he denies. The next time he saw Crystal, she launched into a "tirade of nonsense that lasted twenty-five minutes. I was so shocked at the hate coming out of her mouth that I couldn't respond."

When she stopped, Gene told her, "Crystal, what is the matter with you? I have never said anything about you and I never would. You are part of my family and I wouldn't be talking about my own family."

Both Gene and Beverly say that, after one of these episodes, Crystal would soon return to normal and act as though nothing had happened. She would give them a hug at the door and march the children out to say goodbye.

David could only shake his head when he was alone with his parents. "He'd always say, 'Now you know what I have to live with,' " Beverly said.

To the Brames, Crystal was at best a brat who'd been spoiled by her doting parents; at worst they feared she was mentally ill. They thought there was nothing more telling than the magnet Crystal kept on her refrigerator: I DESERVE EVERYTHING AND I WANT IT DELIVERED.

"That was Crystal, right there," Gene says.

As far as money is concerned, Jane Brazell, David's sister, says she had the exact opposite impression than the Judsons did; in fact, she thought of Crystal as a spendthrift who went to extravagant lengths for birthdays and Christmas. "It would take the kids forty-five minutes to open their birthday presents. It was so ridiculous it was sickening," Jane says. "Why would a little five-year-old girl need thirty-five Barbie dolls? David wanted his kids to have everything nice but not to that extent. Everything was overboard. The normalcy was not there with Crystal."

At Christmastime, Jane says, Crystal would have not one but three Christmas trees, one for the family room and the other two in the kids' bedrooms with expensive

Disney ornaments on them. "Before she took the trees down, she would take pictures of them so she could decorate them in the exact same fashion the following year."

To Jane, it was not at all surprising that Brame put his extravagant wife on a budget, and if she bristled, so what?

David wanted to approve the larger purchases so the credit cards were in his name but, says Jane, there's no doubt that Crystal got what she wanted. To prove it, Jane produced the couple's credit card bills that show purchases—small, medium and large—from Nordstrom, Target, Party World, Mervyn's, Toys "R" Us and even Seasons on the Bay, the store in Gig Harbor where Linda Lee Clark claimed to see Crystal counting her nickels. It wasn't all nickels apparently because, a few months before they broke up, in November 2003, Crystal spent $758 and $352 on Christmas trees and decorations.

There's no doubt the Brames were locked in an extraordinarily contentious marriage marked by odd behavior on both sides. And their neighbors in Gig Harbor could not help but notice. Marty Conmy, who lives on Eagle Lane across from the Brame house, considered Brame someone "with zero personality," and he knew something very strange was going on with his neighbors. He remembers one time when, as he was outside his house playing basketball with his son, Crystal came running out of her house.

"She was very frantic. Her young son was just a toddler at that time and he'd knocked over a lamp and had nicked the wall," Conmy remembers. "Crystal kept saying that her husband would be home soon and he was going to be very angry. It was gonna be horrible. Her reaction seemed way out of proportion to what happened."

Another neighbor who was also outside calmed Crystal down and helped her patch the hole, but the incident made Conmy begin to take special notice of the Brames.

It wasn't long before, one summer's night, he heard yelling coming from across the street. He peeked out the window to see Crystal pounding on the door and screaming to be let in. As he walked over to see if she needed any help, the door opened, she went in and the door slammed shut. "A few minutes later, the garage door opened and their car came out. Brame was driving and Crystal was sitting next to him. They looked straight ahead and, as the car passed, the little girl, who was in the backseat, turned her head and looked at me with a very sad, sad look. She had the saddest eyes I've ever seen," Conmy recalls. "It was a troubling incident. There wasn't anything violent but you knew it had the tone, the feeling that something was not right."

After that, Conmy and other neighbors made a pact that they'd keep their eye on the Brame house. But behind closed doors, the marriage was worse than even they suspected.

9

"I Don't Want to File a Police Report"

The tensions in the Brame household became more and more unyielding; Crystal grew weary of bending to David's will and David was sick to death of what he considered her "weird" behavior and violent mood swings. It was clear something had to give and in September 1996, it did. But it was not Crystal who went to the police claiming physical abuse—it was David.

David reported that on two occasions that year, Crystal attacked him; he told fellow police officers about the incidents at the time and documented them carefully. The question is, why? Did Crystal really attack David, as he claimed? The Judsons believe that David was leaving a documented record because he feared Crystal would someday file for divorce and he wanted to counter whatever claims she made. In any event, David kept detailed handwritten notes of the incidents that he later gave to a police buddy for safekeeping. Until years later, after she filed for divorce, Crystal never once called the police to report that her husband had abused her in any way.

On September 15, 1996, Brame wrote that he was having trouble putting together a car seat for their daughter Haley. This is David Brame's version of the day:

> With the two-year-old Haley present, Crystal kept up a barrage of sarcastic and profane criticism. Throughout the day and into the evening, she refused to drop the matter. Finally, at 11 p.m., I went to bed. As soon as I lay down, Crystal came into the room, turned on the light and announced that she had things to do in the bedroom. I retreated to the living room couch. She followed and turned on the light, announcing that she wanted to watch some television. This went on for another hour or two during which I repeatedly said that I had to go to bed as I needed to get up early to go to work the next morning.
>
> Finally, in desperation I warned Crystal that if she didn't stop haranguing me I was going to leave [the house]. She continued her verbal assaults, then began punching and hitting me. Because she was so angry and volatile, I gathered all three of the service revolvers I kept in the house, put them in my gym bag and headed out the door. On my way out, Crystal shouted, "If you leave, it'll be the biggest mistake of your life!" I drove in my police cruiser to my parents' house to spend the night.

Crystal immediately called her mother.

"She was crying, frantic and very afraid," Patty said. "I kept asking her, 'What happened, what happened?'"

Crystal was sobbing; it had gotten very ugly. Even worse, Haley had seen and heard the whole thing. "We had a fight and . . . he said, 'A bullet in both your heads would take care of both of you.'"

"Call the police."

Crystal picked up the phone but hesitated. She knew

David would go ballistic if she made an official report but she was scared and dialed anyway.

The call was not taped by the Gig Harbor police; the officer on duty asked if she wanted to make a report or have a car sent over and Crystal told them no. She said she had not been physically hit and she did not want a car sent over. The duty officer then informed Crystal that because Brame was a Tacoma city cop, he would patch her in to the Tacoma police department.

Temporary Sergeant David Fischer was in the TPD's communications center working the graveyard shift when Crystal was patched through.

"She was almost hysterical," he recalls. "She was crying. I asked her to slow down and tell me what was wrong."

Fischer reports the following exchange:

"My husband and I had an argument. He's a police officer in Tacoma and he left the house with all his guns."

"Did he assault you, ma'am?"

"No."

"Did he threaten to hurt you?"

"No," Fischer claims Crystal said. "But he took his guns."

"Yes, ma'am, do you know where he went?"

"I don't know, maybe to his parents' house."

"Do you think he intends to hurt them?"

"No."

Fischer privately thought Brame had done the right thing by removing his weapons from such a volatile situation. He told Crystal that he would call the Gig Harbor police and have a car sent over to her house to check on her. He remembered one other thing about the call— Crystal made it clear she did *not* want to file a formal report against David:

"I don't want to get him into trouble. Please don't tell anyone I called 911."

"Yes, ma'am," Fischer said, but he knew what he had to do.

The moment they hung up, he immediately called the night shift duty lieutenant. It was a female cop named Catherine Woodard, a tall, imposing, no-nonsense blonde whose nickname within the department was "Big Bird" because of her resemblance to the Sesame Street character. Fischer didn't know it but Woodard was a friend and a confidant of David Brame's. He told her about Crystal's call and she immediately said, "I'll handle it."

That's the last Fischer ever heard of the matter.

But that wasn't the end of it. David was livid that Crystal had called the police, because a report of domestic violence could derail his career. He later said that he considered Crystal's emergency call "an extreme betrayal of the trust between husband and wife, not to mention a threat to my livelihood."

The next morning, Crystal said he confronted her and told her never to do that again. "Don't bite the hand that feeds you," he said. "If I don't eat, nobody does."

Just thirteen days later, another major fight erupted, this time over furniture. Crystal wanted to spend $5,000 on a bedroom set from Schoenfeld's furniture store and Brame refused. Crystal became enraged, according to Brame, whose handwritten notes describe what happened:

> She charged at me with clenched fists and punched me on my back and shoulders. She hit me on the back because I turned my back to avoid more serious injuries. She then ripped my T-shirt at the right shoulder area . . . she retrieved some cosmetics and she began throwing them at me.

Crystal, he said, continued to pelt him with refrigerator magnets, nearly breaking a window. He says she then proceeded to curse and yell at him for "ninety minutes" while he held little Haley in his lap. At that point, he says he had enough and took preemptive action. He went to the Gig Harbor cops but did not file a formal complaint. Instead, he kept his own notes on the incident, the last line of which is: "I do not [his underlining] want my wife arrested or prosecuted (although I understand the law). I want our marriage to work and I want counseling."

While Brame was at the office of the Gig Harbor police department, he placed a phone call to another longtime friend on the force, Officer Norman Conaway. By now it was four p.m.

Conaway, who died in 2003, kept handwritten notes from that conversation: "My wife answered the phone and said, 'It's D. A. [Brame's nickname] and he sounds terrible.'"

Conaway took the phone. "It's happened again," Brame said. "I don't know what to do."

"I could tell immediately that he'd been crying. 'Where are you?'"

"GHPD"

"Okay, sit tight, I'll be right there."

When Conaway arrived at the Gig Harbor police station, a sergeant showed him in. His friend looked horrible.

"D. A. took off his glasses and covered his eyes with a hanky. You could tell he'd been crying. He had to calm himself for several minutes before he could even talk. I noticed that his T-shirt was torn around his right shoulder blade area. The material was stretched out and it appeared to be a fresh tear."

"It happened again, she went nuts on me," Brame said.

Brame recapped the argument about the furniture.

He mentioned that he didn't want to file a report on Crystal; he wanted to keep the marriage alive. Conaway convinced him to keep careful notes of the incident and the one from September 15 and to file an "informational report" with the Gig Harbor cops. Brame agreed and eventually gave the handwritten notes to Conaway for safekeeping. The informational report was not filed but years later, the Gig Harbor police were able to come up with an "incident report form." It reads in part:

> Brame concerned with possible escalating problems with his wife Crystal. Brame states his wife has become increasingly hostile (verbally) towards him and has made threats to "destroy his career" with false accusations . . . Brame plans to move from the residence later this night and may request civil standby.

David Brame did not move. Instead, he went home and, from there, called his best buddy on the force, Bill Meeks, and asked him to take a videotape of his injuries. (Meeks later claimed he lost the tape or his kids had recorded over it.) Meeks said he "absolutely" believed the injuries were made by Crystal and still recalls how "vicious" they were. Meeks urged Brame to have her arrested but, when Brame refused, Meeks implored him to at least report the abuse to then-Interim Chief Ken Monner. Brame took his advice. Monner was sympathetic and suggested that the Brames go into counseling. In his handwritten note of the incident, Brame claimed that he wanted to but that Crystal refused.

Looking at these incidents in hindsight, it's hard to believe that Brame would be so calculating that he would have falsified both incidents with Crystal, going so far as to call friends in the department, cry in front of them and file a report. Two other cops, trained to take witness statements, had no doubt that Brame was telling the truth. And yet, Crystal's family believes it was all an elaborate ruse to preempt any abuse complaints Crystal might file.

But of course the Brame family believed David. And they had a further reason to feel that way. In June 1998 Brame showed up at his mother's house with more scratches on his neck and deep black-and-blue bruises on his upper arm, right near his bicep. Brame told his mother that Crystal had attacked him in a fit of anger and he asked Beverly to document the abuse. She agreed, taking photographs of the injuries as Brame stared deeply into the camera. If he was embarrassed, his eyes don't show it. Crystal later said that Brame had caused the bruises on his own by dropping weights on his arm.

The pressure, meanwhile, was rising on the Judsons to do something about all the stories Crystal was telling them about Brame's controlling nature. Around this same time period, Crystal had committed a now long-forgotten transgression against Brame and he was demanding a written apology. She refused and complained to her father. Lane Judson picked up the phone and called Brame at work, demanding that he stop hounding his daughter. Gene Brame recounted the conversation as his son related it to him:

"She hit and scratched me, Lane—in front of Haley."

"Well, she was raised not to hit."

"But she did. I swear to you. She goes into these rages . . ."

"Oh, does big you get hurt by little Chrissie Boo?" Lane teased.

Brame apologized but Lane says David begged him to keep the conversation a secret. Brame was walking a tightrope. He desperately tried to control Crystal and her movements but, if her behavior exploded into violence, he knew it could derail his career. In one sense, Crystal had his future in her hands even though she felt like the one being controlled. When she realized the truth, it would all come crashing down.

Crystal's Oasis

Debbie Phillips still remembers the first time she saw Crystal Brame walk through the front door of the Oasis Tanning Salon. "It was the first of March 2001," Debbie remembers. "I saw her come storming down the courtyard, marching quickly, and wearing this bright pink lipstick that she liked. She had a great smile, a wonderful smile, very bubbly."

The Oasis is not much to look at; it sits in the middle of a strip mall in a commercial section of Gig Harbor that is decidedly not beautiful. But it is convenient if you happen to live in Gig Harbor and so, back in 2001, Crystal's sister bought her a lifetime membership for $150. It turned out to be the gift of a lifetime, because Crystal and Debbie hit it off and it became much more of an oasis for Crystal than the name was actually meant to imply.

Crystal did not have a slew of close girlfriends. She blamed Brame and his controlling nature; his family blamed it on her "crazy" personality. In any case, Crystal said she had lost touch with most of her high school and college friends and the Judsons say that Brame didn't allow her the time to develop friendships with the mothers of her children's friends.

The best thing Crystal had going was an e-mail relationship with an old grade-school friend, Lori Hamm. The two didn't talk much but they did e-mail each other constantly. Hamm noticed something in the e-mails that galled her—it was the way Crystal referred to her husband. "She was too careful with what she said," Lori remembers. "She never talked about how much she loved him or what fun they had together. It really annoyed me that when she had to have a hysterectomy, he wouldn't help her around the house or with the kids during her recovery. He was always 'too busy.' We always talked about getting together but I always had a feeling that he wouldn't approve. She didn't talk about other friends besides her sister."

Crystal had tried to befriend Linda Lee Clark, the shopkeeper at Seasons on the Bay, but it only went so far. Clark is much older than Crystal and she had a store to run. "You could tell she was looking for someone to be friends with," Clark said. "I don't think she had a lot of friends. She'd become isolated." Clark knew what Crystal wanted and did her best, but there were always customers and other sales help around so, other than complaining how cheap her husband was, things never got too private. Intimate secrets were never revealed.

But all that changed inside the Oasis. Debbie Phillips recognized a kindred spirit in Crystal—a "fellow abused woman." There is no doubt Crystal loved going to the Oasis Tanning Salon, because in an eighteen-month period she visited more than two hundred times. At first, it was because it was twenty minutes of peace in an otherwise hectic day. She could lie in one of the tanning beds and not think about her husband, her children or her problems. "This was her twenty minutes of peace or serenity where there was nobody watching her, seeing her undress," Debbie said. "It was almost like sanctuary for her and that's the reason why she came tanning no matter snow, sleet, rain, shine—she was here. She needed to talk to somebody. She was able to have that here, that time to talk with a human being and that friendship, that secret friendship."

Little by little, Debbie drew Crystal out by talking about her own troubles with her own ex-husband who had left her. Crystal slowly began confiding in her, telling her things she had never told anyone—intimate things. She told Debbie that Brame was a terrible lover, that he showed her no love or compassion. "She said she lay there and took it. In fact, she told me it was almost like being raped," Debbie says. "It was 'Prepare yourself, Ethel, because here I come.' There was no kissing, no foreplay. It was very forceful, very angry, pulling of hair, very rough, rough. And it wasn't enjoyable. It wasn't meant for her to enjoy it in the first place. She was just the tool. David was a pervert but nobody knew that."

Crystal and David Brame, by many accounts, had a very complicated sex life. For his part, David Brame was classically conflicted. He was fond of quoting scripture and letting people know he was a Christian, but he had a sexual appetite that he could never quite satisfy or understand. It was like a beast he was wrestling with, and toward the end of his life, he was desperately trying to come to terms with it, even going so far as to seek treatment for a sexual addiction. One reporter who covered this story said that Brame reminded him of the Judge Turpin character in the Stephen Sondheim musical *Sweeney Todd,* who whips himself while watching a young girl undress. Pain and pleasure at the same time—that about summed up David Brame's feelings about sex.

Crystal told stories about what went on in their intimate moments and Brame once mentioned to his father, "You can't believe what goes on in that bedroom."

Crystal went into a bit more detail, telling trusted confidants that David would sometimes handcuff her to the bed and leave her there after sex; other times, he choked her to the point of unconsciousness to heighten the erotic pleasure. It's unclear who initiated this behavior. Whenever either of them mentioned their sexual antics, whoever was doing the telling tried to blame the other. What is known is that, after her death, investigators found, in David's desk, nude photos of Crystal that had been shredded. No one knows who did the shredding but the FBI lab put those photos back together, according to a source who says the photos were not shot by a professional. They were taken in the Brame home and showed Crystal posing in front of her Christmas tree in nothing more than a Santa hat and boots. Investigators also found an application she'd made to appear in *Playboy* magazine; it was unclear if it had been sent out. Also curious is the disappearance of nearly all the couple's family videos. What was on them? No one knows, but someone went to the trouble of destroying or hiding them.

Crystal also told Debbie that she and David had gone on vacation to the Desert Shadows Inn Resort in Palm Springs, California. An upscale nudist resort that caters to first-timers, Desert Shadows makes nudity seem, well, natural. It proudly offers "the ultimate stress-free nude vacation in a beautiful clothes-free setting perfect for the discerning naturist. There simply is no place like this in the world! Acres of meticulously landscaped grounds behind secluded gates offer panoramic views and sunshine year 'round—only one mile from downtown Palm Springs, California!"

How or why Brame got it into his head to vacation at a nudist colony is not known, but he must have enjoyed it. He and Crystal returned there three times while the Judsons watched the children. Certainly there is nothing illegal about it and despite the common misperception, nudist colonies are not necessarily swap meets for swinging husbands and wives. But maybe Brame didn't know that. Brame did know that a fellow officer, who went on to achieve a high rank within the department, was a member of a "lifestyle" club not far from Tacoma. The club was called New Horizons and bills itself as one of the largest swingers' clubs in the country and it is a place where consenting adults have group sex and swap partners. Again, there is nothing illegal about it but perhaps Brame did not want to experiment so close to home.

In any case, the first time Crystal and David vacationed at the Desert Shadows Inn was August 2001. Crystal and David met Sara and Brett Larson (not their real names). When they first met, they said that David was strutting around the grounds au naturel while Crystal was more demure, sitting around draped in a towel. She was friendly, as always, and told the Larsons that this was their first trip to Desert Shadows. The couples hit it off and spent some time together. They told the Larsons they were from Seattle and they made arrangements to meet there again a couple of months later, in October.

Debbie listened in astonishment as Crystal tearfully recalled what happened next. Crystal told her that in September 2001, David called Sara and Brett Larson at their home in New Mexico. She didn't know about the call until later and was aghast.

Brett recalls that David asked him, "I've been thinking. What do you think of Crystal?"

"Seems like a good lady. Very nice."

"Well," David said, and hesitated. "I think Sara is pretty nice also."

"Thanks."

"Do you, uh, well, I have a proposition for you."

Brett had vacationed at many nudist colonies. He was pretty sure he knew what David was about to ask and he was interested. After all, Crystal seemed like a loving woman and was very attractive.

"Well, what do you think if the four of us get together next time we're there?" David asked.

Brett laughed. "Are you asking what I think you're asking? You want to swap Crystal and Sara?"

"Yeah, but I thought it would be more like a foursome, like we'd all be together."

"You into that?"

"Yeah."

"Are you experienced?"

"I've never tried it, if that's what you're asking, but I want to. I've been fantasizing about Sara since we met."

"Really? Well, you know, I'd be there too."

"I know."

"All right then, I'm interested. I think Crystal's pretty nice too and I know Sara would be interested. We've done it before."

That night, when David got home, he related the phone call to Crystal.

"There's no way I'm doing that," she told David.

"Oh yes you are."

"No, I'm not. This goes against God," she said. "It goes against everything I believe. Why do you want these things anyway, David? Am I not enough for you?"

"No, you're not good enough. I want more."

The two fought, but the next month they were back at Desert Shadows. David greeted Brett and Sara as old friends when he saw them. But David turned quiet and sullen when the Larsons turned down their invitation to dinner; they were scheduled to meet another couple, but Brett said he hoped they could get together later. David was angry and he blamed Crystal for being cold. He thought Brett and Sara could see that Crystal was not interested. They fought and David left Crystal in the hallway crying.

That's when Sara and Brett came by. "She was really upset and was crying so we invited her to our room. We didn't want to make a scene and she told us that David would probably be listening."

For the next two hours, Crystal poured her heart out to these strangers. She told how David controlled every penny she spent and how he watched what she did with her time. "She basically told us David was abusive and controlling and she was afraid to go back to her room."

The Larsons told Crystal she could spend the night in their room with no strings attached, but she knew David would be extremely angry so she finally got up and left.

David, meanwhile, was angry, but he also seemed distracted by something going on at work. He had just heard that the current chief, James Hairston, had announced his retirement.

11

"An All-American City"

By September 2001, the city of Tacoma sent out a brochure to police jurisdictions across the country. TACOMA WASHINGTON, AN ALL AMERICA [sic] CITY SEEKS A POLICE CHIEF, the pamphlet announced. In a featured pull quote, City Manager Ray Corpuz was quoted as saying, "Our next police chief must be a skilled ethical leader, someone who is unquestionably committed to community service and continuous improvement."

Among the qualifications:

- Has unquestioned ethics, integrity and values
- Has highly developed skills and is sensitive and empathetic to others, builds trust and possesses good listening skills
- Is a good mentor who can grow and train a motivated staff

It didn't sound anything like the private David Brame, but almost no one outside the Judson family knew that man. And the public David Brame, well, he seemed perfect. But Brame was far from being a lock for the job. For one thing, Mary Brown, assistant human resources director for the city of Tacoma and a seasoned veteran of civic infighting, would be overseeing the selection process and she had no love for David Brame. Fact is, she hated him. They had crossed paths when Brame was a vice president of the Police Union and she didn't like him at all. In fact, Brown was later quoted as saying, "He was a pile of slime."

In order to keep things fair, all candidates had to submit to telephone interviews by city council members, answer a list of sixteen questions and be interviewed by four separate panels, including the public, heads of departments and Police Union Locals 6 and 26. It was to be an exhaustive search and the final decision would be made by none other than City Manager Ray Corpuz, the most powerful official in town, who was rebuilding downtown Tacoma block by desecrated block.

It was a grueling application process but in many ways, it was an attractive job for a lot of reasons. Tacoma is a midsized city of two hundred thousand people, and the chief's $130,000 annual pay was generous for the area. It was a terrific opportunity for a sharp-eyed cop on the way up, a place to get experience running things on your own, a classic stepping-stone type job that could lead to bigger and better things.

In the past decade, Tacoma has been trying its best to bury its ignominious past. In a roll-up-your-sleeves style of civic pride, the city announced it was undergoing an urban renaissance, and darn it, that's just what it did. Ray Corpuz had worked hard in his eleven-plus years in office to attract glamour projects and is largely credited with revitalizing a section of downtown. There is a new building for the Tacoma Art Museum, a new branch of the Washington State History Museum, and the centerpiece—a state-of-the-art building housing the Museum of Glass, featuring works by Tacoma native Dale Chihuly. Across the street from this cultural center sits a branch of the University of Washington and next to that are old warehouses being converted into art shops and apartments.

The city was changing for the better, Corpuz knew, and it was time to get someone new, someone more professional to run its police department. It's worth mentioning that Tacoma has a city manager form of government and, even though there is a mayor, he's more or less a figurehead. The real power lies with the city manager and, heading into the new millennium, Corpuz had held that position for more than a decade, cementing his power. Corpuz would make the ultimate choice of who would be the next police chief, but there didn't seem to be any reason to worry. So far, his achievements were impressive, at least to some.

"Ah, it's all a bunch of artsy-fartsy stuff," says John Hathaway, Tacoma's answer to Matt Drudge. "There're still potholes eight inches deep just off downtown."

Hathaway is a lot like Drudge. He may cut a semi-comic figure but there is the soul of a crusading reporter behind his affected look. And, like Drudge, when Hathaway doesn't like you, well, that's that. And he didn't like Ray Corpuz. Hathaway believed Corpuz was corrupt and a liar and was not afraid to say so. For his money, Hathaway wanted the Tacoma city council, your classic dysfunctional small-town government body, to assume the power that was rightfully theirs. Corpuz served at the council's pleasure but its members didn't seem aware of that; instead they were content to let Corpuz run things as long as they got something for their neighbors. That's the way it had been in Tacoma since Corpuz assumed power and Hathaway didn't like that.

Hathaway might work at a bowling alley, but he considers himself a journalist first and sends out "breaking news" alerts when he feels he has a scoop worth reporting. "My sources are impeccable," Hathaway says, and while that may be an overstatement—and certainly the Tacoma *News Tribune* doesn't think his sources are so impeccable—he is very plugged in with certain people. His Internet column gives Hathaway an aura of being a player, which is what he wants more than anything. As he likes to say—without any prompting or humility—"I'm the man who knows too much."

It should be no surprise that his act wears thin on a lot of people in Tacoma, including the editorial writers at the Tacoma *News Tribune,* who cannot find anything good to say about Hathaway. Even some of the reporters—all too young to have been schooled in the days when colorful characters like Hathaway would have been their city editors—often turn a deaf ear to his ramblings.

But, as Ray Corpuz geared up to find Tacoma a new police chief, Hathaway was paying a lot of attention and dogging the process every step of the way. He was working the story, looking for something dark, something dirty.

For the latter half of 2001, Corpuz along with the Tacoma city council and Mayor Bill Baarsma conducted their search. Thirty-two police officials from around the country wanted the job, and there were a couple of good internal candidates besides Brame. One of them was Catherine Woodard. Tacoma has never had a female police chief, and there were those inside the city government who felt that Woodard was just what the new Tacoma needed. Brame, ever the political animal, knew that Woodard was his primary competition and he needed to knock her out, so he supposedly offered her a deal before she could even submit her name: don't compete with me and I promise I'll make you my assistant chief. Woodard, who later said she was always a bit intimidated by Brame but denies cutting a deal, never put her name up for the chief's job, leaving Brame as the top inside choice.

After running the gantlet of interviews and question-naires, four candidates were chosen and David Brame was among them. But that pool was quickly whittled down to two when two of them dropped out for personal reasons. The only ones left standing were Patrick Ste-phens, deputy chief of the Cleveland police department, and Brame, the hometown favorite and, it seemed to many, the natural choice. Brame had joined the Tacoma police department in 1981, following his father and brother onto the force (another brother still works for the Pierce County sheriff's office). In fact, Brame liked to joke, "Tacoma hired us on the family plan. It was cheaper that way."

But the handsome Brame had achieved far more than any of his relatives. Brame moved up the ladder because he knew how to massage egos; politicians praised him and newspaper people wrote that Brame seemed like a breath of fresh air. He was even a vice president of Police Union Local 6 and they went to bat for him, let-ting Corpuz know that he was their guy. (In fairness, the union later told Corpuz that they would support Ste-phens as well but by that time Brame was the front-runner.) The rumor is that Local 6 only threw their sup-port to Brame because, a couple of years earlier, he helped them get a big raise for their members. How big? Mary Brown said it was equivalent to a "blank check."

Brame and Stephens were the two contenders left standing and, after a final round of answering questions from the public, Corpuz in December 2001 interviewed both men one-on-one. Brame was the ultimate insider who knew Tacoma and how it operated while Stephens was the outsider. He had impeccable credentials but Corpuz did not know him very well. And Corpuz once before had picked an outsider for the chief's job: Phillip Areola, the former police chief of Milwaukee. The choice was a disaster. Areola got into public shouting matches with police officers—most notably Bill Meeks—

and even remarked publicly that the department was filled with corruption. The situation was so bad it was close to boiling over. After Meeks spoke out against some police budget cuts at a public forum, Areola jerked him off the podium and told him, "I'm taking you to the woodshed." The media lapped it up and Areola later confided that the public attention led to his ouster as chief.

Corpuz was wary of making that mistake twice but Patrick Stephens seemed like an outstanding choice, though less popular than Brame.

Corpuz was intrigued but had a question. He asked Stephens what he would do with Brame if Stephens got the nod. His answer was simple: Brame would have to go. Stephens correctly saw that the Tacoma PD was filled with internal bickering and he wouldn't leave his chief rival in place to undermine his authority. Yes sir, Stephens said, if he got the top job, Brame was a goner.

That was a difficult answer for Corpuz. David Brame was the popular choice—the newspaper loved him and had named Brame one of its top twenty people to watch in the South Sound. Should he be fired through no fault of his own, after all the good work he'd done?

Just a day or two before Corpuz was to make the final decision he received a visit from Mary Brown. She had news from a high-ranking police officer who had told Brown that Brame's marriage was rife with problems of domestic violence. The officer refused to be identified.

"Do you have any proof?" Corpuz asked.

"No," Brown said.

"Okay," he said, and that was that. He would not derail such an important choice because of an anonymous tip.

Corpuz decided that he could not choose Stephens because then he'd have a new mess on his hands—the firing of David Brame, the hometown hero.

That was too high a price to pay, so Corpuz chose

Brame. On January 16, 2002, Corpuz sent David Brame "a conditional offer of employment" to become Tacoma's next police chief at a "starting annual salary of $132,412.80, $63.66 per hour." The condition was that Brame had to move within Tacoma city limits by June 2003.

Why did Ray Corpuz ultimately pick David Brame? Corpuz' words provide the best insight into his thought process. In the press release naming Brame, Corpuz referred to him as "a trusted insider" and later told a crowd that picking Brame was "a natural choice, a comfortable choice for me." A lot of people thought Corpuz went with the safe choice, the cop who knew the way things worked in Tacoma.

12

Hail to the Chief

And so on January 17, 2002, some three hundred friends, family, cops and retired chiefs gathered in the Tacoma Dome to celebrate what many saw as the "coronation" of a hometown hero. When David Brame got up to speak, few had any doubts that this indeed was the right man. That day, David Brame looked like a million bucks. His uniform was bedecked with three stars on each shoulder epaulet and those shoulders were broad. As handsome as he was, he looked like he could literally carry the city on his back.

"There's absolutely nothing wrong with the Tacoma police department that cannot be fixed by what's right with the Tacoma police department," Brame told the eager crowd. "And what is right with the Tacoma police department are the working men and women that give it their all, shift in and shift out."

Crystal and her family, who were used to a much more subdued Brame, were astonished at how gregarious he appeared. The David they knew barely spoke to them. On Christmas and birthdays, he would barely say hello to his in-laws before disappearing into another room to either close his eyes or stare off into space. Anything, it seemed, rather than talk to them. Julie Ahrens joked that she wanted to go to the ceremony to hear what his voice sounded like. Crystal's godmother, Judy Hellstrom, said, "I couldn't believe it. I was amazed and thought he was just an awesome speaker. I mean he didn't talk when we were together. We pretty much never heard anything from him."

Indeed, Brame came off like *The Natural;* everything he did and said was on point. He even turned to Crystal and his two children, who were onstage, and said, "They're my bookends. They keep me up. They're my anchors; they keep me well-grounded in life."

It was an impressive performance by a man at the top of his game. It was all coming together for David Brame and he knew it. He gave a good speech, said all the right things and left everyone with a warm feeling.

And then, after all the speeches and the ceremonial matters, the moment came for Crystal to pin the chief's badge on her husband. Everyone watched as Crystal, looking prim and proper in a blue suit, reached up to her much taller husband and pinned the badge to his chest. The only problem was, she couldn't do it. There was an uncomfortable shifting of seats as Crystal fumbled badly while she tried to pin the badge on him. It might have been nerves or it might have been something else—a subconscious signal, perhaps, that appearances could be deceiving and that Crystal thought everything onstage was a lie.

Seated nearby was Crystal's mother, Patty Judson. She was not at all surprised that Crystal was having so much trouble pinning the badge on Brame because, Patty says, the truth was almost too much to bear. "It hurt me to see them up there looking like a happy couple. I knew better."

After what seemed like an eternity, Crystal got the badge on Brame, they exchanged a brief kiss and the band played on.

A few moments later, Crystal got a nice surprise of her own. Catherine Woodard, Tacoma's new assistant chief, strode to the podium with a bouquet of flowers. "Behind every successful man is a successful woman," Woodard said, handing the flowers to Crystal, who was clearly charmed. She later sent Woodard a note thanking her profusely for the white roses "and speech of recognition you gave. I appreciated it more than you know! . . . All your special *touches* were *noticed* and *greatly appreciated* [Crystal's emphasis]."

Crystal genuinely looked happy and Brame picked up his son, David Jr., who spoke into the microphone: "Thank you."

The scene could have been a Norman Rockwell painting: a happy American family at the pinnacle of success. A handsome husband and father, a pretty wife and mother and two gorgeous and well-behaved kids, one boy, one girl, on a stage in front of adoring family and friends. Crystal confessed to her parents and sister that, now that everything was going so well for Brame at work, she hoped he'd become the husband and father he'd never been. David Ahrens, Crystal's brother-in-law, put it best: "She didn't want to say it but she was hoping he'd become more human."

Just a few miles from the Tacoma Dome, a woman watched with astonishment the ceremony playing out on her television set. Sally Masters (not her real name), a slim forty-five-year-old schoolteacher, simply could not believe it. Masters and David Brame had once been friends but that was a long time ago. Their friendship had ended badly and now, looking at her TV screen, she could barely comprehend how the man she knew had somehow been appointed the city's new police chief. She considered driving down to the Tacoma Dome to make a public scene, to tell all she knew about David Brame. But the more she watched his speech, the more she realized that no one would believe her, and she didn't want to be put into that position yet again. She didn't need it. She'd rebuilt her life and didn't need to drag David Brame back into it. Truth is, she was afraid of Brame. Just a couple of months before, he'd appeared at the Starbucks where Sally bought coffee each morning. She'd turned around to see him in line a few people behind her; he didn't say a word but their eyes caught for a moment and it was chilling. No, Sally didn't need Brame back in her life, especially now that he was more powerful than ever.

She knew she was in a minority. All of Tacoma seemed in love with David Brame, so pleased that this native son had gotten the top police job. She wondered if a man could truly change—or was he living a sordid private life that was hidden? Sally turned to the television again, but this time her eyes locked not on Brame but on Crystal. What was it like to be her? She didn't look happy pinning that badge on. She looked nervous, scared. I wish I could help her, Sally thought. Maybe she's the one I should reach out for. She'd listen. She knows. I can tell by looking at her.

But Sally knew she'd never have the courage to do that, at least not at the point she was at now. Her time would come; she'd work up the nerve to take on David Brame, but not yet.

She punched the remote, shutting off the TV, and picked up her guitar. Now she tried one more time to write the song she was sure would release her demons. The words weren't coming, so she picked up her acoustic guitar and strummed the tune. It was a quiet, sad tune. She thought someday she might be able to finish writing the way she felt about David Brame but the words did not come this night, just as they had not come for a long, long time.

David Brame had won again, she thought. He always wins.

1 3

The Godfather

A lot of men are obsessed with the classic film *The Godfather,* the ultimate testosterone story of men who live by a twisted code of honor and do what men must. If you cross the line, well, you might end up like Moe Greene with a bullet square in the eye. It's not unusual to hear grown men who can't quote a single line of Shakespeare recite the movie's key lines verbatim, lines uttered more than thirty years ago by Marlon Brando and Al Pacino. David Brame was one of those guys.

"Brame was kind of obsessed with *The Godfather* movie. He talked about the movie a lot. He could quote from it and used it in our bargaining, our union stuff," said Tacoma police detective Barry McColeman. "I could never remember that kind of shit. I couldn't even remember who the different guys were or the characters' names but D. A., he was obsessed."

Given Brame's interest in the film, McColeman, long considered one of Brame's "guys," decided that a nice present for the new chief would be an autographed photo of Michael Corleone. He searched the Internet and found a photograph, allegedly signed by actor Al Pacino, who of course played Michael, the youngest Corleone. McColeman spent $75 on the present and then asked his wife to get it framed.

McColeman, who started in the Washington State Criminal Justice Training Academy in 1981, the same year as Brame, said the newly minted chief was so happy with the gift that he hung it in his office. A lot of cops wondered about the propriety of a police chief idolizing a gangster, even a fictional one, but Brame didn't care what anyone thought. He was living out his fantasy and was about to take care of his enemies nearly as ruthlessly as Michael Corleone. Sometimes he even watched the movies in his office; he had two complete sets of all three *Godfather* movies in his desk.

The Tacoma police department, like every police department in the United States, had its share of cliques but in Tacoma, they were called "racing teams" or "swimming teams." Brame's men were known as the Davidians or D. A.'s Team. Aside from McColeman, Brame had Assistant Chief Catherine Woodard on his team, as well as his closest buddy on the force, Captain William (Bill) Meeks, the beefy former college football player nicknamed "Meatball."

David Brame's rivals were known as the Meinemites, the Mount Tahoma Mafia, the Mine-Mines or simply the Dark Side, as Brame himself called them. Police Captain Charles Meinema, who detested Brame, led them—informally, of course. He had seen for years how Brame treated his enemies and he knew that Brame led by "intimidation." Asked in a deposition to describe Brame's management style—and this deposition was taken *before* Brame became chief—Meinema recalled it as being "domineering, tyrannical, bullying." Meinema's men included "Iron Mike" Darland, a deputy chief. Darland was admired by many in the department and he would have made a perfect police chief except for Ray Corpuz. It was thought within the department that Darland would have been too much of a threat to Corpuz, so

Corpuz neatly put the brakes on Darland's ambition. Corpuz made a college degree a requirement for the job; Darland had only graduated from high school. Eventually Darland retired after he decided he could not continue under Brame's dictatorial rule. He was killed in May 2003 when he apparently had a stroke while on his motorcycle. His death was a morale-crusher to a lot of Tacoma cops because "Iron Mike" was a beloved figure.

The intense dislike these two groups had for each other was palpable, and if you were on one side, you were against the other. It sounds incredibly juvenile, or like the Jets and the Sharks from the movie *West Side Story,* but the two camps of cops were not joking. In 1999 Police Lieutenant Joe Kirby, a Meinemite, went so far as to sue the city of Tacoma for employment discrimination. In his $10 million lawsuit, he enumerated some very nasty rumors about Brame and Corpuz, charges that were to take on new meaning after April 26, 2003. Kirby was a close confidant of John Hathaway's, so it was no surprise that as David Brame eventually began to crumble, Hathaway was there every step of the way with one damaging story after another.

But that was still more than a year away. At this point, in January 2002, David Brame's rule was at full throttle and the Meinemites were worried.

Brame liked to say, "If you're not on my side, you're the enemy," and that wasn't just an idle threat. One of the holdover assistant chiefs when Brame took over was Ray Roberts, a well-liked veteran of the department. Roberts had a lot of friends but Brame wasn't one of them; he wanted his own team in place and Roberts was from the previous administration. But the greatest sin Roberts had committed—at least in Brame's estimation— was when Roberts submitted his name for the chief's job. Whatever other reasons Brame had for disliking him, this one was fatal. Roberts had to go. Brame called him in and bluntly asked him about his career goals.

Just as bluntly, Roberts, a twenty-nine-year-plus veteran, said, "Put in thirty years and leave with my head up."

Roberts had a paraplegic son in college and wanted to get the largest pension possible; that was triggered by serving thirty years on the job and Roberts already had more than twenty-nine years in. Reaching his goal was just a matter of time—and not much time at that. Brame nodded and the talk moved on to something else. But then, a few weeks later, Brame again called Roberts in and this time the boss had something to say.

"I'm demoting you to captain effective August fifth," Brame said.

The date was significant; it was one month before his thirty-year anniversary. Brame was letting him know who was in charge. Roberts could hang around and get his thirty years but it would cost him in pride and money. If he retired as a captain, his overall pension would be reduced by a total of $200,000. If he left immediately, he would not get his thirty years in and he'd not be eligible for an upcoming 8 percent pay raise. It was a point of pride because no cop wants to leave 30 days short of such an important milestone.

Brame didn't give Roberts any reasons for the demotion so Roberts had to ask.

"Why?"

"Because I can."

It was a chilling moment, worthy of Michael Corleone himself. Brame had vanquished an enemy and spit in his eye besides. Roberts took the hit and retired before getting his thirty years in; he missed out on the 8 percent pay raise but, by leaving before being demoted, he made sure his pension wasn't $200,000 lighter. It was a bitter ending to a career he had loved and devoted his entire adult life to. Brame got what he wanted—Roberts was out the door and no longer could be a rival.

Soon enough, "Iron Mike" Darland followed Roberts

out the door. He retired on his own, telling friends, "I can't look guys in the eyes anymore. I keep seeing all this going on, good police officers being screwed because they weren't blind or obedient to Dave Brame."

The public, of course, never saw this side of Brame. Early on in his tenure, the Tacoma *News Tribune* interviewed Gene Brame, David's father. He was hardly a neutral observer but what he said was echoed by much of the public—and in the newspaper's editorials—soon after Brame took over as chief. "He is the best-liked and loved police chief that Tacoma has had for a number of years," the elder Brame said. "David's overall plan was to have the most wonderful police department in this nation and he was well on his way to doing that."

There's no doubt that, in the public's eyes, Brame was the right choice at the right time. For the first time in many years, Tacomans were feeling good about their city. The new Museum Mile downtown was nearly complete and things were looking up. There was almost a giddy excitement about Brame and the future. With a hometown boy in charge, everything seemed in place for Tacoma's long-awaited renewal. Weeks after Brame's appointment as chief, voters on February 4 passed a $34.3 million bond measure to build four police substations and a new headquarters.

"Thank you, citizens of Tacoma," Brame said in a press release. "It's beyond our wildest dreams."

In October 2002, Chief Brame even had a moment on the national evening news broadcasts. It seems the snipers who had terrorized Washington DC, John Allen Muhammad and Lee Boyd Malvo, had practiced their deadly craft in the backyard of a Tacoma home. The national news media was voracious for any angle on that story and descended on Tacoma to see what they could learn. Chief Brame held a press conference to announce that, thanks to ballistics, Muhammad and Malvo now were suspects in a previous killing in Tacoma and also may have used their weapons to vandalize a synagogue. The murder victim was a twenty-one-year-old mother who died of a single gunshot wound to the head.

Chief Brame again managed to come off as the man in charge at the press conference. "Although the suspects are in custody," he said, "we believe it is very important to bring closure to this case and to the Cook family."

But no one knew what was going on behind the scenes until the Tacoma *News Tribune* later reported that Brame had actually dropped the ball on one key aspect of the story. Aides suggested that Brame check police reports to see whether shots had been fired in or around the house Muhammad and Malvo reportedly lived in. Brame said he would check the next day and had no answers for reporters' questions. At the same time Brame was saying he knew nothing, neighbors of the men in Tacoma were going on national TV saying they had reported that someone had been firing a high-powered gun in the area well before the snipers went on their deadly spree of violence. But that was not reported until much later. At the time, Chief Brame just looked like the golden boy once again.

He was a man on the move, pushing his agenda forward. He created a Professional Responsibility Bureau to oversee internal affairs investigations and soon after, he formed an auto theft task force to stop the rash of auto thefts afflicting Tacoma. "We've got to get it on," the dashing new chief told the newspapers. Soon after, Brame's newly created task force busted two groups of car thieves linked to hundreds of thefts. Editorial writers at the *News Tribune* were impressed: "[These initiatives] show imagination and a refreshing willingness by the new chief to do what it takes to improve the department's performance."

Within the department, however, David Brame's vindictive actions against his enemies had everyone on edge, and subordinates complained privately how "arrogant" he was. On the home front, Crystal practically wept when she read what a good job her husband was doing.

The Gatekeeper

Besides Crystal, and of course Beverly Brame, there was one more woman who got to know Chief David Brame better than anyone, and that was Jeanette Blackwell, the chief's administrative assistant. Blackwell, a forty-something African American woman, had been serving chiefs in that position since 1996. She was the gatekeeper to the police chief, sitting right outside his office door. But the truth was, she was much more than that. "She ran that department," said one investigator from a different agency. Blackwell worked for at least two chiefs other than Brame, so she had something to compare him to—and what she saw, she didn't like. She had never seen a police chief behave the way Brame did. For starters, she felt that Brame's public persona was just a big act.

"He led people to believe that he was very, very humble," Blackwell said. "I had believed him also until I was working with him very closely and realized how arrogant he was. He would refer to small town chiefs [who were visiting for a conference] as 'just lucky dogs.' He'd say 'They're not really chiefs, they're just lucky dogs.'

He had no respect for them. It was very embarrassing, very horrible."

At the same time, Blackwell said, Brame put on airs to convince people he was still the hometown hero. "He didn't want people to call him 'chief.' He'd said, 'I'm still D. A. I grew up here.'"

But Blackwell was observing Brame close-up, and she especially took note of the way he treated the two secretaries who worked for her in the police chief's office. "He didn't even acknowledge them. They had pretty much no relationship. He acknowledged them when he walked in the door but that was it. They're here and that's where they're gonna stay. It was very uncomfortable."

And Blackwell soon learned more about David Brame than she ever wanted to: Brame constantly used her as a sounding board for personal issues. It seemed that achieving his lifelong dream job offered no respite from his contentious marriage. She said his feelings toward Crystal fluctuated wildly. "One day he'd say, 'She's crazy and she's been crazy from day one,' and the next day he'd say, 'She's the love of my life.'" Brame told Blackwell early on that he was going to be getting a lot of calls from his wife, and indeed he did. "Crystal was a talker, that's for sure. She'd keep me on the phone for twenty minutes every time she called, just talking about her kids and what she was gonna do that day.

"He talked about how abusive she was towards the kids and how she cussed them out every single morning and that he was the real buffer," Blackwell remembered. "There were several days that he would come into his office and call me in there and he'd say, 'Close the door. I've just got to wind down. Rough morning at home.' And then he'd tell me, 'I physically had to shield Haley this morning 'cause she's [Crystal] swiping at her with the brush and trying to hit her.' It was very important for him to relay any kind of morning issues that they had."

Blackwell certainly didn't take what Brame said at face value; she'd seen firsthand how Brame operated and the way he manipulated those who worked under him. But still, she did have some doubts about Crystal. More than once, she told investigators, "I heard it with my own ears. One of her kids would call—usually her daughter—and Crystal would be screaming and yelling in the background."

On other occasions, Brame would go out of his way to praise Crystal to Blackwell, telling his assistant just how good Crystal looked in a bikini. "She was his beauty queen, you know, she was just gorgeous," Blackwell said, practically wincing at some of his stories. She repeated them to illustrate just how mixed Brame's feelings were for his wife. "He shared some of their lovemaking stories and how she got on his nerves. He said they were being intimate one time and she just talked so much. She kept talking, talking, talking and he just got up and walked away. I believe he said, 'I was erect and just got up and threw my clothes on and said, "I can't do this." ' And she didn't miss a beat and kept talking, talking, talking . . ."

Blackwell couldn't believe what she was hearing and told Brame to respect her boundaries, that there were some aspects of his life that she just did not want to hear about.

David Brame had a Jekyll and Hyde personality but not many people saw both sides; he was delightfully charming to some, diabolically evil to others.

At this point in his life, he still had his Hyde side under control and, publicly at least, Brame was saying all the right things as the city's new police chief. In February 2002, just a month after being appointed chief, he issued his "Mission, Vision and Values Statement" for the police department espousing "honesty, integrity and ethical behavior, compassion and empathy, respect for the law, accountability in all actions and dignity for all persons."

His memos were full of good intentions that seem all the more hollow given the way he was behaving at home. Consider this gem from an April 2002 memo on community policing: "Understand that happiness is not based on possessions, power or prestige but on relationships with people you love and respect. Successful people are loyal, honest, and self-starters . . . take responsibility for every area of your life. Be bold and courageous. When you look back on your life, you'll regret the things you didn't do more than the ones you did."

Clearly, Brame was a tortured man because he knew—even if almost no one else did at that point— what a contradictory life he was leading.

Back on Eagle Creek Lane, life was getting progressively harder for Crystal. If she'd had any hope that Brame might grow more "human" with his ascension to chief, those hopes were soon dashed.

He claimed to love and respect his wife and kids but he seemed to have forgotten how to show it; instead, he bathed in the accolades that poured in for the allegedly great job he was doing. At the 2002 Daffodil Parade, Brame was an honorary grand marshal and spent the day waving at residents cheering him on. His ego was getting bigger and bigger but he was getting none of that adulation at home; the arguments between him and Crystal were growing more and more violent. Just days after the parade, not long after he issued that departmental memo about honoring relationships with the people "you love and respect," Crystal told friends that they'd gotten into a horrendous fight.

He had decided that she was having an affair. (In fact, he once described to Blackwell how he had caught Crystal in bed with another man "who had much bigger equipment," but that story appears to have been a figment of his overactive sexual imagination.) Crystal told her family that Brame pushed her against the back wall of the bedroom's walk-in closet and began choking her until she started gasping for breath. Brame caught himself before going too far.

The next day—April 24—was Crystal's thirty-fourth birthday. She was blown away when she answered the door and found a deliveryman carrying flowers. She opened the card and read, "From your secret admirer."

"Crystal didn't have a secret admirer," Lane Judson said sometime later. "Those flowers were from Brame. He was playing games just like he always did."

One of the other games Brame apparently liked to play also was on Crystal's birthday. He had gotten into the habit of buying her a limited edition lithograph by Thomas Kinkade, the Christian artist who specializes in inspirational paintings of landscapes that illustrate his "world of beauty, peace and hope." Brame knew that Crystal did not care much for the artist but *he* liked him, so what did it matter what she thought? Brame liked the way they looked in the house on Eagle Creek Lane and over the years, it filled up with Kinkades.

On April 24 he came home and berated Crystal once more for her alleged affair, and they got into yet another argument. The very same scenario played itself out four times in 2002, according to Crystal's divorce papers. Crystal and Brame would get into a horrible fight, he'd choke her and the next day, flowers from "a secret admirer" would appear. Crystal never called 911 nor did she report Brame. He was now in the most powerful position he'd ever held and her parents believe she held back for two reasons: she didn't want to get Brame in any trouble that could hurt his career—he'd warned her many times about that earlier 911 call—and she was afraid that no one would believe her because, for all intents and purposes, Brame now *was* the police, at least in Tacoma.

*　　*　　*

Brame was especially busy his first year in office but not always with official duties. When he wasn't berating Crystal or issuing official pronouncements, he was using up a lot of energy putting out sexual feelers to the women he came in contact with each day. He'd tried talking about sex with Blackwell and had been rejected outright. He next tried to see how far he could go with Gwen Kopetzky, a recent divorcée who worked as the personal secretary to City Manager Ray Corpuz. Kopetzky, it turned out, had an interest in law enforcement and one day approached Brame for his help.

"Chief, I was wondering if you could set up a ride-along for me. I hear all about police work all the time and I'm curious to see what it's like on the front lines," Kopetzky told him.

She later told investigators that she truly was just being friendly and curious but Brame no doubt saw opportunity knocking.

BRAME: No problem, I can help you out with that. How about Friday night?

KOPETZKY: That sounds good.

BRAME: I'll have one of the guys show you around but I want you to do me a favor.

KOPETZKY: Sure.

BRAME: I want you to page me when you're done. I'd like to hear how it went, all right?

KOPETZKY: Sure, but it might be late.

BRAME: That's okay.

KOPETZKY: You sure I won't be interrupting if I call after ten? You might be doing something with Crystal and the kids.

BRAME: Don't you worry about that. Just page me, even if it's midnight. Maybe we can have coffee or something, all right?

Kopetzky didn't want to alienate him but she thought he was acting strangely. She agreed to page him even though she had no intention of doing so. She'd make up some excuse.

The next Monday, Kopetzky walked into an executive forum, an important government meeting with a lot of people. She knew Chief Brame would be there but didn't really give her snub on Friday night a second thought. She thought he'd just let it go.

But she figured wrong. Within minutes of her arrival, an angry-looking Brame was at her side.

"What happened Friday night?" he demanded.

"Nothing. The ride-along was great. It was really interesting. We stopped a drunk driver . . ."

But Brame wasn't interested in hearing about mundane police work. "That's not what I'm talking about. Why didn't you page me afterwards?"

"Well, you know, it was late for you and your family and I had other plans. I'm sorry. I didn't think it was that big a deal."

"I was looking forward to hearing about it. Look, I'm busy now but what if we have lunch later this week, say Wednesday, okay? You owe me."

"Okay."

A couple of days later, they met for lunch at the restaurant on the second floor of the downtown Sheraton Hotel. Even in Tacoma, there were far better places to eat lunch, but Brame knew that on the floors above them were hundreds of rooms with beds. He might get lucky, you never knew.

"If people were to see us here having lunch," he told Kopetzky, "they might assume we were having an affair."

Kopetzky didn't like the way the conversation was going and didn't respond.

"They couldn't prove it. We could just say we were here having coffee," he continued.

Kopetzky later told friends that Brame wouldn't let it go and that his comments were getting more and more "inappropriate." She resolved to herself never to be alone with Brame again.

The chief was not happy. He had all this power and was beloved by at least some of his men but he wasn't getting anywhere with the opposite sex. He was fighting with Crystal all the time, his secretary thought he was rude and arrogant and now another secretary had rejected him. But he wasn't giving up so easy. He had his eye on a female officer in the department who was so attractive, so sweet, so womanly, so perfect.

"You'll Have the Time of Your Life"

David Brame first noticed Linda Watson (not her real name) back in December 2001 when they were both working out of the substation on Thirty-eighth Street. He was an assistant chief on the cusp of being named chief of the department and Watson was a patrol officer working out of the same building. She had joined the department back in 1993 but Brame had never really sized her up, not like he did on this day. Watson, sort of a Sandra Bullock type, is, in the eyes of many, one of the most attractive women in the department. "She's not like a lot of other female cops," says one investigator. "She hasn't grown hard and clipped her hair real short."

Like Crystal, Watson is a brunette with shoulder-length hair, and Brame seemed to have a thing for brunettes. She's five feet nine inches tall but she looks even taller because she has long legs and is "well-endowed," as one cop said. Men notice when she walks into a room. Even Assistant Chief Catherine Woodard would later remark, "She had what Brame wanted."

And he set out to get it but, as usual, his approach was anything but smooth.

"One day I was coming down the hallway," Officer

Watson remembers, "and his door was open and he saw me and he hollered out my name. I backed up thinking, 'Oh my God, what did I do?' I had never had any contact with the guy except for pleasantries. I mean none. And he asked me into his office and he told me, 'Close the door.' "

Watson was nervous and thought she was going to get chewed out for something she'd overlooked.

"So I hear you're studying for the detective position," Brame said.

"Yes, well, I'm trying anyway. I mean it's a priority but it's hard to find the time to study. I'm a single mother."

"You have kids?"

"Just one, a daughter. She's six."

He smiled at her and she remembers thinking that he seemed genuine and nice. "Got a couple of my own. Seven and four. They're a handful at that age."

"Yeah, I know what you mean."

"So how are you studying for the test? I mean what method are you using?"

She shrugged. "I have things written on recipe cards. The old-fashioned way, I guess. I mean, I'm making it a point to study real hard. It's my goal to do well on the test."

"If you need any help, I have a computer program that I've used and it really helped me."

"Thanks, it sounds interesting."

Brame was being nice but . . . Watson later acknowledged that she was thrown by the whole conversation. She wondered about the attention. She knew men; they'd been all over her her whole life, and she later told someone that she had Brame pegged as "just another horny guy." But that was later. Right now, she was still sitting in front of him trying to figure him out when he suddenly shifted gears.

"What are your long-term goals in the department?"

"Right now I know I'd like to make detective and stay on days for my daughter's sake. After that, I'm not real sure."

"We talked a little more," Watson said later, "but he seemed nervous and said that if I was interested in talking anymore about the study process to get ahold of him. I thanked him . . . and that was the end of that."

She thought it was a bit odd that Brame was offering to help her out of the blue but thought maybe he was just being nice. Still, she asked a coworker what he thought of the conversation, if he thought she should take the assistant chief up on his offer. "He said, 'Absolutely,'" Watson remembered. "'No one has risen through the ranks faster than David Brame. If he has any advice to give you, take it.'"

Watson set up a meeting on one of her days off to talk about the test and arranged to meet Brame at the café inside Nordstrom's department store at the Tacoma Mall. She was a little uneasy about the meeting because it was nowhere near where they worked, but it set her mind at ease when she showed up that day and Brame was there with another captain. "I knew then it was just all on the up-and-up."

Watson recalls the conversation being "nice" but in retrospect, one thing struck her: "Brame did 99 percent of the talking." But he encouraged her and told her about his own experiences and how he had failed one test but kept persevering. She came away impressed, thinking he was a real professional who wanted to help people in his department. The whole conversation was about what he could do to help her, and he never asked her a single personal question other than some inane thing about her Christmas shopping.

Watson couldn't know that Brame had already targeted her as someone nonthreatening enough to his wife that maybe this time Crystal would sanction Brame's long-stated desire for some group sex. He greatly wanted to get Crystal and Watson together and apparently, just by chance, the two women met for the first time in November 2002 in the Tacoma Mall parking lot. Watson was on patrol in her police cruiser, working on some reports with her head down. When she looked up, there was David Brame standing just outside her patrol car window with his young son up on his shoulders.

Watson lowered her window.

"Hi," he said. "We were just doing a little shopping and I spotted you in your car. This is my wife, Crystal, my daughter, Haley, and this guy up here, that's David. Say hello, David."

"Hi."

"Hi there," Crystal said. She held up the bag she was holding. "Big sale today at Nordstrom's. Have you been?"

Watson chuckled. "Not on duty, ma'am."

They all laughed at her little joke.

"The little girl was looking into my car and staring at me. She looked a little bit shy," Watson said later, recalling the event.

"So . . . do you want to be a police officer like your dad when you grow up?" Watson asked Haley.

"I don't know. Maybe."

"Well, I hope so, because if you do then maybe me and you can eat donuts together. I know a really good place the other cops don't know about."

Haley giggled.

At that point, Watson thought they were a nice-looking family and that Brame was a supernice guy and had all the earmarks of becoming a great chief. "And that was it. It was a nice contact and they left and that was it."

But that wasn't it for Brame. According to Crystal's friend Debbie Phillips, Brame began asking Crystal about Watson every chance he got. " 'What do you think of her? Did you like her?' You know, that kind of thing," Phillips said. "She always put him off. I remember she said, 'David, why am I not enough for you?'"

Brame, meanwhile, was working on Watson to see what she thought of the idea of the three of them getting together. Another opportunity presented itself when Watson asked to see Brame about some shift changes that were coming up. At that point, Watson was on the day shift and had heard that she might be put onto the graveyard or overnight shift. With a six-year-old daughter, it would be tough to find babysitting and be as much a part of her daughter's life as she wanted to. Brame had been friendly to her and he was now chief. Maybe he could do her a favor; she decided to talk to him about her problem. She called Jeanette Blackwell and asked if she could see Brame for ten minutes. Blackwell gave her an appointment that would have taken place in two weeks' time. But Watson didn't have to wait that long, not at all.

"About half an hour later I got a page from her and it said, 'The chief can see you in his office immediately.'"

Watson went in and laid out her case, asking for any insight he might have. Brame listened to her but at the end, he moved his chair closer to her. She was getting nervous because the ever-vigilant Blackwell had told her the chief only had ten minutes for her before his next meeting, but here he was, acting like he had all the time in the world. "He puts his hands behind his head and he says, 'So what do you like to do with your off time?'"

Watson was nervous and talked about her daughter some more. She was getting increasingly antsy when Brame began talking about how he had season tickets to a local theater and there were times now and again when he couldn't use them.

"If we're ever unable to use them, I'll give you a call and pass them on to you."

"That's really generous. I appreciate that."

Brame seemed not to notice Watson's eagerness to

get out of his office, or more likely didn't care. "You know, Linda, I think you're gonna do really well in this department. I think you're gonna go far. But what you have to know, if you really wanna get far, are the Twelve Steps to Success."

Brame pointed to a poster he kept on the wall. Watson was practically rolling her eyes about the Hallmark-card quality of his "advice" but didn't want to upset him. She forced herself to sit still while he began reading the poster aloud.

"He starts to read each of these Twelve Steps to Success and after every step, he'd read the first one, he'd comment on it. I'm getting really worried 'cause I'm in there about a half hour now and his secretary said he had another appointment."

Watson didn't know it but Brame had all the courage of a high school boy asking a girl to go for a walk. He was building up to something, screwing up his courage, until he finally asked her out to lunch.

"You know, I have some information about the test that you may find useful. Maybe we can have lunch sometime."

She wondered why he just didn't tell her the information that moment and instead made a little joke: "Even the chief has to eat." She gave the chief her cell phone number, and they made a date to eat lunch the following week at a restaurant on Puget Sound with the perfect name for what Brame had in mind—Shenanigan's.

Watson was off the day she had arranged to have lunch with the chief; she had dropped her daughter off at school and had a few hours to kill before picking her up. Brame thought that would be the perfect time to sound her out about his desires. She had no idea what was coming.

"So we go sit down. The server seats us at the table and he asked to be moved to another one that was quieter. I should have known right then," Watson said.

She was very nervous, especially because Brame was so quiet. Watson tried to fill in the conversation gaps, asking Brame about his Thanksgiving plans and if he had thought much about her child care problem, if perhaps he had any new information to give her. She didn't think so but she was hopeful. "He had really no additional information," she says. "And then the whole thing just kind of took a shift."

"So tell me what you like to do on your off time."

Weird, Watson thought. Didn't we just have the exact same conversation last week?

He didn't wait for her answer.

"Well, let *me* tell you what you like to do. Let me tell you about *you*."

Watson was growing exceedingly uncomfortable as Brame began to reel off personal information about her. But Brame either didn't notice her discomfort or, more likely, didn't care. He kept going, telling her not only where she went to high school but also where she worked before she started in the police department. It was clear he'd been reading her personnel file in detail, but then he added something that was not in her file.

"Let's see, last year you celebrated your thirtieth birthday by attending cooking school in New York."

He smiled and looked very satisfied. Watson remembers being very shaken; Brame had gone well beyond just reading her file. He'd been spying on her, talking to people who knew her. What's more, she couldn't understand why he was telling her all of this. She thought he probably was trying to flatter her with attention but he was coming across as kind of a weird stalker.

"You know, Crystal and I talked about you after we ran into you at the mall that day," Brame said.

"Oh?"

"Yeah, she thought you were attractive and seemed nice and, well, I guess I agree with her. She thought you might be the kind of person she'd like to get to know better. I was thinking that maybe we could all go to the Fifth Avenue Theatre some night and maybe have dinner."

"Your wife doesn't want a third wheel."

"That's where you might be surprised. I know she looks like the typical wife but she has a wild side. She likes to try new things. I think you and she have a lot in common.

"You know," Brame continued, "Crystal and I have fantasized about bringing someone else into our bed. We've talked about having a threesome and we both thought you might be interested. You can get to know her a little better if you like. It's been a fantasy we've always had but we've never acted on it."

Watson, to say the least, was floored. She remembers being shocked, not just about what Brame was saying but the way he was saying it. "He laid the whole threesome thing on the table. It was like it was a business plan.

"I was stunned and I was so uncomfortable," she says. "I mean, how do you respond to that?"

She responded by sliding out of the booth and putting on her jacket. "It's about time for me to go pick up my daughter."

"That's fine, but now you keep that detective's position in mind."

That's when Watson knew exactly what Brame was saying. "It all became very clear."

At that point, Watson had taken the detective test and finished second among the test-takers; however, Brame had the option of picking any one of the top three finishers for the job that was open. It was clear from what Brame was now telling her that, if she went along with what he wanted, the job was hers. Brame had put the carrot in front of her and made her reward very clear.

Watson was shaken. She was dazed as she stumbled out of the restaurant into the sunshine, and the smell of the water nearly made her puke. "I went right out to my car and got on my cell phone and I called my mom. And I said, 'You are not going to believe what just happened.' And I filled her in on the whole thing. I couldn't believe it."

Watson remembered something else Brame had told her the day he was going through the Twelve Steps to Success with her. He'd mentioned that he only wanted people in the department who were loyal, and if someone crossed him, he would make sure they paid for it. And with her looming child care problems and desire to avoid the overnight shift, Watson had given Brame a clear and easy way to punish her. The choice was clear: cooperate with Brame's insane plan to have a three-way with him and Crystal and become a detective, or spend years on the overnight shift away from her daughter.

Watson sought counsel from her mother and then her sister, and finally she told her boyfriend what had happened, asking them to help her figure a way out of the situation. "My mom asked me, 'What are you going to do?' So I reviewed my choices. I considered going to Ray Corpuz but I really did not feel that he would believe me. 'Hey Ray, guess what Chief Brame wants me to do.' It was unbelievable even to me. What everybody thought of this man and what he was suggesting, they were just so opposite.

"And that's when the phone calls started. Nearly every weekend, he would call my house, he would call my cell phone. He would suggest we get together, that I come over to their house. He wanted me to come to Seattle with them, to rent a suite at the Four Seasons for him, his wife and me. I mean it was just every weekend. I would make up lie after lie to get out of it. I took time off from work that I didn't need to take off. I told him I was out of town. I'd take a Friday off. I just tried my best to avoid the whole deal."

Just when Watson thought it couldn't get any worse, it did. She picked up the phone one day because the number on her cell phone read PRIVATE. Of course, it was Brame, who had blocked out his number when he realized she wouldn't take his calls. "He wanted me to talk to his wife. And so his wife got on the phone and we talked very briefly. I actually feigned that I was losing the cell connection just to end the call 'cause it was like, this guy is too freakin' much. I didn't even believe this."

But Brame was persistent and he had Crystal call again. "I always got the impression that he was listening or looking over her as she was conversing. He clearly wanted this deal to happen very badly for whatever reason, whatever his deal was. She always sounded nervous. She was kind of high-strung almost in her conversation, her communications. At the end of the conversations she would always say something, she would toss it in real fast, like 'You know I really hope we can get together. I think it would be a lot of fun.' Something like that and then the conversation would end."

Crystal told Debbie Phillips that the very idea of a three-way was anathema to her Christian upbringing. "And she was, 'No, I'm not gonna go in for threesomes, or wife-swapping, or any of the rest of that,'" Phillips said, quoting Crystal. "And I agreed with her. It's like, 'No, that's not who you are.'"

But Brame didn't notice that both Crystal and Watson were not even lukewarm to his sexual fantasies. He told Detective Barry McColeman that both women were interested.

"Dave said that Crystal was very interested in the threesome. Seemed to make her really hot and it sounded like it was going great guns," McColeman said. "Dave didn't say where or how or anything else but he said he had found someone that was interested in that— a female that was interested in joining in. He said that he'd had several lunches with her and that they had talked about it.

"He said Crystal called this other female and they

seemed to hit it off on the phone okay. And they talked about maybe getting together and going shopping and kind of getting to know each other a little bit."

Watson was so distraught that she stopped answering her phone. Not that it mattered; Brame was her ultimate boss and there was no way to avoid him forever. At the end of 2002, Watson got word that she was indeed being promoted to detective, even though she'd rebuffed Brame at every turn. She breathed a sigh of relief but not for long. Right after she got news of her promotion, Brame ordered Jeanette Blackwell to get Watson on the phone. She did, and patched Watson through. Brame congratulated her and got off the phone in less than a minute. But then the chief buzzed Blackwell.

"I want you to call Detective Watson and ask her what she thought about me calling her," Brame told Blackwell.

Blackwell thought that was weird but rather than come right out and say so, she asked Brame why.

"I want to get a feel for her, how she felt about me just calling her," Brame said.

Blackwell didn't believe what she was hearing. "I just thought, 'What a stupid request.' "

"You're the chief," she told him. "You're gonna make her so nervous. And what am I gonna say to her?"

"Just ask her what she thought about me calling," Brame said.

A minute later, Blackwell called Watson. "Hi, Linda, it's Jeanette."

"Yes?"

"What did you think about Chief Brame calling you?"

Watson didn't say anything. She was sick of Brame but didn't want to start complaining about him to his personal secretary. She had to be very careful what she said, so she didn't say anything. Blackwell could sense that she was uncomfortable with the conversation. "Did I say something wrong?" Blackwell asked.

Again, Watson said nothing for a few uncomfortable minutes. "Well, I guess it was nice. Is he doing this for everybody?" (There were two other officers being promoted along with her.)

"Well, usually the assistant chief calls to say 'Congratulations,' but I guess this time he wanted to do it himself."

"Okay, well, thanks," Watson said. And with that she hung up.

She couldn't shake Brame. Her swearing-in should have been a great day but Watson knew that Brame would attend. In fact, he'd already told her that he planned to bring Crystal to Watson's swearing-in ceremony "because they wanted to watch me and go home and fantasize about positions. He told me—I remember the exact words—'You'll have the time of your life.'"

Watson was living a nightmare and decided that she would not invite anyone—not her family, friends or boyfriend—to her big day. She had told her mother, sister and boyfriend about Brame and didn't want to take a chance that they would react negatively when they met him in person. "I didn't have one single person at my swearing-in ceremony. I didn't have my family, and if anybody knows anything about me, they know how important my daughter and my family are. He took something that should have been probably the proudest moment of my career and it just made it so . . ."

She trailed off, not having to say the obvious. Blackwell was at the ceremony that day and, because of Brame's odd behavior, she had an inkling that something might be going on between Brame and Watson. Blackwell and another acquaintance approached Watson, congratulated her and then asked why her family wasn't there. "And I told them this story that wasn't even true, that my sister had been in a crash and that she had a broken leg and the whole family was there with her."

Watson's boyfriend was getting more and more fed up

with Brame and what he clearly saw as harassment and a violation of Watson's civil rights. "His tolerance level for this wore out real quick and he told me, he said, 'You need to go to an attorney. You need to see somebody. You need to do something.' " But Watson was afraid to do anything. She knew the culture of Brame's police department and knew that once she crossed him, her career would effectively be finished.

In January 2003, Brame traveled to Quantico, Virginia, to attend a two-week training academy at FBI headquarters. Watson was relieved he was leaving Tacoma; maybe she'd get a couple of weeks of peace, clear her head and figure out what to do. Little did she know what Brame was thinking. He'd decided that while he was away, Crystal and Watson would get together, hit it off and the fuse would be lit. Even from Virginia, he browbeat Crystal to call Watson. She told her sister, Julie, about one such conversation.

"I want you to call her," Brame said.

"Screw you," Crystal said. "I'm not calling her."

"I told her you were going to call her," Brame said.

"Why are you doing this? All I want is you."

"Don't blow it," Brame said coldly. "You better call."

Exasperated, Crystal dialed Watson's number but she wasn't home and Crystal left two messages to satisfy Brame that she'd called. But he kept at her and she called again. This time, Watson was home with her boyfriend; they had just finished dinner. There was no way Crystal was going to ask for the favor that Brame wanted. Not that it mattered. Weeks before, Brame had already told Watson about what she calls "his master plan."

"Crystal and I would meet him at the airport, pick him up, bring him downtown, we'd all go out to dinner and go to the Four Seasons with that whole suite deal again. You know, he wanted us to rent a room and have a little fun. He was really pushing her to call me."

When Crystal did get Watson on the phone that night, she didn't know what to say so she rattled on about everything under the sun except the threesome. "She talked for so long about everything. It was, the toilet was broken, the light switch needed repair, one of the kids was sick. The whole thing was getting really ugly to me. It was a bad situation. That's when I really made up my mind, I don't care if this guy gets pissed off. I was so tired of it all."

When Brame returned, Watson ran into him at a meeting and pointedly told him that she was really busy. He backed off and didn't call her again until late February 2003. By then, the events that Brame had set into motion were out of his control.

"Every Man's Fantasy"

By the first week of February 2003, Crystal Brame had had just about enough of her husband.

It was bad enough that David had choked her—several times—in the heat of an argument, but that was only the beginning of the abuse, according to what she was now telling friends and family. Brame, she said, had taken to threatening her life on a daily basis. One night, after yet another fight, she'd refused to sleep in the same bed with Brame and had sought the relative safety of the living room couch. In the middle of the night, however, she awoke to find Brame standing over her, staring down at her.

"David? What are you doing?"

"Let me ask you something, Crystal."

"Yes?"

"Do you think you'd have a heart attack if you woke up and I was standing over you with a mask on and a butcher knife in my hand?"

"Are you crazy?"

"Not as crazy as you."

"I'm going to report you, I swear."

"Go ahead. Who would believe you? I'm the chief of

police, or maybe you forgot that. No one will believe you, Crystal, so you go ahead and do whatever you want."

He smiled, turned and walked back into their bedroom.

All during this time period—from February 2001 to February 2003—Crystal was increasingly on edge, her nerves frayed from the ongoing threats and games. At one point Brame allegedly told Crystal, "It is every man's fantasy to strangle his wife."

Much later, when David Brame's family heard this story, they chalked it up to another of Crystal's delusions. "She said a lot of stuff that wasn't true," Beverly Brame said. It would be easy to dismiss the statements of a grieving mother, except that more than one police investigator told me that they felt Crystal was more than a little prone to exaggeration. It's important to remember that by the time Crystal related these stories, she was getting ready to file for divorce and clearly hated her soon-to-be-ex-husband.

But there is no doubt that David Brame clearly wanted to have a threesome with Crystal and Linda Watson. We know that because of everything Watson told investigators and because of what Brame told his police colleagues.

But Crystal had no idea that Tacoma police detective Linda Watson wanted nothing to do with the idea. Brame had told Crystal that he and Watson were already having sex even without her participation. It was totally untrue but Crystal did not know that, and Watson said nothing about sex during their awkward phone conversations. For all she knew Crystal was agreeable to the idea of a threesome, and Watson was not going to tell the chief's wife that she thought her husband was insane.

It's no wonder that, with all of this going on in Crystal's life, her mother, Patty, thought her daughter "looked sick all the time." She no longer had the erect posture that she'd honed years before in ballet class. These days, she was hunched over and looked afraid and just "miserable," Patty said.

In the weeks leading up to February 2002, Crystal told her parents that she was having severe stomach pains; she had been to the doctor but couldn't figure out the cause. Crystal casually mentioned to her parents that Brame, who normally would not lift a finger to help her, had taken to bringing her a Coke each time she complained. It was totally out of character.

It got Lane to thinking. "So he brings you what, like a can or bottle of Coke when your stomach hurts?"

"No, he brings me the Coke in a glass, one of those blue glasses we got from Tupperware. He's actually kind of sweet about it."

But Lane didn't think it was so sweet; in fact, he didn't think anything about Brame was sweet. He knew too much. "Do you ever see him pour the Coke into the glass?"

"No, he just brings it in when I'm not feeling good."

"How long has this been going on?"

"I don't know. He's done it a few times," Crystal said.

Lane was getting increasingly agitated. "That's kinda weird. I mean, he didn't lift a finger last year when you had the hysterectomy."

Crystal knew her father was right.

"You know, now that you mention it, the Coke does taste a little off."

It dawned on Crystal what her father was getting at. Could there be a connection between the pains in her stomach and the Coke? Was Brame poisoning her? Crystal remembered something Brame had told her a couple of months back; he said he had the keys to the police forensic locker. The rest of the night, Lane, Crystal and Patty speculated about whether Brame was poisoning Crystal with arsenic or some other chemical. Crystal made an appointment to see Dr. Gary W. Nickel, who tested

Crystal for the presence of common poisons including arsenic. The results came back negative but a second appointment was set up for more extensive checking.

Lane Judson was getting more and more worried about the safety of his daughter, and both he and Patty were pressuring her to move out and file for the divorce. Crystal told them about the night she awoke to find Brame standing over her, asking her if she'd have a heart attack if he had had a knife and a mask.

Lane Judson had heard more than enough. There was no more use in talking to this guy, he told Crystal. It was time to get out, not just for her sake but for the children as well.

On February 7, 2003, the Brame neighbors on Eagle Creek Lane once again heard yelling and screaming coming from the Brame house, but this time the argument seemed to have a different pitch. There was a touch of hysteria in Crystal's voice. The neighbors didn't find out until later what the fight was about but when they did, they were scandalized. Once again Brame was pressuring his wife about sex, but this time there was a new twist. Crystal told relatives that he had offered her up to a retired police officer celebrating a birthday. Wouldn't the guy like Crystal to perform oral sex on him for his birthday? And while she took care of his buddy, Brame would sit back and watch. It could have been another of Brame's wild ideas that had no basis in reality, but he presented it to Crystal as a fait accompli; if she wouldn't join him in a threesome with Watson, well then, he was going to loosen her up one way or another. Crystal was disgusted by the idea but she knew what it was all about—Brame was exerting another form of control, telling her that she was his slave and had to do whatever he wanted.

What Brame didn't know was that Crystal had been talking openly to her sister about getting a divorce since

December and this time, she meant it. The Brame marriage was in its death throes; Crystal apparently had made the decision to leave Brame and she was not going to bow down in front of him any longer. This night, when she heard Brame explain his idea for a bizarre birthday present to a retired cop, she lashed out, telling Brame flat out that she was leaving him soon and would get as much of his money as she could.

"You will never leave me," Brame told her. "No woman will ever leave me."

"You just wait and see."

As always, Brame's thoughts were on his money, not his children. "I'll kill you before you see any of my deferred comp," he said.

It's hard to imagine—in the heat of a marital argument—that a husband would shout down his wife about something as arcane as "deferred comp," but Crystal swore to her parents that it was true.

At this point, Crystal was just waiting for her divorce attorney, Joseph Lombino, to file the papers with the court. In their discussions, she already had made one tactical decision: she would file in King County, not Pierce County where they lived. Even at the end of the marriage, Crystal was still thinking of Brame, although there surely was more than a hint of self-interest in her thought process. She told her family that she was filing in King County to keep the divorce as quiet as possible. She figured that the name "Brame" was not nearly so recognizable up near Seattle. But she also had something to gain by not publicizing the divorce: if Brame kept his job, he kept his $132,000 annual salary, and some investigators think that was a not unimportant factor in her decision. "She wanted him to keep his job because he made a lot of money," one cop said.

The night of February 15 was upon David and Crystal Brame. Neither knew it at that point, but this was to be the last major fight they would endure under the same roof. This particular fight had all begun a month earlier when Assistant Chief Catherine Woodard called Crystal to extend a personal invitation to a dinner being held in celebration of the appointment of two new assistant police chiefs, Richard McCrea and Don Ramsdell. The dinner would be held at Anthony's Restaurant, not five minutes from the Brame home in Gig Harbor. At that point, Woodard and Crystal had a good relationship. Fellow cops describe Woodard as "a mother hen" type, and it was she who had remembered to bring Crystal flowers when Brame was appointed chief. The two women would phone each other from time to time and Woodard had even bought Haley and David some small presents. Crystal was very appreciative of Woodard's thoughtfulness and had written her a couple of warm thank-you notes.

But this time Crystal declined Woodard's dinner invitation. Fellow officers knew the marriage was troubled, but most had no idea how far it had deteriorated. All they knew was that Crystal had removed herself from any official duties of being the chief's wife. "You just could not get the two of them together," said Jim Mattheis, the department's spokesman.

Brame knew far in advance that Crystal was not going to attend the dinner that night, but it still got under his skin. She was just not listening to him like she used to. He recognized the change in Crystal and he didn't like it. He thought he had her under enough control that she would never file for divorce, but he had noticed that she now was standing up to him during their spats. In early February, Brame had confided to his personal assistant, Jeanette Blackwell, "Something is going on. Something's coming down the tube. I can feel it."

So on the night of February 15 Brame pushed Crystal to attend the assistant chief's dinner, and he pushed hard. He tricked her into going into their walk-in closet to look for his favorite blue turtleneck and when she did, he stuck his department-issued .45 caliber Glock up to her face and said, "Accidents happen."

Crystal was terrified. Her lawyer had warned her not to rile Brame up, but he'd done it to himself. He was as angry as she'd ever seen him. The divorce papers were going to be served on Brame in little more than a week and she had to keep her cool. But she would not put her fingerprints on the Glock no matter how much he pressed, and when he left, she slumped to the floor of the closet thankful that nothing more had occurred. She could not take any more of this. She wasn't just worried about herself. Their children, Haley and David, had witnessed a lot of fights by their parents but now it was happening nearly every day.

The moment David left, Crystal called Julie. She and husband Dave hustled over, and Crystal handed them photo books and videotapes she wanted out of the house. She and the children would be gone soon enough, but it was time to begin passing along some precious mementos in case David learned she was about to serve him with divorce papers. There was no telling what his reaction might be, but she knew it would not be good.

"I'm Here Alone in an Empty House"

On February 24, 2003, Crystal Brame woke up in David Brame's bed for the last time. The couple was in the last desperate hours of their marriage. Joe Lombino, Crystal's divorce lawyer, had informed her that the process server would deliver the divorce papers to Brame that day. She should have been relieved, but she was nervous and apprehensive. She knew what a controlling person Brame was and she was terrified of what he might do. She did everything in her power that morning not to arouse his suspicions about what was about to happen. It worked; he left the house without incident and Crystal immediately called her parents for help moving out of the house on Eagle Creek Lane.

Patty and Lane Judson hurried over and helped their daughter take as many clothes as they could carry. There was no way they were going to take everything; they wanted to make sure they did not run into Brame. Usually he worked long hours, but Crystal was taking no chances. They frantically cleaned out drawers and took what they could and raced over to where the Judsons lived, a beautiful gated community of upper middle-class homes in a development just north of Gig Harbor called Canterwood.

Call it a cop's intuition but, for whatever reason, Brame did go home early that day, arriving at his house somewhere around two p.m. The house was strangely empty and, once he saw that some of Crystal's clothing was gone, he knew what had happened. Immediately he called Jeanette Blackwell, his assistant.

"I'm here alone in an empty house if you know what I mean," he told her.

Jeanette was not surprised. She'd been privy to a lot of phone calls between the two and had sometimes heard Crystal screaming on the other end of the phone.

"He was just devastated. I could hear him opening cabinets and drawers and slamming stuff."

At 2:20 P.M. Brame called his in-laws, the Judsons, at their home. He knew Crystal would be with them. The couple talked and Brame pleaded with her to return back home. "He told her he loved her," Patty said. "He told her he knew that she was very upset with him but he thought they could work it out."

Brame sounded desperate and, despite everything Crystal had been through, she was still overcome by emotion. "He repeatedly asked me to come home and told me that he loved me. He told me not to cry so hard and not to be so upset."

She refused and cut him off, saying she had to pick up David Jr. at preschool. They agreed to talk that evening.

At four p.m. Ed Lund, a local process server, knocked on the door and gave Brame the bad news in the form of the divorce papers. Later, Lund would say that Brame did not exhibit any anger, just resignation. "It was pretty routine," Lund said. "In fact, he seemed to know I was coming."

The divorce papers filed with the superior court clerk in King County at 8:36 A.M. on February 24, 2003, are, for the most part, fairly standard in their demands, but of course, seeing Crystal's declarations spelled out in black and white hit Brame hard. Crystal was asking for half of Brame's annual salary, demanding more than $5,300 per month; she also wanted Brame to pay her lawyer's fee of $7,500. In the declarations, she lobbed a couple of personal punches at Brame but, all in all, it wasn't too damning. She asked that his mother not be allowed any contact with her children because, Crystal alleged, she had struck the children in the past. She also mentioned that she was concerned for her own safety and alleged that Brame kept his .45 caliber Glock on a shelf where the children could reach it. Finally, she asked that he eventually move out of the family home so she and the children could move back in.

By six that night Brame was back on the phone with Crystal, who was still holed up with the children at her parents' gated community. "He was crying and told me that he was not alone, that he had called the Tacoma police chaplain [Bill Bowlby] to come over to our residence to be with him," she said. "He asked if I would come over and talk and I said I would."

Crystal agreed to meet Brame back at the home on Eagle Creek Lane as long as Bowlby was there. They met for an hour and discussed the marriage. Bowlby took the Christian approach, reminding Crystal of her marriage vows.

"I know you have feelings for David, as he does you. I'm sure you thought long and hard about this decision but maybe things can be worked out. Can you call it off for six weeks while we all meet for family counseling?" Bowlby asked.

Crystal wiped away her tears. "No, I can't. This was the hardest decision I have ever made in my life but I think it's the best thing for me and the children. I just want all of us to be safe and happy. David, it's better for all of us this way. It is."

Crystal went on to tell Bowlby all about David's many sins. She was clearly fed up, not only with David but with the police chaplain as well, whom she considered an ally of David's. She mentioned how her husband had tried to lure her into threesomes and foursomes, how he'd admitted adultery with women subordinates and prostitutes. "What does your God say about that?" Crystal asked.

She returned to her parents' home, emboldened by putting Brame in his place. In her mind, there was no going back.

BOOK II

LIFE WITHOUT CRYSTAL

"Pull Yourself Together"

The house on Eagle Creek Lane was now empty.
There was nobody to make David Brame dinner, no
children clamoring for attention. For the first time in a
long time, Brame was alone every night with just his
thoughts. Like a lot of men in his situation, David Brame
found himself falling into the black hole of divorce. His
days became focused on meeting with his children, finding a lawyer to represent his interests and spilling his
guts to virtually anyone and everyone he came across in
the Tacoma police department. As for actually running
the police department, well, that no longer seemed to
be high on his priority list.

"The change was very dramatic in regards to his work
performance," said Jeanette Blackwell. "He was not getting anything done. He had an excellent group of assistant chiefs that were running the department. Without
them, nothing would have gotten done.

"Crystal filed in February and for about two weeks it
was just kind of bad because he hadn't shared too much
with anyone. He was still getting stuff off his desk because I was just basically babysitting him. And then once
he started sharing little bits and pieces of his divorce, he

just gradually began to deteriorate. His assistant chiefs were picking up the ball and just taking care of everything.

"He was just not functioning as the chief of police. He ate, slept and drank Crystal Brame. There was not much work being done."

According to Jeanette, Brame was too distraught to even eat most days or to take care of physical appearance. The man who once told the mirror "I love me" now couldn't get it together to comb his hair. "He started losing weight and he would come to work looking like hell. There were a couple of times I went in there and closed the door and said, 'Go in the bathroom. Comb your hair. Brush your teeth again because this is not gonna work. You've got meetings to go to.' He was canceling meetings. I was like, 'You cannot skip this meeting again. You're making the whole department look bad.' It was really sad. He was having people waiting in his office area for thirty, forty minutes, sometimes an hour. He was in there with people just sharing his life story."

One of those people behind the closed doors was Brame's longtime friend and colleague Bill Meeks. At one point, Brame called Meeks in, and he looked especially bad.

"He just started crying. He told me Crystal wanted a divorce and he didn't want to be known as a 'two-time loser,'" Meeks said.

Meeks was far from shocked. He'd heard Crystal screaming one time when he called Brame, and he had once videotaped Brame's injuries, allegedly at the hand of Crystal, as far back as 1996. Meeks told Brame to stay focused on his job and he would get through this but, during the meeting, Brame couldn't stop sobbing.

For her part, Jeanette took the tough love approach with Brame. He used her as a sounding board for some of Crystal's juicier revelations that he was afraid would come out. Brame confided in Jeanette about his desire for a threesome and asked her what she thought. "You sound like a man who wants to entertain a third person in your bedroom," Jeanette said diplomatically. She really didn't care about his personal troubles, only how it came to affect the department.

"I said, 'Pull yourself together. You're not being a chief.' "

But the divorce completely took over his life; it was all he talked about, all he thought about. Jeanette could see that he was thinking not only about his reputation but the hit that his bankbook was about to take. "Money was everything in the world to him," she said. "It was everything."

In one memorable conversation, Brame told Jeanette, "I love Crystal and I want her to have everything she needs to take care of the kids but . . ."

"But what?" she asked.

"Well, you know, I've got to save $5,000 a month. That's my goal."

That was all Jeanette needed to hear. "You know what? I don't want to hear any more from you about what you need to save. Five thousand a month! Do you know what I make? And I am a single mother raising three kids by herself. I don't want to hear about your problem saving $5,000 a month. A month! Don't even go there with me."

"But Jeanette, listen to me for a second."

And then Brame whipped out a pencil and paper and showed her his expenses and how this goal might still be possible, how he'd figured everything out. Brame had tears in his eyes and Jeanette could see there was a lot more going on here than just money. But she still didn't want to hear it and was brutally honest with him.

"Okay, mister, dry it up. You've got an appointment and nobody wants to see you crying over money. Get it together."

Jeanette is a tough cookie and solidly grounded, so she was shocked by how needy Chief Brame had become. She was sick of him talking to her about his problems, especially when she had her own life problems to deal with and he could care less. She tried to be a good listener but Brame tested her patience. One night she was driving in her car when her cell phone rang, as it did nearly every night in this period after Crystal walked out. "This is how bad it got. I was driving one of my children to the emergency room one night and he called me on my cell phone and said, 'What are you doing?' I said, 'Driving my child to the emergency room right now.' He didn't miss a beat. He said, 'Well, let me tell you what happened to me today.' So I talked to him the entire time and my child is lying over in the back and unbeknownst to me she'd got a cyst that is rupturing. She's in severe pain but I'm driving and I'm talking to him. I get to the emergency room and get her loaded up on a wheelchair. I finally have to say, 'I'm at the hospital now. I have to go.' And he never once asked me what it was about."

Blackwell wasn't Brame's only wet nurse. That role also fell to Assistant Chief Catherine Woodard, the "mother hen" of the department. She looked out for everyone and now it was Brame's turn, even though she later confided to some that she found him to be a "cocky, know-it-all, arrogant and vindictive person who supervised by intimidation and fear and demanded blind loyalty from his subordinates." Woodard felt trapped. She thought she had no choice but to help Brame do everything because he seemed so helpless.

Woodard was used to taking care of people and she felt she owed it to the department to take care of Brame. She was reluctant but got sucked into Brame's neediness to an astonishing degree. Over the next two months, she made out a grocery list for Brame, helped him move a bed and a bed frame into the apartment he eventually rented and picked up his car to fix a flat tire. She was going so far above and beyond her job title that the rumors were flying that she and Brame were having an affair, a rumor that she denies to this day. But there's no doubt Woodard got much too involved in Brame's life and divorce—serving as an intermediary between Brame and Crystal—and it later became one of the biggest regrets of her life.

19

"You Were the Mother of the Children"

From the moment she walked out of the house, Crystal kept a detailed diary of everything that happened between her and David Brame. It is a remarkable document that shows—from the inside—the breadth of her emotions, the depths of divorce, the sadness at the onset followed by increasing bitterness and anger. That first week, Brame peppered Crystal with phone calls and there was a lot of crying on both ends. He had had her under his thumb for so long that he didn't know what to do without her. There was a void in his life. He begged her to come back, said he was a changed man, that he wanted them to be a family again, but it clearly was too late. Crystal had made up her mind, but she did have feelings for Brame and allowed him small visits during which he would come by and hug the kids and even put them to bed.

David said he had really underappreciated me and that all the marriage problems were all his fault and he didn't blame me for leaving . . . he said he only wanted to be married to me and that he was a fool to want other women. He continued by saying that he had the perfect wife and the perfect life and that he threw it all away for nothing.

That entry was made on February 26, two days after Crystal had moved out. When Brame realized she wasn't coming back right away, he asked that they work out visitation for the children. Crystal agreed to let him take the children every other weekend even though she hated to do it. The first weekend in March loomed large. On the night of February 28, Brame arrived at the Judsons' house in Canterwood to take the children away with him and back to the only home they'd ever known. He arrived more than an hour late, which Crystal noted in her diary.

> He was to arrive at 6 p.m. and instead arrived at 7:10 p.m. stating that he just couldn't make it on time. He gave no reason why he was so late . . . David Jr. started to cry and wanted Mommy to come with them to go home. I started to cry also as this was extremely difficult to say goodbye to our children for the first time. This would be the first time David would have ever had the kids by himself overnight in their lives. David Sr. told me: "Look what you are doing to the kids. Look what you've done to our children by filing for divorce."

It was the first of many ugly scenes to come. They continued to stand outside the car, Brame berating Crystal in front of the children and demanding that she order them a pizza that would be delivered by the time the three of them got to the family home on Eagle Creek Lane. It was surely a renewed attempt by Brame to establish control but Crystal told him she wasn't taking orders from him any longer. He glared at her as he drove away with the children.

That weekend was contentious; Brame seemed to

spend more time on the phone demanding Crystal come home "where you belong" than he did playing with his kids. On Sunday, March 2, Crystal agreed to visit David while David Jr. was sleeping.

He started explaining why he wasn't a good husband and that he had failed as a father. He repeated he was a terrible husband and that he didn't know how to keep a wife . . . he said HE WOULD DO ANYTHING TO GET ME BACK [Crystal's capitals].

It's unclear if she was really considering it, but she presented her two "deal-breaker" demands: neither she nor the kids would ever have any contact with his mother again, and she wanted more than $100 every two weeks. He refused the request about his mother, telling her that "blood is thicker than water and that's my mother."

As for her demand for money:

He said we could maybe negotiate a little more money—however, I lived (meaning me) a privileged lifestyle by getting to have $100 every TWO WEEKS! He told me that actually I was even more lucky than I realized since really I get $216 per pay period (every 2 weeks) because there are 26 pay periods in a year and that dollar cost averages out to technically be $216 per month!

Like his argument over his "deferred comp," it seems inconceivable that any man would make this argument while trying to win back his wife. Perhaps Brame was not thinking clearly or more likely, he was thinking about the one thing he really cared about—money. The meeting continued to degenerate until both of them were screaming at each other. [Crystal inserted the capital letters in the following excerpts.]

He started YELLING AT ME! I WILL PICK THE VENUE FOR THIS DIVORCE, NOT YOU. I'M MOVING IT TO PIERCE COUNTY SO I CAN HAVE PEOPLE I KNOW IN COURT AND YOU WON'T STAND A CHANCE. IT WILL BE THE CHIEF OF POLICE'S WORD AGAINST YOU. YOU ARE JUST A HOUSE-WIFE. I WILL RAKE YOU OVER THE COALS BEFORE ALL THIS IS OVER. HE TOLD ME THAT I HAD BETTER DROP THE DIVORCE NOW . . .

I AGAIN REMINDED HIM TO PLEASE JUST LEAVE ME ALONE AND RESPECT MY WISHES THAT I JUST WANT TIME AND SPACE AWAY FROM HIM. HE TOLD ME THAT HE WOULD NEVER LEAVE ME ALONE!

Brame followed through on his threat. The following day—March 3—after the children were returned to the Judson home, Brame called Crystal at ten thirty at night. Alone in his house, Brame had been turning the divorce over and over and, in his mind, he could not figure out why Crystal had left him. She wrote down her version of the conversation.

He told me, "You need to give me one reason why I am losing you. You will always be my true love and I will NEVER let you go! Do you get that, Crystal? NEVER MEANS NEVER! I spent two years and three months and 10 days dating you and you LEAVING ME WILL BE THE COSTLIEST MISTAKE YOU'LL EVER MAKE WITH ME! . . . I will always be there knocking on your door even when you are old or away from me . . . I'll always be there. You'll be sorry till the day you die."

If Crystal ever had any doubts about whether or not to leave Brame, they grew weaker with each phone call and contentious meeting. Even when Crystal broke down and included David in her plans for the children, she came away frustrated. One day in March, she invited David to his son's belated birthday party. David promised to attend but instead used the day to go to the local credit union and change the requirements for writing a check or taking out money. From then on, two signatures would be needed so that Crystal could no longer withdraw money by herself. Now it was all-out war. Brame even pulled out the answering machine on Eagle Creek Lane, saying he was sick of messages from her and the kids.

They argued bitterly over the children's basic needs. Haley had gone up two shoe sizes and Crystal asked him if he would contribute to the cost of new shoes. He told her to produce the receipt for the shoes. She did so and, with Crystal's parents standing there, he supposedly issued a deadly threat. The exact words in Crystal's journal were:

David said, "Before I give you or the children even one dollar, I will see you dead first."

From there, it only got worse, especially the allegations concerning Haley. Crystal maintained in her journal and ultimately her divorce papers that Brame had enjoyed sleeping in the same bed with Haley, who was eight years old at the time of the divorce. (There is no corroborating evidence to suggest this was true and may have been an allegation included in the divorce papers to make David look worse than he already did.) Crystal was determined to put a stop to that. After all, as far as she was concerned, Brame was a pervert for wanting to involve her in threesomes and foursomes with other women and couples. On March 14, 2003, Crystal wrote that Haley herself brought up the matter as she was about to go to her father's house for that weekend's visitation.

> Haley told her dad, "Dad, you know when I come to stay with you this weekend I have to sleep in my own bed. You know that, right?" Her dad replied, "Oh darn, because that was the one thing I was looking forward to most." The children walked out to leave and Haley stopped and threw her arms around my waist and cried really hard, stating she wanted to stay with me and her grandma and Papa Judson. I told her everything would be okay and I would call her and she could call me anytime.

It's difficult to know what to make of this entry or the inclusion of Brame's sleeping habits in later divorce papers. Did Crystal really think anything untoward was going on? And if she did, why didn't she report it to social services or refuse to allow Haley to go with her father? The Judsons too have alluded to this "strange" behavior in interviews but have never said outright that they thought he was abusing Haley. Was this just the sort of thing that some mothers include in their divorce papers to embarrass their husbands, especially ones that hold public jobs? There are no answers but, for everything else Brame later was accused of, he was never accused of being a child molester.

On March 16, Brame dropped off the children as scheduled but refused Crystal's request for more money for the children. He told her he wanted to speak to her alone, not in front of Patty, the woman he privately referred to as the Barnacle because, as far as he was concerned, she was a barnacle on their marriage. Crystal told him if he had anything to say, he could say it in front of her mother.

I told him that both my parents were aware of HIS OTHER WOMEN, HIS WANTING ME TO PARTICIPATE IN THREESOMES AND FOURSOMES AND EVEN TO DO IT IN OUR HOME WHERE OUR BEAUTIFUL CHILDREN ARE. HIS THREESOMES INCLUDING DETECTIVE LINDA WATSON, AN EMPLOYEE OF HIS! A COUPLE FROM [NEW MEXICO] WHO REFUSED AND AN AFRICAN AMERICAN RETIRED POLICE LT. DAVID KNEW I WAS VERY AGAINST ALL OF THIS, AND THIS WAS ONE OF THE THREE MAIN REASONS THAT I FILED FOR DIVORCE.
DAVID'S RESPONSE WAS, "I DON'T GIVE A SHIT, I DON'T GIVE A SHIT. I DON'T GIVE A SHIT!" HE KEPT REPEATING IT.

As crazy as it seems, just one day after that outburst, Brame was apologetic and again begging Crystal to return home. His seesaw ride of emotions continued when, on March 17, Crystal and her mother dropped by the Eagle Creek Lane house to get some schoolbooks that Haley had left behind. Brame tried to separate Crystal from her mother and maneuvered her so that her back was facing her mother. In that position, Brame turned loving one more time.

He kept trying to whisper to me to call him, that he loved me, and rubbed my ring finger on my left hand (I had not worn my wedding ring since he was served with divorce papers on 2/24/03). We

left the house immediately. (I had tried to explain
some of Haley's math homework to him when he
was rubbing my finger—of which I pulled my hand
away immediately.)

Throughout these weeks, both Brame children, as always, were witnesses to their parents' fights. Haley is a
quiet child by nature while David Jr. is more
rambunctious—your typical five-year-old boy—and he is
the spitting image of his father. The children were pawns
for both adults.

On March 26, 2003, Haley called her father and told
him in no uncertain terms—even for an eight-year-old—
that she did not want to visit or see his mother. Crystal
wrote what Haley said to her father:

She [Beverly Brame] is mean to her and little
David and Haley went on to say not only didn't
she want to go but that her dad couldn't make her
go either! Once Haley said this comment her dad
cut her off immediately and hung up on her.

But two days later, Brame did indeed take the kids
over to see his mother. Haley called Crystal from her
paternal grandparents' home and was trying to tell her
something, but all Crystal could hear was Brame in the
background.

I heard HER DAD SAY, "TELL YOUR
MOTHER THAT IT IS FUN AT GRANDMA
BRAME'S AND YOU TELL HER NOW."
HALEY, BEING THE OBEDIENT CHILD THAT
SHE IS, TOLD ME AS HER DAD SAID. HALEY
WHISPERED TO ME THAT SHE WANTED TO
TELL ME SOME THINGS LATER.

In late March Brame finally agreed to move out of

the family home, and he put a down payment on an apartment in the Gold Pointe development in North Tacoma. It was only a few miles from Gig Harbor, but you had to travel over the infamous Tacoma Narrows Bridge and in every sense, it was a world away.

Brame was angry, very angry, and yet another major fight broke out over the children. They were with Brame when he called Crystal and told her he didn't want her talking to them any longer while they were in his care.

> He told me that unless I was willing to talk about reconciliation, then I was NOT GOING TO BE ALLOWED TO SPEAK TO THE CHILDREN. HE CONTINUED BY TALKING AGAIN SO LOUDLY THAT MY PARENTS COULD HEAR HIM SAY, "YOU WERE THE MOTHER OF THE CHILDREN." I told him, "I still am the mother of the children." His reply was, "NO, CRYSTAL, YOU WERE THE MOTHER OF THE CHILDREN. YOU USED TO BE THE MOTHER OF THE CHILDREN."

Brame then egged Crystal on, telling her he'd let her know soon if he was going to allow her "permission" to get a divorce. She told him she didn't need his "permission." Crystal was growing increasingly frustrated and she was about to take the gloves off.

20

Take That!

In late March 2003, Crystal Brame filed a "supplemental declaration" with the court and told the world all about her life with David Brame. It makes her initial filing seem very mild by comparison. In these new divorce papers, she really let loose. She told the court how Brame had stuck a gun in her face and said, "Accidents happen," how Brame had warned her he would kill her before she would see any of his "deferred comp," how she had asked for money for Haley's shoes and Brame had told her, "Before I give you or the children even one dollar, I will see you dead first." She said that in one fight Brame had pointedly reminded her of their wedding vows: "Crystal, do you remember our wedding vows, you know, 'till death do us part'? I'll let you go when you're dead."

And that was just for starters. Crystal went on to inform the court of Brame's desires to bring other women into the marital bed, including his desire to have threesomes and foursomes. She also accused him of having an affair. Her lawyer, Joseph Lombino, later added even more declarations from Crystal's family. The ones from Julie and David Ahrens were particularly biting. Dave

Ahrens said he was worried about the personal safety of his sister-in-law and his niece and nephew. Ahrens noted that Brame typically left loaded firearms within the reach of the children.

And Crystal didn't stop there, telling the court how her budget was limited to $100 every two weeks, how Brame had choked her on four separate occasions during the past twelve months, how he threatened her during another fight by saying, "All I have to do is take the palm of my hand and drive your nose up into your brain and the fragments will scatter into your brain and you will be dead." If there was ever a doubt Crystal hated Brame's mother, Beverly, the divorce papers put that to bed. Crystal recounted in detail the entire story of how her mother-in-law had struck her young son. She told the court that David Jr. lived in fear of Beverly Brame and how he once refused to hug his paternal grandmother. "Her outrageous reaction to him was that she shook her finger in his face and told him, 'I will hit you anytime I want, whether you like it or not.'"

Crystal included a list of personal property she wanted to keep once she moved back into the family home and which items Brame could have for himself. It went into the most mundane detail, the kind of detail that makes any divorce sad and sordid. Brame could, if he so desired, keep "a fair share of dishes (the everyday dishes of the Allegro Blue pattern)." Crystal wanted a floor lamp but said Brame could keep the "two blue and cream striped wing chairs." The list went on and on. She wanted the old video camera and the treadmill; he could have the Weber kettle barbecue, charcoal and "some wood" for the fireplace.

David Brame, of course, fought back. By now he had hired attorney Ann Meath and, in his divorce papers, he portrayed Crystal as an unstable mother who had fled the "family residence with the children without prior notice." He tried to come across as the reasonable one with the stable job. "My wife is unable to control an often ferocious temper. I believe that she is emotionally unstable in ways that I am not equipped to diagnose." He told of a time when Crystal was unable to reach him at work and instead sent a 911 page to his pager. It was their personal code for emergencies. When Brame called Crystal back, he said she was distraught because Haley had broken the television's remote control. "[She] was literally screaming, 'How the hell do you expect me to turn the television on?!!' "

Brame then enumerated the various beatings he'd endured at Crystal's hands during that fateful September of 1996. He also included the photographs his mother had taken of an ugly bruise on his arm that he claimed was caused by Crystal back in 1998.

Brame told the court that Crystal's deposition was full of lies that she'd made up in order to hurt him personally and professionally. "She has made several threats that she will destroy my career," he wrote. "The most recent occasion was on Sunday, March 2, 2003, when I told her that my attorney was going to move for a change of venue to Pierce County. Mrs. Brame responded that she was going to drag me 'through the mud.' She added, 'Prepare to lose your job.' "

Brame went on to accuse Crystal of physically attacking their children. "What is far worse than all of this is the impact of Mrs. Brame's uncontrollable anger on our children," he wrote. "Tragically, Mrs. Brame has also unleashed her fury on our children more times than I can recall. Typical of her personality, she blows the smallest incident out of all proportion, hysterically berating the children for the slightest perceived offense. When really provoked, Mrs. Brame will go after the children, raining blows upon them. I have literally had to wrap my body around Haley's in an effort to shield her from Mrs. Brame's pummeling."

Was there any truth at all to Brame's allegations of Crystal's abuse toward the children? There is no proof that she ever struck them, but there is little doubt that Crystal was high-strung, or to use the current vernacular, "high maintenance." Brame's personal assistant, Jeanette Blackwell, had heard her screaming at the children when they would call their father, and years earlier a close friend of Brame's, who asked to remain anonymous, told me he had called Brame's house one evening and could hear Crystal screaming and yelling "like a maniac" in the background.

But to shopkeeper Linda Lee Clark and many others, the idea that Crystal would ever do anything to hurt her kids in any way, physically or mentally, was beyond belief. "She was a great mother to those kids," Clark said. "They were darling and she loved her children."

Furthermore, Clark found the allegation that Crystal had lashed out and actually injured David Brame to be patently ridiculous. "She's a tiny person. The accusation that she injured him is almost laughable. He controlled her to no end. In the two or three years before the divorce, she looked very strained as though she were extremely nervous."

But not everyone saw Crystal as the shy, retiring type. Catherine Woodard also mentioned that Brame on various occasions seemed cowed by Crystal's nearly out-of-control temper and recalled that Brame had told Woodard he sometimes was afraid of Crystal. Woodard remembered one incident from 1999 when Brame was still an assistant chief. The Seattle police asked for assistance in dealing with the activists who were rioting during the World Trade Organization's conference. Brame was scheduled to go to Seattle to help out but Crystal told him he could not go because she had to do some Christmas shopping; she demanded that Brame stay home and watch the children. Brame was beside himself but stayed home despite the street riots going on in Seattle.

Brame used the divorce papers to refute every story Crystal had ever told regarding him and his family. As you might expect, he put on a rigorous defense of his mother. He included a note Beverly had written him upon his first anniversary as chief. In her own handwriting, Beverly tells David how proud she is of him and what a handsome man he is. Then she goes on to write, "David, you may always hold your head high because you will survive and conquer. I love you and Haley and David Jr. with all my heart and wish Crystal didn't hate me. I don't know what I've done but the third and last screaming outrage was the last. At my age, I don't need that anymore. I felt bad as I loved Crystal from the start."

Surprisingly, Brame did agree in principle to give Crystal and the children nearly $5,000 per month, a bit below what she had asked for but still a substantial sum.

There was one more surprising item on Brame's list. For someone so concerned with his reputation and the contents of the divorce papers, he insisted that the divorce be moved from King County back to Pierce County, where he and Crystal lived.

Detective Barry McColeman, one of Brame's closest friends in the department, said Brame wanted the change of venue because "his attorney told him that King County was much more favorable to women in property settlements . . . Dave said his attorney told him that the reason she filed up there is because all the attorneys know that they are more favorable to women as far as property and custody issues go.

"He said, 'Bullshit, let's bring it back to Pierce County.' "

He also thought that his being the chief of police would carry a lot of weight with the judges in his home county. A change of venue hearing was set for April 10.

21

"She Was in a Cocoon and She Got Free"

As bad as David Brame was looking physically since Crystal moved out—colleagues describe his hair turning gray and his face growing gaunt—the Brame divorce was having the opposite effect on Crystal. Certainly she too was living with the stress of being involved in such a highly contentious divorce but physically, the only effect it was having was positive, at least according to family and friends. Suddenly, they said, Crystal told them that she felt more alive than she had in years. "It was like a tremendous burden had been lifted off her shoulders," said her godmother, Judy Hellstrom. "She was suddenly like the Crystal we knew when she was growing up, bubbly all over again. And interested in things again, like going to law school. That was her ultimate plan once she got on her feet—to go back to school and become a lawyer."

And the change was more than just mental. "There were people who didn't even recognize her," said her mother, Patty. "Crystal ended up looking just like she did when she graduated from college. She told us she felt free. It just turned around so quickly that people could not believe what she looked like."

"We felt like we had our old Crystal back," said her father, Lane. "She told me many times after the divorce, 'Dad, I'm free.' And even Haley would tell us, 'Papa and Grandma, I'm free now.' "

That phrase became Crystal's mantra during the divorce. She told anyone she would come across that "I'm free now. He doesn't control me anymore." Neighbors like Marty Conmy also noticed the astounding difference in Crystal. "Before, she was hunched over like she was hiding something but literally, after she left him, she walked taller like she had nothing to hide. The difference was incredible."

Debbie Phillips, Crystal's tanning parlor confidant, said the change in Crystal was so noticeable that it began to bother Brame. "He saw she was getting stronger and stronger, that's what David got angry at. He was becoming more and more flustered and more and more angry because he started to see her become happy," Phillips said. "It's kind of amazing that when you get out of an abusive situation, you become happy. She smiled all the time. There wasn't a time that she didn't walk in and smile and just be able to be so relaxed.

"Her whole demeanor just totally changed, her whole outlook on life. She actually had something to look forward to. She was looking forward to little David going to school full time. That would allow her to go out and get a job or go to law school like she wanted. Even being able to go to the movies by herself. She was able to do that for the first time in, like, ten years. She told me, she said, 'Debbie, it was just great. It was such freedom.' And that's the word she used all the time. She'd say, 'I am so free. I don't have anybody screaming and yelling at me. And guess what? I can balance my own checkbook.' And I said, 'Well, of course you can.' "

Crystal told Phillips everything just like she always had. She told her how she was now able to go out and buy new undergarments. Her own had become shredded and she never had the money for new ones, but now she could go out and buy new ones and feel good about herself. "And I watched her whole self-esteem and her whole outlook change. She didn't always have her head down anymore. It was held up high, you know. She'd say 'Hi Debbie, how you doing?' and her shoulders were back and I could see that she was really, really happy and I was so proud of her. I just knew she was going to thrive like a butterfly because she was in a cocoon and she got free."

Crystal began spreading the word that she was getting divorced and got back in contact with some old friends, including grade-school friend Lori Hamm. Crystal had never confided in Hamm, probably out of embarrassment, but Hamm knew something was wrong with Crystal's relationship with Brame. "When he got promoted to chief of police for Tacoma, she wrote me and told me that he had been selected and I wrote her back about how proud she must be of him. I never got a response to that statement," Hamm wrote in an online diary.

"In mid-February, I came home after running some errands and noticed I had a message on my answering machine. It was Crystal talking a mile a minute about not e-mailing her at the house, she had left David, how he had had affairs, threatened her, and she wanted me to call her at her mom and dad's. I immediately called her back and she spilled her guts and talked like she never had before, which is something for Crystal, because she was always one that could talk but now she sounded so alive and free. She went into great detail about all that she had gone through and that she had been hiding it for years, how she had not even told her parents or sister the depth of it until she left him. They knew he was controlling but never the daily horror she had to endure with him."

Crystal was going through the same ritual with other

friends and acquaintances. One day Crystal, with her mother, walked into Linda Lee Clark's gift shop with a big smile on her face. "She told me, 'I want you to be the first one to know. I moved out and I filed for divorce.' And I hugged her and had tears in my eyes and thought, thank goodness. I told her how proud I was of her because I knew she was frightened and finally it just spilled out of her, and even her mother said she heard stories she had never heard before. She told he had threatened her and that she lived in fear. I hugged her again and told her, 'I am just so proud of you,' particularly in the position her husband was in," said Clark.

But Crystal wasn't spilling her guts just to old friends; she was telling virtually anyone she came across the sordid story of her divorce. In that respect, she wasn't too much different than her soon-to-be-ex-husband. Neighbor Marty Conmy had never really known Crystal well. He had witnessed some odd behavior and screaming matches but had never had a heart-to-heart talk with her. Basically, they knew each other just to wave hello and goodbye. Whenever Conmy did talk to her for any length of time—like the time he tried to buy an old table and chairs from the Brames at a garage sale—he noticed that Crystal always seemed nervous and "she spoke in less than clear sentences. Her thoughts were scattered."

But in mid-April, Conmy emerged from his house one day to find Crystal and her mother across the way. He waved at them and walked over to express his sympathy for Crystal's divorce, which he'd heard about from another neighbor. "She came right up to me. Her manner was completely different than I'd observed. She's a small woman and she had always been hunched over. She always seemed to be trying to make herself look even smaller. This time her shoulders were back. Her arms were out and she spoke clearly, confidently, in complete sentences. And what she had to say to me was really mind-blowing."

Conmy considered himself just a very casual acquaintance but suddenly Crystal was treating him like much more.

"How have you been?" Conmy asked casually.

"Since I left David, I've been great," Crystal said. "You wouldn't believe what it was like living in that house. I know I've never been much of a neighbor but I want you to know that things are going to change. David was a monster. He controlled everything I did. Every time I went to the store, he looked at the odometer. He wanted the change and a receipt for every purchase to make sure I wasn't squirreling away any money. It was just a horror living with that man. Can you believe that he weighed me every day to watch my weight, to make sure I didn't gain too much?"

Conmy was taken aback and didn't know what to say; he certainly had never been on such intimate terms with Crystal and didn't know what to make of the way she was now behaving. It was 180 degrees different from the way she'd behaved when she and David Brame were living together.

"Well, I'm sorry . . ."

"And that's not all," Crystal interjected. "You would just not believe what he wanted me to do. He wanted me to get involved with him and other women and have threesomes and foursomes. That was really the last straw and when I said no, he backed me into a closet and put a loaded gun to my head and he told me that 'accidents happen.' "

"Crystal, I'm sorry. I had no idea."

"Oh, I know, I know. We looked so normal and all but it was anything but."

"I hope everything goes smoothly for you from now on."

"Well, I was hoping that too but it doesn't look like that's going to happen. In fact, we're getting a restraining order against him, so if you see him in the neighborhood near this house or anything, please call 911 and report him to the police."

"You want me to call 911 if I see him near the house?"

At that point Patty, who had been standing next to Crystal, jumped in. "Right, call 911."

Conmy could barely process what Crystal was saying. Threesomes, death threats, calling 911 on a guy who was the chief of police. It was all too much. He thought to himself, this woman has obviously been living in terror all these years. I guess now I understand why she always seemed so frantic.

"I'm hoping to be a good neighbor in the future," Crystal said. "I just want my life to be normal again."

"Well, be safe, Crystal. Just be safe. Let me know if I can do anything to help you."

Those were the last words Conmy ever spoke to Crystal. He turned and went back into his house and told his wife, "You are not going to believe what I just heard."

22

Mind and Body

Free from David Brame's control, Crystal was getting emotional support from her friends but sought out professionals to help repair her mental and physical health. Her lawyer, Joseph Lombino, referred her to psychologist Dr. Maxwell Knauss of the Allenmore Psychological Associates in Tacoma. On April 4, Knauss submitted a letter to Lombino that eventually made its way into Crystal's divorce folder. He had only seen her four times but it was enough, Knauss wrote to the court, to form an opinion. It is the only record of what a trained professional saw when he spoke to Crystal Brame and heard her story. The caveat is that he was hired by Crystal's lawyer.

The letter and subsequent events show that, although Crystal looked and felt better than she had in years, she still feared her husband greatly. Crystal felt that he knew far too many important people in and around Tacoma and Gig Harbor. When they first met, Crystal told Knauss that she still held out hope that her husband would become more reasonable. Dr. Knauss wrote:

> This reportedly has not occurred and Ms. Brame states that the death threats have continued and

that she has decided to file for a restraining order. Recently, Ms. Brame told me, "I hope a restraining order will help. I fear he will come after me and kill me. He has threatened me so many times. David has said, 'I will never let you leave me. No woman will leave me. I will see you dead first.' "

Crystal reeled off the assortment of controlling behaviors Brame had exerted over her—monitoring her weight, watching how many miles she drove the car, giving her very little money—and she enumerated once again the times she said Brame had choked her or threatened to shoot her.

Dr. Knauss described Crystal as being well-dressed and groomed but her state of mind was something else. He wrote:

Her mood has generally been characterized by mild to moderate anxiety and occasional hopelessness and dejection . . . she has been physically tense in sessions and reports difficulty relaxing. Her speech has been mildly accelerated . . . her concentration has appeared mildly impaired.

Ms. Brame denies either suicidal or homicidal ideation, planning or intent. She admits being very preoccupied with and ruminating over fears that her husband may try to kill her if she goes forward with the divorce and attempts to return to the family home.

Knauss administered the standard psychological tests: the Beck Depression Inventory II, the Beck Anxiety Inventory, the Minnesota Multiphasic Personality Inventory 2 and the Millon Multiaxial Clinical Inventory III.

The testing results characterize Ms. Brame as an insecure individual who has low self-esteem, de-

pendency issues and is very attuned and sensitive
to other people's opinion of her. These test results
indicate a woman suffering from a generalized
state of anxiety, tension and apprehension. She
may have been preoccupied for an extended period
of time with feelings of depression, guilt and
hopelessness . . . she believes that she is being plot-
ted against and that other individuals are attempting to influence her to make her believe that
she is crazy.

In layman's terms, the tests confirmed what Crystal
had been telling everyone: she thought her husband was
bringing the power of the Tacoma police department
down on her, and, after a decade of being controlled
and threatened by her husband, she was depressed and
frightened.

Ms. Brame also achieved testing results found in
individuals who have experienced life-threatening
events producing intense fear or feelings of help-
lessness. Individuals confronted with this type of
life-threatening trauma often experience chronic
symptoms of anxious arousal (e.g. hypervigilance,
elevated startle response, panic attacks), emotional
numbing and avoidance of circumstances associated with the trauma.

Knauss diagnosed Crystal's problem as "adjustment
disorder with mixed anxiety and depressed mood" and
said he could not yet rule out "posttraumatic stress
disorder."
Then he laid it all out in plain English and let the
court know just how serious this case was:

Specifically, Ms. Brame's major fears are that if
she proceeds with the divorce process, her husband

will use his power and resources to destroy her reputation, will continue to pursue her and retaliate against her for years or will kill her, leaving her children to grow up without their mother.

She appears to me to be very dedicated to her children . . . she impresses me as being remarkably free of bitterness towards her husband and understands the need for the two of them to collaborate in parenting their children during the process of and after the divorce.

Tanning parlor owner Debbie Phillips, who has a lot of street smarts and is good with people, told Crystal in no uncertain terms to stay away from Brame. He was, she said, dangerous. "He was like a five-year-old boy with a gun and a bad temper," she said.

Crystal was doing what she could for her nerves and psyche but Debbie Phillips was afraid she wasn't doing enough. Debbie had been privy to all Crystal's allegations against her husband and she also knew Brame personally as he was a frequent visitor to her tanning salon. She knew the type of man he was. "He never really smiled unless you forced a smile out of him," she said. "He was very distant, very, very cold. He showed absolutely no emotion, very strict. You could see that in him."

Debbie warned Crystal that she had to protect herself physically. Crystal was slight and losing weight every day; David Brame was losing weight also but he still towered over her by a good eleven inches and outweighed her by at least eighty pounds.

In her search for solutions, Crystal came across Bill Kortenbach. Bill is a fifth degree black belt in the martial arts who teaches at the Gig Harbor Karate Academy, a storefront self-defense school located in yet another strip mall in Gig Harbor. But Bill thinks a lot about personal safety and has started an eight-hour course called "Full Force Adrenal Response" that he teaches once a month for anyone concerned about his or her physical safety. It should come as no surprise that the class fills up with women, a lot of them abused, a lot of them either in the middle of a divorce or already divorced. The class is a combination of martial arts skills and street smarts; in another context you might say that Bill teaches you how to fight dirty. Bill believes that knowing how to handle yourself can greatly improve your confidence and self-esteem. That's where his philosophy comes in: "When your life is on the line, when you're being attacked, you have to do anything you can to survive."

Bill started the course a few years back after a woman, one of his karate students, was attacked and told him afterward that, as soon as the man put his arms around her, she immediately forgot most of what she was taught. All that karate training did her little good. Bill says that incident convinced him that he needed to teach a type of self-defense that would be "hardwired" into your subconscious so you don't need to think about what to do—you just react. For example, if someone grabs you from behind, you just leverage your weight to throw him over or smash down on his foot without giving it a second thought. It's just what you do when put into that situation. To achieve the desired result, Bill came up with a course that is as intense as he is. He's only five feet six but he has eyes that hold your gaze and he speaks with an intensity that reveals he is a true believer in self-defense. If he weren't built of solid muscle, Bill would be just the kind of guy bullies would pick on. He wears thick glasses and has a flattop crew cut and, if you didn't know any better, you could easily mistake him for a techno-geek. His personal story is the kind of classic "skinny guy gets the sand kicked in his face" that goes all the way back to fitness guru Jack LaLanne. Bill was a skinny kid in school who was picked on, who had no self-esteem and who was doing lousy in his classes. Then he discovered karate and "I went from flunking out to getting straight A's within six months," he says.

Today, Bill is a devotee of security expert Gavin de Becker, who wrote the best-selling self-help book *The Gift of Fear*. The book espouses the philosophy that it's okay to trust your instincts. If you are being followed when you walk down the street and you feel odd about it, you must do something to change the dynamic. De Becker says you must trust your own internal feelings; they will guide you and may very well save you from dangerous situations. Listen to yourself above all else. Bill can reel off quotations from the book nearly as fast as he can flip you onto your back, and he knows what page the quotes are on without looking. He admits that he's more or less memorized the de Becker book. "Everyone in America should read that book," says Bill. "It would save a lot of lives."

Bill teaches his course at the Gig Harbor Karate Academy once a month. It lasts for eight hours and attempts to "hardwire" reactions to violent behavior. He has volunteers dress in protective bodysuits so they don't get injured; he calls them "ghouls." Before a single student arrives, Bill blackens the windows of the karate school so that it's pitch-dark inside. He instructs his students what to do and how to react to an attack, and then he unleashes his ghouls on them. The students never know where they're coming from or whom they're going after. When they attack, the whole class shouts in approval while students pummel, gouge, kick, punch, stomp and do everything possible to escape the attack or to put the ghoul on his back. The poor ghouls take a beating but Bill says they understand—it's all done to eventually save a life.

It's unclear exactly how Crystal heard about Bill's class, but David Jr. takes karate lessons at the school and it's likely that she read a flyer or talked to another mother who knew about it. In early April, she paid Bill a visit.

"She was sitting in my office and, as she told me her story, I could feel the waves of fear coming off her," he says. "You cannot fake that level of terror. She was scared for her life."

As she talked, Bill says that occasionally "the fear would lift like the clouds parting and the sun shining through." That happened mostly when she was talking about her children or her new life. Whenever she returned to speaking about Brame, "a shadow passed over her face."

When she finished laying out her case, Bill latched on to what he considered the most important part of her story. "Her husband was a person of great standing in the community. He was the chief of police; he had a lot to lose. His whole career was at stake. This man had resources and power and if that power was threatened, his livelihood would be threatened and he was going to fight back to save it."

Bill agreed to take a down payment from her for his next course that would be taught on April 27, but for the first time, he warned her against taking it. "This woman's life was in danger. I could see that."

He said he gave her the best advice he could under the circumstances. He fixed his penetrating gaze on her and said, "Crystal, if I were in your shoes, I would go to the bank, withdraw as much cash as I possibly could and I would take my children and disappear."

Crystal seemed startled. "That's not an option. I grew up here. My parents are here. My sister. I've never lived anywhere else. He should be the one to move."

"Well, maybe that's so but you're the one who needs to be careful. He's got a lot of power in this area."

Bill said Crystal was adamant about not running away. "I'm not gonna let him chase me away from everything I know. It's not fair and I won't do it to myself or the children. I'm getting a restraining order against him and in the meantime, I'll take your course. I'll be all right."

Bill's instincts told him she was taking a great chance but there was nothing else he could do.

"Well then, I look forward to seeing you in the class on the twenty-seventh."

"I'll be there."

She wrote him a check as a deposit and got up to leave. "Be very careful. Make sure you're never alone with him," Bill warned.

"I'll be all right," she said. "I have a lot of people who love me. Thanks for your advice. I'll see you on the twenty-seventh."

Bill stood at the window and watched her drive away. Just then, the clouds finally gathered up the strength to rain.

23

"Prepare to Lose Your Job, David"

While Crystal was busy getting her life together, David Brame was watching his fall apart. He alternated between being utterly depressed and fighting back but, somewhere along the line, he decided he wasn't going down without a fight. He'd answered Crystal's divorce papers with his own defenses and allegations of her physical abuse and was hoping a change of venue would bring the case back onto his turf, his power base— Tacoma. In the meantime, he began to keep his own diary. Unlike Crystal's neatly typed journal, Brame's musings were handwritten either on a yellow pad or on stationery from the Doubletree Hotel chain.

David's diary begins with these fateful words, allegedly spoken to Brame by Crystal:

> "I'm a good little actress, David, and I'm going to ruin your career.
> "Prepare to lose your job, David. I'm going to drag you through the mud."

If we're to accept Crystal's notes at face value, then don't we have an obligation to see David Brame's in the

Beautiful Gig Harbor.
(Courtesy of the author)

Downtown Tacoma with the city's imposing Tacoma Dome.
(Courtesy of the author)

The Brames during happier times.
(Courtesy of Gene and Beverly Brame)

David as a
loving father.
(Courtesy of Gene
and Beverly Brame)

The enigmatic John Hathaway.
(© Gayle Rieber)

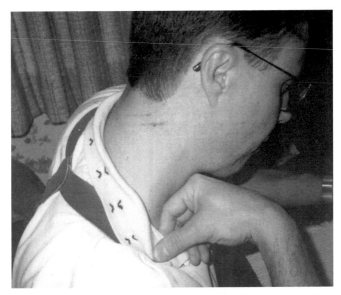

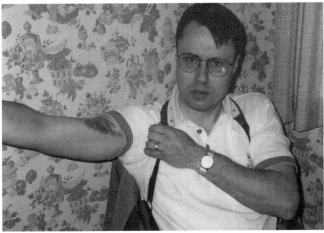

The recorded evidence of the physical abuse David alleged Crystal inflicted upon him. (Courtesy of Gene and Beverly Brame)

David Brame becomes chief of Tacoma Police on January 17, 2001. (Courtesy of Gene and Beverly Brame)

An awkward Crystal fumbles as she pins the chief's badge on David at the official swearing-in ceremony.
(Courtesy of Gene and Beverly Brame)

Area beside Crystal's car where she collapsed.
(Courtesy of Pierce County Sheriff's Department)

The blood-spattered pamphlet titled "What Children of Divorce
Really Need" that Crystal received from a class she took just
about an hour before the shooting.
(Courtesy of Pierce County Sheriff's Department)

Crystal's car after the shooting.
(Courtesy of Pierce County Sheriff's Department)

View of Gig Harbor from the cemetery where Crystal is buried.
There is no mention of the name "Brame" on her headstone.
(Courtesy of the author)

same light? He could have been writing them for the court case but, then again, the same could be said for Crystal's notes. Again, Brame's notes—written in an odd sort of haiku style—highlight the day-to-day heartbreak of divorce, this time from the husband's point of view. On March 23, Brame writes of a forty-five-minute conversation he had with Haley:

Haley asks me questions:
Why don't you love Mommy?
Why do you make her cry?
Why don't you give her money?
Why did you call me on your cell phone yesterday?
Where were you yesterday?

The way Brame saw things, most of his conversations depict him as reasonable and Crystal as contentious; of course, there was a lot of water under the bridge on either side.

CDB [Crystal DeEtte Brame]
Angry over frozen savings acct.
Why am I doing this to her and the kids?
She has no $; has to pay her atty [attorney] Tuesday
CDB confused; I said I want reconciliation and counseling, she said my atty says otherwise
[Crystal] Mentioned my mother hasn't called or even tried to contact/come out and see kids for a couple of months this yr.
Tried to talk to me about placing restrictions on my mother (not leaving kids alone w/her)—I wouldn't discuss
Said I threw wedding ring on bathroom counter, I corrected her—she saw it on counter

I said she hasn't worn hers for 4 weeks, me just 1 week

She said I was going to clean the house out—I said no way—she's been taking things, not me

Said my mom is happy about divorce—I said Mom and Dad are grieving

She asked where I was going to live—I told her of my security deposit [Brame had just put a deposit on an apartment in the Gold Pointe development in North Tacoma]

She said w/divorce I could go off w/other woman Linda Watson—why did I need 3 beds

I told her I want reconciliation

She said that she didn't know what she wanted

I said I loved her—finally she said it albeit reluctantly

Said I was going to slam the door in her face and not keep the door open

Brame portrays himself as wanting to get back together. Of course, given what she went through, Crystal is very reluctant. What's missing from Brame's writing is any sort of anger. The notes are written in a "just the facts, ma'am" style that's perhaps more comfortable to police officers. There is very little emotion, especially when compared to Crystal's writings which revert to capital letters and exclamation points anytime she wants to express her frustration with Brame.

On March 26, at "2040 hrs.," Brame writes that he is returning Haley's message. It seems very evident from this entry and others that Crystal was using her kids to get information from Brame.

Spoke w/both kids

Asked Haley if I could speak to Mom (CDB) re: her accident. [Crystal had discovered a small dent in her car and thought Brame had been following her and was sending a message, although there is no proof of that.] H said C did not want to talk

Haley asked me why I called her on the cell phone and she asked where have I been and why have I been getting home late

She asked why I don't love Mommy

Haley said that she does not want to go around Grandma Brame; she treats her mean; she doesn't like her; she does not want to see her this weekend and I can't make her see Grandma Brame

It was apparent that Haley paused between these statements as if someone was coaching her or telling her what to say or possibly reading to her

Brame dutifully recorded the times and dates of all phone calls, including those he had with his kids. Haley seems mostly to ask him to bring her clothes that were left at the family house in Crystal's haste to get out of there. David Jr., just five years old, genuinely seems to miss his father.

Weds messages
8:10 a.m. David—Dad, have a good day.
7:48 p.m. David—I love you. Bye.
Haley—go to bed in a few minutes (CDB in background) by 8 o'clock in a few minutes. Love you.
7:50 p.m. Haley—Why are you using the cell phone all the time and where are you? I love you, bye

On March 27, Brame brings some clothes to Haley at school and asks Crystal to sign their joint tax returns. He ruminates on the state of his life as he waits for them to come over to his car.

I won't give her $ but said she will eventually get $

I will violate order if I take the kids to see M & D at Dad's 75th birthday party.

I wait in the car @ school, when they arrived

Haley waved enthusiastically @ me

She ran to me and I gave her the clothes—she hugged and kissed me

I went back to the car to retrieve the mail and I briefly went back to the school

I then decided to wait in the car—I was in full police uniform and armed

She (CDB) and her mom walked up to the car and I unlocked the passenger side—CDB opened the front passenger door and stood there—her mom was a few feet behind her

CDB and I spoke and she eventually signed the taxes and I gave her the mail

She rubbed my wedding ring finger with her finger and asked me, "David, how does it feel to not be wearing a wedding ring?"

I said "Not good" I've lost 11 #; she said she lost 12 # and she asked me how she looked as she was rubbing her waist; I said "Not good, you need to gain weight."

Patty (CDB's mom) said, "You look real good, Chrissy."

I asked if she would call me, she said why—I said I wanted a chance to speak w/her alone

She said not right now. I said I have to get going to work—I left

Knowing what Brame thought of Crystal's mother, it must have been galling for him to have Patty shadowing his wife's every footstep. At this point, Patty Judson had dropped all pretense of any affection she may have once had for her son-in-law; she wanted Crystal to get a divorce and she would be damned if she'd see them back together.

Later that day, Crystal called Brame again and told him she had some "good news" for him. She had talked to her attorney and it would be all right if the children attended his father's seventy-fifth birthday party.

> We talked nicely for a while—I told her I wanted reconciliation—she said "really" I asked her to stop the divorce process so we can stop the legal arguments; she said she would think about it. It was a very nice conversation and it renewed some hope in me

But that warm feeling did not last long. Just a week later, Haley called her father about a diamond necklace that she couldn't locate and she thought it might still be in the house on Eagle Creek Lane.

> I told Haley that I wanted to talk about other things. She kept asking me, pausing between sentences as if someone was talking to her.
>
> I told her @ least 4x I don't know where the necklace is, that I didn't know which one it is
>
> I believe Crystal is trying to set me up to allege a theft—that I had stole her necklace.
>
> I told Haley I wanted to talk about other things. She said, "Are you going to answer the questions or not?" Haley said, "If you don't, I'll hang up the phone." The phone was disconnected. Either Haley or someone else @ their residence hung up the phone.
>
> I have no idea what they are talking about (Crystal and Haley)
>
> I gave Crystal her jewelry box w/o incident about one week or so ago.

A week later, on April 7 at 8:16 P.M., Haley called
again and everything was normal; there was no more
talk of the necklace. This time Bill Meeks was with
Brame when they called. The call clearly triggered some
memories in Brame because suddenly there appears in
his journal a list of past offenses and odd behavior on
the part of Crystal:

Yelling @ David Jr.
Name calling "little shit," "little asshole"
Told [David's] mom she would keep Haley and
let me have David Jr
Neuroses [Brame was convinced Crystal had ob-
sessive compulsive syndrome because she con-
stantly checked locks, the stove and lights over
and over]
    Looking under changing table
    Door locks
    Stove
    Curling iron
Bill heard conversations when CDB was yelling
at the kids
Calling me names in front of the kids
Obsessed with nap times
Lane threatened me on the phone—called me at
work approx. 1/96
CDB threw a plastic cassette/book holder at me
It hit the bathroom window
Hands behind her back, insinuating a gun
Writing "shit" on newly painted wall
Bill's heard CDB from on the phone—yelling
@ the kids—I held the phone toward him, heard
screaming so he could hear

In the first week of April, just before relations between Brame and Crystal deteriorated even further,
Brame and his father paid a visit to both Haley and

David Jr.'s schools so he could talk to their teachers and tell them about the divorce. He made sure that the teachers knew that as far as he was concerned the children came first. In both cases, he writes that the children were happy to see their father and grandfather.

> Both Dad and I went into class and sat down. David Jr's back was to us and in a minute he turned around and saw me and Grandpa Brame. He immediately smiled and came to me and hugged me and kissed me. He said that he loved me (I loves you Dad). He sat on my lap for a few moments and he hugged and kissed both of us again. I then told him to join his classmates. We gave him one last kiss and he said goodbye as we left. 5 min visit

That night, Haley called her father and again it was clear to David that Crystal and/or her parents were manipulating what the child had to say. The following phone call occurred on the same day Brame and his father had visited Haley's school as well as David's. Because the visits went so well, someone at the Judson household obviously was not happy. It seems clear, yet again, that someone there was using Haley to relay an adult's emotions.

> Haley called, small talk about school; she said she was sick and tired of me coming to her school; I repeated that "you're sick and tired of me coming to your school?"
> Haley said that she didn't mean that; that she forgot what she was going to say to me.
> She then resumed small talk about school and the day's events
> I told her that I missed her—she said "Me, too."

I told her that I loved her and said she loves me too. We then said goodbye.

Small talk w/David, then goodbye.

A week later, Brame made the last entry in his journal; it was the day before the change of venue hearing and emotions were running high.

Saw Crystal and her mom @ Bartell's in Gig Harbor

Made brief eye contact when she first came into the store—we did not speak; she sneered @ me; I looked away. As I paid for my items, the checker said I can help you next—I looked up and Crystal said "OK"—she was about 15–20 feet from me. We made brief eye contact and I left the store. At no time did we speak.

In his personal journal, David Brame portrayed himself as a reasonable man who thought only of the children. In her diary, Crystal Brame painted herself as an angry soon-to-be-ex-wife sick of her spouse's controlling and threatening behavior. Probably neither picture is entirely accurate. Brame was certainly a manipulative manager as evidenced by the career-ending knives he thrust into the backs of his enemies within the department. He was also—it was clear to his friends and certainly to Linda Watson—a clumsy, wannabe lothario.

But what are we to make of Crystal? She never actually reported any abuse by her husband until after the divorce proceedings were underway. Her one phone call to 911 back in 1996 was because she was upset Brame had left the house and taken his guns. She may have been covering up for him, but she specifically told the police that Brame had not threatened her. Was Crystal simply afraid? Probably—but experts insist that in domestic violence cases, there is always a trail of abuse.

Somebody sees it, somebody remembers it, somebody takes a photograph of it. That's what prosecutors look for when considering whether to bring murder charges against a woman who murders her husband and then claims that she was battered.

In 2004, a Houston, Texas, housewife named Susan Wright stabbed her husband 193 times. She claimed she was an abused woman, emotionally and physically. The case went to prosecutor Kelly Seigler, otherwise known as the toughest little prosecutor in the toughest county in Texas. Seigler had believed other women who had killed and later claimed they were battered, but she didn't believe Susan Wright. Why? Because of a lack of physical evidence. Had Susan filed a police report? Had she gone to a doctor with her injuries? Had anyone seen the injuries? Had she taken photographs? In Susan Wright's case, her mother and a girlfriend testified they had seen Susan with a black eye and indeed, she had a large bruise on her thigh when she was arrested. But to Seigler, even that wasn't enough. She prosecuted Susan Wright for murder and won a conviction; Wright was sentenced to twenty-five years in prison.

Compare that case to Crystal's. In her case, there is no physical evidence, nothing except what she told others. In all the later complaints about David Brame, no one brought forth a photograph or mentioned a bruise they remembered or a black eye they saw.

In fact, it was David Brame who had photographs of abuse he said he suffered at Crystal's hands and it was Crystal who was heard yelling at Brame and her children on the phone by people who "had no dog in this fight."

The key to the relationship clearly was control. Brame controlled Crystal in every way possible but she occasionally lashed out. Nevertheless, as long as she stayed in the marriage, the control belonged to Brame. When she left and began speaking openly about their intimate secrets and Brame's bizarre behavior, the power shifted.

Crystal had the children and was gaining power; Brame was feeling more and more isolated and threatened. Their roles were being reversed and that was becoming increasingly more dangerous for Crystal. As Bill Kortenbach noted, David Brame had a lot to lose—his career and the only job he'd ever known.

24

"Big Bird"

Despite being a woman in a mostly male universe, Tacoma assistant police chief Catherine Woodard was well-respected within the Tacoma police department. She was one of the first women on the force and worked in the motorcycle detail before she began rising through the ranks. The fact that her nickname was "Big Bird" was nothing but a sign of affection. And besides, with her close-cropped blond hair and tall stature, Woodard does bear a funny and unmistakable resemblance to the Sesame Street character—so much so that, once you hear her called that, it's hard to get the image of Big Bird out of your head.

And just like her Muppet namesake, Woodard does exude an aura of caring. Maybe the role fell to her naturally because she worked around hardened men for so long, but there's no doubt that she had a good reputation, and many thought she would have been a much better and more thoughtful choice for the police chief's job than David Brame.

Woodard and Brame had a close working relationship and the worse his divorce got, the more he leaned on her, especially when Brame's personal assistant, Jeanette

Blackwell, refused to get involved. It fell to Woodard to give Brame a shoulder to cry on and cry he did. He used her in this two-month period—from mid-February to mid-April—to do his dirty work and relay thoughts and ideas to Crystal in hopes she might stop the divorce proceedings.

If you had asked Crystal Brame her opinion of Assistant Police Chief Woodard before March 10, 2003, she no doubt would have praised Woodard to the rafters. Woodard had been friendly with Crystal since January 1999, when David Brame was promoted to assistant chief. Though they mostly had a phone relationship, Crystal obviously liked Woodard and made it a point to call and wish her a happy forty-sixth birthday. Despite all that was happening in her private life, Crystal put on a good front, telling Woodard how proud she was of her husband's career and all his accomplishments.

It was not surprising, then, that on March 10 Crystal called Woodard at home to discuss her divorce. Woodard was out but her husband, Bill Woodard, took the call and, as usual, Crystal never passed up any opportunity to talk on the phone. She unloaded on Bill in lieu of Catherine. According to detailed notes Catherine took later after speaking to her husband, this is how the conversation went:

"He's [Brame] done a lot of things to me that you and Catherine have no idea about. One time, I was home sick, so sick that I was even vomiting and what did he do? He went out and bought a car! When he told me, I asked why he didn't consult me or ask me about that decision to spend $10,000, and you know what he said? He said, 'Crystal, I've been working a long time and the paycheck says David Brame on it. If I want to go out and buy a car, it's my business.' Can you believe that?

"He's always trying to control me. Anytime I go to any police function, he tells me that I can't dance with anyone else and if I do, I had better be prepared to walk home."

Bill Woodard asked if she'd met with the chaplain, if perhaps they could seek counseling. "I've met with the chaplain," Crystal said. "And I told him all about Dave's affair [at this point, Crystal was convinced that David was having an affair with Linda Watson apart from the suggested threesome] and how he wanted me to have a threesome with Linda Watson. He's sick. Things have been bad since he became chief. You have no idea. Dave's mother even hit David Jr. and the marks lasted three to four days. I don't want them to see her ever again. I told her not to touch my children but Dave, you know how he is. He won't be honest with me or anyone."

At this point, Crystal shifted gears and seemed to re-member why she called in the first place. "I have no hard feelings against Catherine and I hope she doesn't have any against me. The kids love her and you know I just wanted to let her know where we're living now. We're at my parents' home in Canterwood. Let me give you the phone number over here. Catherine can call us here any time. I'll leave it up to her if she wants to call. I know she's friends with Dave. It's up to her."

"Hey, look, Crystal, maybe the two of you can still work things out," Bill Woodard said to her.

"I don't think so. It's been unbearable and with the other women and all, I don't know. Dave told me if it bugged me so much that he was around other women to move on."

"Well," Woodard said, "it's natural for him to be around other women. There are lawyers and Catherine and Jeanette and other department directors."

"That's not it. I'm not talking about those women. I'm talking about 'other women' he's seeing, having affairs with. Look, this has nothing to do with the way I feel about you and Catherine. I appreciate all your support and your support of Dave to be chief. I just wanted to talk to Catherine about this but I'll leave it up to her whether she wants to call back."

Crystal wound up the conversation by repeating all the ways Brame tried to control her. To Bill Woodard, she seemed rational and didn't repeat herself like she often had in the past. She talked about how Brame would not give her any money for new clothes for the kids. "I had to take the kids' outgrown clothes to a recycling center and get a little money for them and he wanted half of that!"

"That doesn't sound like the chief."

"I know. That's the whole point. He doesn't treat other people this way. Why does he treat me this way?"

When his wife returned home, Bill Woodard told her about the conversation. Catherine knew what a contentious divorce the couple was having and didn't want to get in the middle. Still, she felt she owed it to David Brame—her boss—to tell him about the conversation. He immediately ordered her to write everything down.

What's more, Brame said, he wanted Woodard to call Crystal and initiate a conversation about the divorce. He enumerated three points for Woodard to relay: he wanted Crystal to stop using the children in the divorce; he wanted her to consider reconciliation, to know that he had never had an affair; and he wanted Crystal to slow down the legal process or stop it completely.

Woodard agreed and on March 31 she called Crystal at her parents' home in Canterwood. At eight p.m. the phone rang in the Judsons' home and they immediately saw on the caller ID that it was someone from the Tacoma police department. Crystal answered and turned the volume up so her mother, sitting next to her with her ear to the phone, could hear both sides. It was this conversation that changed the whole relationship between Crystal and Woodard and it was a monumental phone conversation for Woodard's career, though of course she had no idea until much later that it would become such an important issue.

In her own handwritten notes, Woodard writes, "The situation between Crystal and Dave seemed volatile."

As Woodard tried to make the points dictated to her by Brame, Crystal interjected, "The first thing Dave needs to do is stop sending death threats. I just want to be happy and safe."

"Crystal," said Woodard, "you are safe. David would never hurt you. He misses you."

"I just want the whole thing to keep moving on. I'm happy I did what I did and I'm not going back."

"Dave wants to get back together with you. Is there any chance you'd consider that?"

"No way. I am never going back to him and you can tell him I said that. Never, never! Not even a one half of one percent chance. He's made his choices and now he's going to have to live with them. I'm happy and I don't need him. I should have left a long time ago. Did you know that he's having an affair with Linda Watson? She's one of your detectives, Catherine, and he promoted her. What about that? He's got Linda now so I hope he's happy."

"He does not have Linda, Crystal. He never did. They are not having an affair. Dave wanted a threesome. He wanted you involved. You know that. I thought you were part of that discussion. I thought you discussed this with him and you were amenable."

"No way," Crystal said. "That's what *he* wants, not me. And there are others he wanted me to get involved with. It was always his sick idea, not mine. I'm just glad to be away from him now. I feel good about my decision. You've got to understand, Catherine, he's not the same man he is at work. If I were married to that man I'd be happily married, but he was nothing like that. I wish. I will always support Dave as the chief but that's it."

"He told me he misses the kids."

"Oh, he doesn't miss the kids, that's just what he likes to say. If he misses them so much, how come he never calls them?"

"I thought he called them every night to say good night. I know he's told me he would like to see them more."

"You're only hearing one side of the story. I understand, I know that Dave is your friend and that's okay. He always told me that if I had a problem with him wanting other women that I could move on and go my separate way, and that's what I'm doing."

"But there are no other women, Crystal."

"You don't know him, Catherine. You only see him at work. I'm getting a restraining order against him."

"Why? He'd never hurt you. He loves you."

"Listen, I don't want to put you in a bad spot. I know you work for him. I think the world of you and Bill. I don't want to make you uncomfortable; that's why I left it up to you to call back or not."

Woodard tried to steer the conversation to something other than Crystal and David.

"How are the kids dealing with all this?" Woodard asked.

"They're fine and they're very happy over here. They're busier than ever."

"That's good. You know I hope the kids don't get caught up in your divorce. It's hard on them."

"It is but I think things will settle down after a while. This is something I've wanted to do for three-and-a-half years."

"What made you finally do it?"

"All the threats and women, but there's something else. I begged David for three weeks before I left to tell me he loved me and he wouldn't do it. Why should I stay married to someone who won't tell me he loves me? I didn't want it to end this way. I didn't want to hurt Dave and that's why I filed in another county. I wanted to keep it quiet. I didn't have the papers served at work. I made sure they waited until he got home. I didn't want to be mean."

Woodard, a good soldier all the way, tried to get Crystal to change her mind. "The whole divorce thing is so cold. Why don't you stop it and the two of you can go to counseling or something?"

"I won't do that. I thought about Dave's feelings throughout this whole thing but he never once thought of mine. He put a lot of hurtful things in his papers. I tried to put his feelings first but he wouldn't do that for me. Do you know what he did, Catherine? Did he tell you? He froze me out of the TAPCA [credit union] account!"

Woodard had already heard the other side of the story from David. "No, he didn't, Crystal. All he did was require two signatures for withdrawal. It helps you too. That's very common for divorces. It happens all the time."

Crystal refused to budge. "No, no, what he did is illegal. Other lawyers told me so. Dave told me he doesn't care about legal papers. He says they don't mean a thing to him. He's not telling you the truth, Catherine. Did he tell you he said that he won't give me any money? He doesn't miss the kids. He tells you one thing and me the other."

"You know, Crystal, I think there's a lot of miscommunication here and that happens when you talk through lawyers. It would be nice if you two could sit down by yourselves and just talk things out."

"Don't you think I've offered to do that? He won't. He's even taking the food out of the house. Don't think I don't know what he's like, Catherine. I know he put you up to this phone call. I'm sure he's having you write everything down so you can tell him everything I said.

I don't want to be set up and used. He made his choices and I can't feel sorry for him anymore. It's over. You just know his side of things and it's all wrong."

"I know he loves you, Crystal."

"Too bad he wasn't faithful then. I'll never go back."

"Crystal, think about the kids. You should put them first."

"The kids *are* first. They're my top priority. They love their mom and they love their dad."

"Don't you think Dave should see the kids more than every other weekend?"

"I'll let the courts decide that. The kids come first but we all have to get through this."

"I understand. Let's talk about this more when we meet for lunch, okay?"

"Okay. Goodbye, Catherine."

"Bye."

In her notes on the phone conversation—which Woodard handed over to Brame—she noted that "Crystal was very pleasant with me but very businesslike in her approach, matter-of-fact and adamant that she's made up her mind and this is it. At this time, I am inclined not to meet her for lunch as I don't see an opportunity to convince her to slow the process and think about what she'd doing. Meeting and/or talking again may be more harmful than productive. I am aware of the hearing on April 10."

Woodard later told investigators that the one thing that surprised her in the conversation was Crystal's version of the events surrounding Linda Watson. Brame had told Woodard two weeks earlier—sometime in mid-March—that he and Crystal had attempted a threesome with Watson. In Brame's version, Crystal was totally willing. Brame even told Woodard that "Crystal will try anything once and Crystal wanted to try a threesome with retired police lieutenant *Jim Robinson*."

Woodard said she was not the only member of the department who knew of the proposed threesome. She said that Brame had also spilled his guts to Detective Barry McColeman, Assistant Chief Richard McCrea, his assistant, Jeanette Blackwell, and City Attorney Shelley Kerslake.

This became a major focus of the investigation that occurred after Brame's death. How could the chief of police tell so many subordinates that he and his wife wanted to have a sexual threesome with someone he supervised without triggering a sexual harassment complaint? Brame not only told his assistant chief of police, he even told a city attorney! At least four city workers did nothing when confronted with clear evidence of sexual harassment. Woodard later told investigators that she didn't do anything for a number of reasons, one of which is that she believed Brame's story that Crystal pursued the idea as much as he had. Why? Because Woodard had spotted Crystal at Watson's promotion ceremony; it had struck her as odd at the time because Crystal never attended those ceremonies. When Brame told her later of the threesome and Crystal's willingness to participate, it all made sense to Woodard and she figured it was all between consenting adults.

But there was another reason Woodard did nothing with the information. She admitted to investigators that she feared Brame. She knew how vindictive he could be and if she crossed him "Brame could demote me to a sergeant or something."

It might have been understandable from Woodard's point of view but it was a cowardly admission. She was, after all, the assigned Equal Employment Opportunity representative for city government whose job it was to handle sexual harassment complaints. Not telling anyone about what was going on with Watson and Crystal was unforgivable.

*   *   *

For Crystal and her parents, emotions were now at
a fever pitch. Every word spoken by anyone remotely
connected with Brame or the divorce was parsed and
examined for hidden meaning. They were especially
upset by that phone call from Woodard. Although in her
notes Woodard portrays the conversation as a friendly
chat that ended well, Crystal and the Judsons had a
much different interpretation. This was, they were sure,
yet another attempt by Brame to strong-arm and scare
Crystal. This was Brame using the police for intimidation. For sure, Woodard was doing Brame's bidding but,
in the clear light of day, it doesn't seem intimidating to
invite someone to lunch and, in fairness, Woodard was
returning Crystal's call.

Crystal and the Judsons did not see Woodard's call as
a friendly lunch invitation though. In fact, the Judsons
attribute two quotes to Woodard from that phone conversation not found in Woodard's four pages of single-
spaced, detailed handwritten notes. They insisted that
Woodard said, "I'm going to be very involved in your
divorce" and later, "Be very careful what you do and
what you say."

Because of that phone call Woodard became Enemy
Number Two to the Judsons and her involvement with
the divorce took center stage. The Judsons even suspected she might be having an affair with Brame. It
didn't bode well for the change of venue hearing on
April 10. Emotions were running high but they were a
long way from the top.

25

Countdown to Disaster:
April 7

It was a Monday night and Brame was still hanging on, living out his depressing days in the family home on Eagle Creek Lane, hoping that this whole divorce thing would just go away. He desperately wanted Crystal and the kids to move back home and forget all about it. He told intimates that he now realized what he had lost but that he was still hopeful there would be a reconciliation.

Each night was worse than the one before. The house was empty and David Brame could feel its isolation closing in on him. He didn't have many friends but he still had a few loyalists within the department he could lean on for support. One of them was Captain Bill Meeks. Meek is a burly guy who has made friends with one too many cheeseburgers. Balding, with a bushy mustache, he no longer looks like the football lineman he once was. But those who know Meeks say he's a good guy who wears his heart on his sleeve. He always had a soft spot for Brame because they are only a year apart in age and started on the force around the same time. He and Brame had been partners and Meeks had had dozens of conversations with Brame; he knew Brame was a bright guy and embraced Brame's vision.

On this night, David Brame invited Meeks to come by and watch the NCAA final game on CBS. Brame had always loved basketball. He played for his high school championship team and, during his early years on the force, he still practiced at the downtown YMCA. Friends say he was so good that every match was one-sided. He could launch jumpers from thirty feet out and hit nothing but net, or he could go inside and whiz by you so fast, you didn't have a chance to defend.

But on this night, Brame the athlete was a thing of the past. He was depressed but still had a bit of wit about him. Meeks sent him an e-mail late in the day offering to pick up a pizza. "Is sausage okay with you?" he wrote.

"Sure, anything that used to be long but is cut up into tiny useless pieces is fine," Brame wrote back.

When Meeks got there, the two ate pizza, watched Syracuse win the national championship and talked intimately about Brame's divorce. Brame told Meeks that it was going to ruin his career.

"Why?"

He hesitated. "I've done some things I shouldn't have done."

"Like what?"

Brame told him about the visits to the nudist colony in California. Meeks was shocked. He'd always thought of Brame as a prude and this was the first time he had any inkling about David's secret life. Still, he wanted to be supportive so he acted nonchalant about the revelation. "You haven't told me anything that's going to get you fired."

"There's more."

"Such as?"

"I'll tell you another time."

"Listen, nothing you've told me tonight is going to get you fired. What's going to get you fired is not paying attention to your job. Do your job."

"Okay, that's good advice. Thanks."

26

April 10

On the morning of April 10, 2003, Brame tried to reexert some small measure of control. Ann Meath, his lawyer, was asking the court that day for a change of venue; Brame desperately wanted to bring the divorce case from Kent back to Tacoma where he had more influence. By then, all the charges and countercharges were in publicly accessible documents filed with the court. They were damning and would have made a front-page newspaper story in any city in the country but so far, none of the reporters working Seattle or Tacoma had come across them. What's more, the Tacoma *News Tribune* for whatever reason, did not report what was going on in the department, despite dozens of police officers now talking about it openly and the rumors running rampant through the department, the offices of Tacoma and even back in Gig Harbor. During this period, there was never a word in the *News Tribune* even hinting at any of the turmoil bubbling right under the surface.

At seven a.m. on April 10, David Brame rounded up the people he would bring to the meeting. All of them worked for him and probably had little choice in the matter. When he walked into the King County Regional

Justice Center at nine a.m., Brame was accompanied by Assistant Chief Woodard, Detective Barry McColeman and Police Officer James Mattheis, who also happened to be the public information officer for the Tacoma police department.

Crystal brought her own support system with her but it was much more personal. Her sister, Julie, and their parents, Lane and Patty Judson, were there for Crystal. Lane Judson remembers being taken aback that his son-in-law had chosen to bring his subordinates. "We were a little surprised," Lane said. "I thought maybe he'd have his mother or dad or his sister or somebody. But he didn't. It looked like pure intimidation. Three cops. He was showing us that he was the power, that he had the cops on his side."

During the hearing that followed, Julie and Crystal believed that Woodard was staring at Crystal to intimidate her. Woodard was very uncomfortable being dragged into Brame's divorce but she felt she had no choice.

There were actually two reasons for the hearing. Besides the change of venue request, there was a request from Crystal's side about finally getting some money for her and the kids. "He hadn't really given her any money for support," her father said. "And when Crystal's attorney said that, his attorney jumped up and said, 'Oh, we'll be writing a $2,000 check right away.' So after a few minutes they decided they weren't going to hear the whole case right then. It was rescheduled for April 18. The judge had not read all the paperwork or whatever. So we were dismissed from court."

But no one left right away. The two attorneys—Joseph Lombino for Crystal and Ann Meath for David— hunkered down for another forty-five minutes going over paperwork. Woodard said that she and the others, including Brame, went to the lobby to wait. Crystal and the Judsons listened in as Meath tried to negotiate some

extra visitation between David and his children. Meath
kept going back and forth between the two sides with
little tidbits of information. Finally, Crystal spoke up and
expressed her frustration. "You know I keep giving up,
giving up, giving up things and he just keeps asking for
more and more and more. And someplace it's gotta stop.

"I still haven't received clothes that I've asked for a
long time ago. I'd like to have some of my clothes."

Meath went out to the hallway to tell Brame what
Crystal wanted: lamps, ice skates and clothes from the
house on Eagle Creek Lane. The two lawyers talked
again about the exchange of the children. Up until that
point, everything had gone fairly well with the ex-
changes. They were always done at the Judson house in
Canterwood where Crystal felt safe, and her parents
were always present when Brame came to pick the children up.

But maybe Meath sensed the seething hostility in the
room. In any event, she advised Brame, "Don't play
games. Don't go alone to pick up the children."

Brame previously had asked Jeanette Blackwell to go
with him to his in-laws' house when he had to pick up
his children, but Blackwell had refused because she was
about to go on vacation to Disneyland with her children.
So when Meath made her recommendation in the court-
house hallway, Woodard spoke up to say that she and
Crystal had a decent relationship. Meath nodded and
said, "Okay, you go." Then Meath went back into the
hearing room to meet with Lombino.

Unbeknownst to Woodard, Crystal and the Judsons
vehemently opposed Woodard accompanying Brame to
their house. It was because of that phone call from
March 31; it had totally soured Crystal and the Judsons
on Woodard. The Judsons thought it was possible that
Brame and Woodard were having an affair. Lane and
Patty voiced their concerns about Woodard and told
Meath that they would stop by the house that weekend

while David was with the kids at his apartment and they would pick up Crystal's things. But that never was communicated back to Brame and Woodard. It appeared to be an oversight in the hustle and bustle of getting things done. Without knowing any of this, Woodard just assumed it was all set; she would accompany Brame the next night to pick up the kids. It was a trip she would forever regret.

27

The Night of April 11

At four thirty p.m. on April 11, Woodard drove her Ford Expedition over to the Brame family home on Eagle Creek Lane. Brame gave her a tour of the house and walked her back to the clothes closet where he had allegedly threatened Crystal's life just two months before. Woodard picked out the clothes Crystal had asked for and put them in a bag. She also collected Haley's skates and some other things. Brame insisted on photographing everything Woodard was taking and then sat down to watch his wedding video. Woodard held her tongue; at this point, she was used to Brame's odd behavior and still lived in fear that any sign of disloyalty would get her busted to sergeant. At 5:50 P.M., Brame had apparently walked down memory lane enough and rose from the sofa. They decided to take his car over to the Judson home, which was only about ten minutes away.

At six p.m, David Brame drove his red Toyota Camry up to the guardhouse at the entrance to Canterwood. Catherine Woodard, dressed in civilian clothes and not carrying her service weapon, sat next to him in the front seat. A few moments before, Patty Judson had called down to the guardhouse and told gate guard Michael

Berquist that David Brame would be coming by and that
he should be allowed in because he was picking up her
grandchildren. Berquist made a note of it and soon
enough, Brame pulled his car up to the gate and told
them he was there to see the Judsons.

"You must be David Brame," Berquist said.

Berquist said that Brame just smirked and nodded.
Berquist looked in the car and saw "a woman with light-
colored hair" but that was it. She didn't say a word.

Berquist made a notation on his notepad and waved
them through. Then he got on the phone and told the
Judsons, "Brame's here."

The Judsons, already on high alert after the show of
force at the previous day's change of venue hearing,
thought Berquist had said, "The Brames are here."

"The Brames? I wonder what he's talking about,"
Patty asked her husband and daughter.

In the two or three minutes it took for Brame and
Woodard to reach the house, Patty, Lane and Crystal
whipped themselves into fervor. Who was in that car
besides David? Was it Beverly Brame, whom Crystal
could not abide? Was it David's sister, Jane? Was it
Linda Watson? Would Brame dare bring "the other
woman" to pick up his children at his in-laws' house?
All sorts of conspiracy theories were in play when
Brame finally rang the front doorbell. One can only
imagine what little Haley and David were thinking as
the adults ran around in such a state.

Patty answered the doorbell to see her son-in-law and
Catherine Woodard standing there. "What are you doing
here?" she demanded of Woodard, who remembers
being startled by Patty's reaction. She still had no clue
how deeply Crystal and the Judsons had come to despise
her. What's more, neither she nor Brame had any idea
that the Judsons had vetoed the idea of her coming to
their house at the hearing the day before. Woodard
thought all of that had been settled and that she was the

compromise choice. Ann Meath, it turned out, had never mentioned that the Judsons and Crystal didn't want Woodard anywhere near their house. At that point, Crystal blurted out, "You're not a Brame. Why are you here?"

"I'm here to support Dave," Woodard told them.

Crystal was extremely angry. Even though Woodard is a strapping six feet tall, Crystal stepped right up to her. "You're here because you're nosey. I think you should leave."

Crystal then grabbed for the bag of clothes that Woodard was holding. Woodard said she was literally taken aback and took a step backward. Crystal shrieked, "Please give me my clothes."

"Sure, let me show you what I picked out," Woodard recalls saying.

But the Judsons heard differently. They swear they heard her say, "I will show you what I've chosen for you."

Both sides agree that Brame didn't say anything. He just stood there. Woodard claimed later that everyone was yelling and running around and that what she thought was going to be a nonevent turned into a one-sided screaming match, mainly on the part of Crystal and the Judsons, who took Woodard's appearance as another of their son-in-law's intimidation tactics. But there was another reason as well. "We didn't want the little children to see their father with another woman," Lane said. He and Patty and probably Crystal had become convinced that Woodard was having an affair with Brame.

At that point, Lane grabbed the bag of clothes out of Woodard's hands and told her, "You're not welcome here. You shouldn't be here."

It was an ugly scene, and it's no surprise that Haley and David Jr. began crying. Woodard later said she was aghast, wondering how a simple pickup had turned so bad so fast. Woodard had her hands clasped behind her back in a stance commonly referred to as "parade rest." Lane thought she was trying to intimidate them again, when in all likelihood it was simply the way she stood. Friends later said that she was known for standing that way. But Lane mimicked her stance.

"Why are you standing like that?" she asked.

"I'm standing the same way you are. Why, is that supposed to be intimidating?"

At that point, Brame and Woodard rounded up the children and led them to the car.

Crystal ran over to the car window and kissed one of the kids. "Close the door," Brame told her. "We're leaving."

Woodard was sitting in the passenger seat and, to the Judsons, she and Brame appeared to be a couple. The car pulled away and Crystal and her parents were left to stew about the encounter. What they didn't see was that Woodard herself was crying as the car pulled out. She had never been so humiliated, and she regretted ever involving herself in Brame's personal affairs. Brame saw her tears but said nothing, and she later told everyone that what really bothered her the most about that night was that Brame never once—then or any other time—told her he was sorry for getting her mixed up in his private affairs.

But that wasn't the end of the incident for Crystal and her parents. As they ruminated on it, they decided that Woodard had been guilty of trespassing and intimidation. They called the gatehouse and spoke to Michael Berquist to see what they could do. Later that night, Patty picked up the phone and dialed 911 and then put her daughter on. It was the first and only time in her eleven-year-marriage that Crystal actually reported abuse to the police. The phone call was recorded; these are the highlights:

CRYSTAL: My husband and I are going through a
divorce . . . My children . . . I have sole custody of
the children . . . The issues are that I'm staying for
security and safety reasons [with my parents] . . .
Because of numerous death threats from my
husband . . . There will be a restraining order entered next Friday . . . Due to several death threats
and people that he works with intimidating me . . .
He is the chief of police for Tacoma. He does carry
a firearm . . .

911: Tacoma chief of police?

CRYSTAL: David Brame, my husband that I'm
divorcing.

911: Oh, that's your husband, David Brame?

CRYSTAL: Yes, this is where the problem lies. He
brought one of the assistant chiefs here, who is now
an unwanted guest who has intimidated and threatened me during this divorce process. And it had
already been made known to my attorney, she was
not to have any further contact with me and has
done this tonight and showed up uninvited as an
unwanted guest at my parents' home.

911: With your husband?

CRYSTAL: Yes, with my husband.

911: Who is the chief of police.

CRYSTAL: My husband, David Brame.

911: Okay, I just wanted to make sure.

CRYSTAL: I'm Crystal Brame. We are in the middle
of the divorce and I have my parents here in order
to exchange the children for my safety because
there has been so many death threats with him. So
I have to have this exchange done in front of witnesses so I'm not one-on-one with him for my own
personal safety.

    He has lied to the guards to get in here . . .
David was supposed to come in alone. He told the

guard that the Brames were here, [indicated] they were a couple. They were not and it was one of his assistant chiefs, a female assistant chief, the one who has also intimidated me.

911: And what's that person's name?

CRYSTAL: That's Catherine Woodard . . . the five-year-old was just beside himself.

911: What exactly did she do?

CRYSTAL: She wouldn't leave the property and also she had some of my personal items of my clothing. It was agreed upon . . . that my parents retrieve my items, enter the home. I'm not going into the home due to safety reasons and safety issues.

911: Okay, did you guys exchange the children tonight? Was it the fact that he brought someone else there and he wasn't supposed to?

CRYSTAL: That's correct.

911: Okay, did any death threats take place tonight?

CRYSTAL: No death threats tonight.

911: Okay, well, I'll get a call in and I will get someone out there to contact you just as soon as I can.

Sergeant Kyle Wilson of the Pierce County sheriff's department was working the graveyard shift when he got word that there was a call he should definitely take a look at. It was a request from Crystal Brame to have someone go to her house so she could report an incident involving her husband, David Brame, the Tacoma chief of police. The report summarized the rest, including the presence of Assistant Chief Catherine Woodard. Wilson decided he would call "Miss Brame" before sending a car.

A "calm" Crystal Brame answered his call and immediately began telling him the history of her divorce and why she was concerned about what had happened. She repeated, as she had many times since filing, her allegations that David Brame had threatened her life and physically abused her.

"Have you ever reported any of these domestic violence incidents?" Wilson asked.

"No, but only because I was afraid he'd lose his job. In fact, I filed for divorce in King County to keep the whole thing quiet but he wants to bring it back to Pierce County."

"Yes, ma'am, but do you have a protective order against your husband?"

"No, but I told you I didn't want him to lose his job so I didn't seek a restraining order, but we're going back to court next week to get one. Things are just getting worse and worse and I've given a diary of all the violent incidents to my lawyer, Joseph Lombino."

"That's a good idea," Wilson said. "Have you ever reported anything to the Tacoma police?"

"No, for the same reason, I was concerned about his job."

At this point, Crystal began talking more and more about Woodard and her involvement and how she and her parents believed Woodard was guilty of trespassing. So far Wilson had not heard anything that made him feel sending a car was necessary. Brame and Woodard were long gone.

"Were there any threats or any death threats or any crimes committed once these two individuals had arrived on the property?"

"No, I don't think so, except that Catherine Woodard would not leave when we asked her to."

Wilson explained that, if Crystal had called while Woodard was still there and if the police could see that they were asking her to leave and she would not, they could arrest her for trespassing. Anything else would likely not stand up in court. As far as Wilson was concerned, this was a borderline trespassing case at best. He further advised her on what she could do to obtain an order of protection and then told her he would not be sending a car out.

"Is there anything else I can do for you?"

"Will you be writing up a report?" Crystal asked.

She told Wilson she wanted to make sure there was a record of the incident that she could tell her lawyer about. Wilson assured her he had the notes in his notebook and that her lawyer could contact him at any time.

Both sides hung up and it seemed that was the end of it. But in reality, it was just the beginning of a night that later would have severe consequences for Catherine Woodard.

Crystal's phone call created a paper trail: a report to Central Dispatch at the Tacoma police department and what was known in the internal lingo of the police department as a CAD (computer aided dispatch) report. Brame got wind of it soon after it was made and he called Woodard around eleven thirty p.m. For Woodard, emotionally spent by the night's events, things were about to get even worse. Brame wanted her to call City Manager Ray Corpuz to explain what had happened at the Judson home. Woodard did just that because she wanted him to hear what happened directly from her. She called his cell phone but couldn't reach him so she left a message.

A friendly captain faxed her the report so she could read it for herself. She was crushed. In her mind, she had only been helping out a distraught boss and for this, she now had some serious explaining to do. That night and over the next few days that CAD readout was passed along from Tacoma cop to Tacoma cop until dozens of officers and other personnel within the department were aware of it. Here was tangible proof of how ugly the Brame divorce was becoming, and it was also proof of something else—Brame was dragging those in the department into his sordid personal affairs.

It was only a matter of time before word of what was going on reached John Hathaway.

28

Saturday, April 12

At ten the next morning—even though it was a weekend—Woodard phoned Ray Corpuz to explain from her point of view what had gone down at the Judsons'. Corpuz, a quiet man, simply took it all in. He said nothing about any sort of punishment for Woodard or Brame. To him, it was probably no more than a misunderstanding.

But Woodard was beside herself. This was not the first time she had approached the city manager about Brame. In particular, she recalled a conversation less than a week before. She went to Corpuz that time also even though she feared for her job and felt she was going out on a limb. She knew Corpuz thought highly of Brame, and there was always the chance that he would tell Brame what Woodard had said. If that happened, she was sure Brame would retaliate. Despite the risks, she went ahead and bluntly told Corpuz that Brame was not focused on his work, that he was making the department look bad.

She even gave Corpuz a concrete example. At a recent meeting of local police chiefs concerning the release of sex offenders, Brame had arrived late and left early, and several other chiefs were not happy with his performance. Other times, Brame had simply not even shown up for important meetings. At their earlier meeting, Corpuz told Woodard that Brame had told him the department was running smoothly and that he had heard no other complaints. Woodard fired back that all the assistant chiefs feared for their jobs and were afraid to speak out. She was taking a chance even meeting with him. Corpuz promised he would speak to Brame.

A few days later, Woodard asked Corpuz if he had indeed spoken to Brame. Corpuz reassured her that he had warned him to stay focused on the department and to strike a better balance between his home and work lives.

On April 12, after telling Corpuz about the latest incident between Brame and his wife, she asked Corpuz straight out, "Do you understand what's going on with David Brame?"

"Yes," Corpuz said, "more than I want to. I've warned him on at least five occasions to stay focused on his job."

After her conversation with Corpuz, Woodard buttonholed Detective Barry McColeman. He had been there when Brame's lawyer, Ann Meath, had agreed that Woodard should go along. Woodard complained to McColeman that Brame was so self-centered that it was no surprise he had not apologized for the upsetting scene.

Later that afternoon, Woodard got a taste of how far the CAD report had circulated. Bill Meeks had heard the "hot rumor" about the incident from other cops, and when he spotted Woodard in the parking lot outside the County-City Building, he simply asked her, "Hey, how's it going?"

Woodard obviously wanted to talk to someone. "Not so good," she said, handing Meeks a copy of the CAD report.

Meeks read it over even though he'd already heard all about it. "This is not good," he said by way of understatement.

"Yeah," said Woodard. "I know."

Meeks silently thanked his lucky stars. Brame had wanted him to accompany him to the court on April 10 but he'd begged off because of a golf date. It might have been him at the Judson home that night.

Despite the whispers that were growing to shouts within the department, there still was nothing in the Tacoma *News Tribune;* the paper and its readers remained blissfully unaware of any problems within the police department or with the new police chief who, according to his underlings, was falling apart on the job.

Brame had always had an overblown sense of his own importance, and the frustration in his private life caused it to overflow. To him, his divorce was the biggest news in the world. Friends within the department—even Jeanette Blackwell—told him time and again to get on with his life and to grow up. Many of them had been through their own divorces and knew its course. Things would get better, they promised. You just had to ride it out. But Brame wouldn't or couldn't take their advice.

That evening, Brame called Bill Meeks at home. He was emotional and obviously crying.

"What's the matter, Dave?"

"I've gotta move outta here. Can you help me?"

In the background, Meeks could hear the Brame children playing.

"Sure I'll help you, but not tonight. You got the kids over there. Go play with them and we'll do it Sunday after you drop them off, okay?"

"Yeah," Brame agreed. He valued Meeks' friendship and wisdom and, as he often did, he agreed with Meeks' assessment of the situation. "That's good advice. I'll see you tomorrow."

Sunday, April 13

By late afternoon, David Brame had returned his children to Crystal at her parents' Canterwood home. Maybe his buddy Bill Meeks was right. Maybe it was time to get on with his life, time to move on. He called those closest to him for help; it was time to move to his own, newly rented apartment. That afternoon, a caravan of family members and subordinates arrived to help him pack up. There was his sister, Jane Brazell; Bill Meeks; and Assistant Chiefs Rich McCrea and Don Ramsdell.

When Jane got there, she couldn't believe what she was seeing. Her brother was mowing the front lawn. The control that David Brame held over Crystal was clearly shifting.

"What are you doing?" Jane asked.

"What does it look like?"

"David, honestly, you're leaving. You don't have to do this."

"Well," he said sheepishly, "Crystal just called and she said if I didn't leave the house in good shape, she was gonna call her lawyer. She insisted that I cut the grass so I figured why not?"

Jane looked at him incredulously and went into the

house to begin the packing. A neighbor came over to offer David his sympathy. "Look, we filed a declaration for Crystal being a good mother but we'd do the same for you if you like. I always saw you with the kids. You're a good dad as far as I can see."

David was touched. "Thanks, I appreciate it. I'll let you know."

The neighbor turned to leave but had something more on his mind. "Hey, Dave, just between us guys, I know that Crystal is kind of loosely wrapped."

David Brame nodded but could say no more. He was all choked up that finally someone had seen it his way.

Back inside, the packing had begun. "It was kind of funny almost," said one of those who was there. "He had this list from Crystal and it was so detailed, it was unbelievable. Like he could take one table setting but that was it. She was getting down to the spoons. It was nuts. There was a bunch of junk there he didn't even want, like an old grill and some weight training equipment, but he didn't want to leave it because he didn't want Crystal to have anything she hadn't written down. It was kind of ugly, your classic divorce situation. But that list, that list was what Crystal was all about. In fact, it was the Rosetta Stone to her personality. I've seen a lot of divorces but I've never seen a list like that."

Referring to "the list," David went room to room, pointing out what could and could not be taken. It's interesting that, no matter how much she disliked the Thomas Kinkade lithographs that David had bought for her, she insisted on keeping them. A present is a present is a present. Brame went along with her demand.

As they all moved through the house, taking this and leaving that, Brame paused in his bedroom. "Hey," he said to McCrea and Meeks, "you guys wanna watch my wedding video? You were a lot thinner."

They laughed but declined. It seemed especially weird that Brame would even consider watching the video of a marriage that was literally being taken apart piece by piece in front of them. They didn't know it but Brame had become obsessed with that video, looking at it over and over again to remember the good times. He'd watched it dozens of times since Crystal had moved out.

"He wasn't all that depressed. In fact, he seemed okay with the move. He could even joke about the place he was moving to, a three-bedroom apartment at a place called Gold Pointe apartments; he called them the 'Up the Creek' apartments," said one person on the scene.

By nightfall, it was all over. David Brame looked wistfully at the house where his children had been raised. It was time to move on whether he wanted to or not. He honked his horn and the little caravan made a U-turn in the cul-de-sac at the end of the street. For the last time anyone knew, David Brame passed his home on Eagle Creek Lane, never to return.

•

30

Tuesday, April 15

It didn't take long for the incident at Canterwood to take on mythic proportions within the department, especially among those in the cliques who hated Brame. On April 15, Tacoma police lieutenant Bob Sheehan, a Brame protégé who worked in Internal Affairs, received an anonymous typewritten letter. It was addressed to "TPD Internal Affairs" but mentioned Sheehan by name. The letter was a bombshell: a group of "concerned officers" was demanding that the department investigate its own chief and assistant chief. The letter showed clearly how widespread the knowledge was of Catherine Woodard's visit to the Judsons' home just a few days earlier, and it reiterated the essence of the now-infamous visit, focusing on one key point:

> *Many of us patrol officers are extremely disturbed, offended, but not surprised by the allegations brought against Chief David Brame and Asst Chief Catherine Woodard today, 4/11/03. We would all be very interested to find out if Chief Brame and Asst Chief Woodard used their badges to gain ac-*

cess into the private community for personal reasons.

We, as officers, demand that Chief Brame be investigated with the exact same fervor, lust, enthusiasm and diligence that you have shown when investigating patrol officers. We demand that if you are not able to do this in an unbiased fashion, which we all know you won't be able to, that you turn over the investigation to a law enforcement agency that will be UNBIASED [sic] in their investigation. Rest assured we are not fans of Chief Brame, and we will do everything to see that this incident is broadcast on the news and put into the papers. We will also be advising these news agencies that you will be attempting to cover this story up, which we, who have lost faith in this department's inept administration, know will happen.

For once it would be nice to see the administrators "practice what they preach" and maybe try to live up to the standards set down in the glorious letter we all received from Chief Brame.

Signed,
Concerned Officers of TPD

Obviously, Brame's enemies within the department wrote the letter; it was a shot across the bow. Sheehan recognized the letter for what it was: a political hot potato. He knew that Brame considered loyalty "a very, very big thing" and Sheehan wasn't going to handle that letter if he didn't have to. Sheehan passed the hot potato up the chain of command to Assistant Chiefs Richard McCrea and Catherine Woodard. In his memo to the file days later, Sheehan wrote that Woodard told him it would be inappropriate for her to supervise an investigation into herself and told Sheehan she would alert City Manager Ray Corpuz about the situation. Also informed were Internal Affairs Detective Tom Davidson and Sergeant Bob Blystone of the department's Professional Responsibility Bureau, the department revitalized by Brame.

With so many bigwigs involved, it stood to reason that something would be done. At the very least, why chance having the disgruntled cops take the story to the press? But that's not the way things were done in the city run by Ray Corpuz. It was a key moment in what became known as the disastrous "Brame affair." Corpuz had a chance to investigate and take some punitive action, to at least step in and warn Brame—the man Corpuz had appointed barely a year before—but instead he did nothing.

Sheehan outlined in his memo the official city response to the officers' incendiary letter: "There would be no investigation per the city manager. This was due to the fact that the complaint was anonymous."

31

"The Man Who Knows Too Much"

Like a lot of gadflies, John Hathaway rubs people the wrong way. While he has his supporters, there's a general sense of "who hired this guy anyway?" whenever his name comes up. *That,* and a lot of eye-rolling.

Cops tend to feel the same way about him as the public. After I'd interviewed one top cop about Hathaway, he pulled me aside to make sure I didn't use any of the positive things he had to say. It would, he explained, put him in a bad light with a lot of other cops.

But not all. Hathaway has some close friends on the force. One of them is Lieutenant Joe Kirby, one of the Meinemites, a member of the "racing team" headed by Captain Meinema, a man who harbored a longtime grudge against Brame. Kirby is very much a maverick, having sued City Manager Ray Corpuz and Brame back in 1999 over employment discrimination within the police department. Kirby finds a lot to like in Hathaway and the feeling is mutual.

So Hathaway has his friends on the force and it's probably not surprising that, after Ray Corpuz told Internal Affairs that there would be no investigation into Brame's and Woodard's visit to the Judson home, some

important papers miraculously made their way literally
to Hathaway's doorstep. Those papers were part of the
public record and available to anyone.

It was still Holy Week when Hathaway stepped outside of his small apartment on East Thirty-fourth Street
to fish his daily copy of the *News Tribune* out of his
newspaper tube, only to find something else waiting for
him—a copy of the Brame divorce papers.

This was no mere tidbit of news; it was more like
"Deep Throat" paying a visit to Woodward and Bern-
stein. Hathaway could not believe what he was reading.
"This guy was the chief of police and he was threatening
his wife with a department-issued gun. I mean, come on.
There were a lot of ugly things in those papers; they
made me sick to my stomach."

Hathaway began his reporting; he e-mailed Brame for
a comment. None ever came, but that didn't stop Hathaway. He was well known to the city leaders and easily
got through to Mayor Bill Baarsma, who at first didn't
believe what Hathaway was telling him. Baarsma felt
divorce was a private matter and told Hathaway so.
Baarsma had known Brame since he was a student of
his at the University of Puget Sound and had lobbied
hard to have him appointed police chief. His response
echoed Corpuz: a lot of things get written up in divorce
papers that are not true.

Hathaway thought the papers at least deserved a public airing so, as he frequently does, he assumed the role
of his alter ego, Paul Malone—"keeper of inside dirt
supreme"—and began writing a sarcastic column pre-
tending to be a fictional 1940s columnist dishing the dirt.

Holy Thursday, April 17

Around five thirty p.m., David Brame paged Bill Meeks, who was already at his home on Fox Island, having left early to beat the rush hour traffic across the Tacoma Narrows Bridge.

"Where are you?" Brame asked.

"Home, watching the Mariners."

"Oh, jeez, I wanted to talk to you."

"Do you want me to come back in?"

"No, what time are you getting in tomorrow?"

"What time do you want me there?"

"I don't know, what time do you get in?"

"David, you name a time. I'll be there."

"Okay, how about eight?"

"Okay, I'll be in your office at eight tomorrow morning. See you then."

Good Friday, April 18

David Brame was late. Bill Meeks sat in his office for forty-five minutes waiting until he showed up. He breezed in, apologizing. Meeks could see something was on his mind.

"How are you doin', Dave?"

"Not good. I'm worried about the kids. I don't want to be a weekend daddy. I want to be involved in their lives."

"It's gonna be all right. You just gotta get your head straight and concentrate on your kids when they're with you. They'll be all right too."

"Okay, good advice. Anyway, I've made a decision. I want you to be one of my assistant chiefs."

Meeks was hesitant about accepting the job because he'd been in a mini-scandal of his own the year before. The Tacoma Police had raided a drug warehouse and, among other things, they'd seized baseball hats that read: "Yes Greenhouse." Meeks had grabbed one and had worn it to a department meeting. Lt. Joe Kirby, a member of the clique that hated Brame, filed a complaint and reported Meeks for having stolen contraband. Brame ordered Meeks to stop wearing the hat and to get some retraining. Because of that incident, Meeks felt he had been frozen out of Brame's inner circle for about a year.

Brame's offer to make Meeks an assistant chief meant the end of what Meeks called his "penance."

"Are you sure you want me?" he asked Brame.

"Yes, what's past is past. So do you accept [my offer]?"

Meeks thought about it; he was a terrific writer and he knew Brame needed him to write his pronouncements to the staff. He accepted the promotion.

"All right, congratulations," Brame said, shaking his hand. "We'll announce it on Monday but I want you to do me a favor next week."

"Sure."

"I have to go to a seminar Tuesday through Friday. I want you to be acting chief while I'm out of town."

"Oh jeez, Dave, I have a golfing trip planned to Arizona on Wednesday but I could fill in Tuesday."

"Okay, okay. I'll have Catherine fill in starting Wednesday then. Just keep it quiet until Monday, okay?"

"You got it. Thanks."

Throughout this period, David Brame continued to live his double life. On one hand, he was the doting dad worried how his kids would react to the divorce; on the other, he was still on the hunt for women.

And he had never stopped thinking about newly promoted detective Linda Watson. Brame's calls to her had tailed off as his troubles had mounted, but now that he was alone all the time, he began calling again.

Watson, meanwhile, had been concentrating on her new job and basically just trying to avoid the chief. At least her life seemed to be returning to normal. "I'm thinking things are finally getting better and then in mid-

February he starts pressuring me to have lunch with him again," she said.

By then, Watson was used to Brame's obnoxious behavior and just kept making and then canceling one lunch meeting after another.

Watson made more excuses and blew Brame off, but he wouldn't quit. He paged her again and again. On Friday, April 18, his pages were so frequent that she finally called him back.

The moment Brame heard her voice, he said, "Crystal's gone off the deep end. She's telling everyone that we were having an affair. We need to meet."

Watson was shocked. There had never been any affair and Crystal should have known that, but Watson couldn't blame the poor woman—her husband was a crazed sex fiend in Watson's opinion.

"What are you talking about?" Watson asked him.

"I can't talk about it right now," he said. "We just need to meet. We need to work out a plan."

She knew they had to have this out and was admittedly curious to hear more. "Fine."

"How about if we meet at your house?" he asked.

"No way. I'll meet you somewhere in Tacoma for lunch or whatever but we're not meeting at my house."

"No, we can't do that," he said. "We can't meet in public because if anyone sees us together, that will validate everything she's saying. It's either gotta be your place or my place."

"Well, it sure as hell isn't going to be my place."

"Then come over to my place."

Watson didn't know what to do but she wanted to at least hear Brame out. "Okay, okay, where do you live?"

"She kicked me out of the house. I'm over at the Gold Pointe apartments in Tacoma."

"I'll be there in an hour and you can fill me in on what's going on."

An hour later, Watson knocked at Brame's front door. She had not seen him since January and could not believe the change in his appearance. "The guy looked horrible. He was thin and just didn't look too good."

Brame asked her in and immediately launched into every aspect of his divorce. "What was supposed to be one hour turned into three hours. He sat down and I sat down and he ticked off every accusation that she made. And he made it clear to me that it was important for me to understand that she was not credible and that his story was the true story.

"And then he goes on to tell me that she's named me in the divorce proceedings." (This was not true but at that point it's hard to say what Brame was thinking. Maybe he was just looking for a way to see Watson again and he was sure this would do it.)

Watson stood up. "You've got to be out of your mind. What are you saying?"

In Brame's weird version of events, Crystal had grown angry that Watson would not agree to the threesome. Brame said that Crystal had specifically gone to Watson's promotion ceremony to check her out and then had been upset when Watson wouldn't agree to three-way sex. Crystal, Brame said, had become convinced that he and Watson were already having an affair and had cut her out. She was so jealous that she had named Watson in the divorce papers. Watson could not believe what she was hearing from Brame.

"It's you and me against Crystal now because she's gonna say these things and make us both look bad," Brame told Watson.

"I was so mad, I told him, 'You don't know me from anybody.' How could you put your career on the line for this? It's just out and out inappropriate. You don't know how mad I was at that point," Watson said. "He just sat on the couch and started crying."

"You must think I'm a terrible guy," Brame said.

"I think you're a guy who has awful judgment and I think you're gonna make a lot of people experience a whole lot of pain for no reason. I don't deserve this. What are you gonna do to make this right?"

Brame told her he planned to move the case to Pierce County where he was powerful enough to have the records sealed. He told her that he'd had another case sealed but didn't go into details.

At that point, Watson had had enough. She felt sure he was crazy and that the media surely was going to get hold of the papers. Brame had been crying in front of her for three hours. She stood to leave. Brame moved toward her, but she blew by him and stalked out of his apartment, refusing to so much as shake his hand.

Easter Sunday, April 20

At this point, an increasingly desperate Chief Brame was leaning more and more on longtime coworkers like Detective Barry McColeman. McColeman started training to be a police office for Tacoma in November 1981, one month before David Brame. They were never the best of buddies early on in their careers; in fact, McColeman describes Brame as a "ghost" in those early days, someone who came and went and left little imprint. "I remember him being in the academy and then I remember working night shifts and at that time we'd rotate shifts every three months," McColeman told investigators. "It seemed like right when he came back from the academy that he went into crime prevention and then he got promoted to sergeant. So he didn't have a lot of credibility in patrol with the other patrol officers as far as he wasn't one of the go-getters out on the street or anything."

But the two got to know each other better when they became involved in the Police Union. In fact, McColeman was one of the cops who had heard the story of Brame's first marriage from Brame himself. "Dave was home sick one day and his wife said she had to run to the store and he got his robe on with his pajamas—this is him telling me about it—and he said he followed her and she went over to this other officer's house. And he went up and knocked on the door and confronted them and then that was the end of the marriage. It wasn't a physical confrontation. He went over there and knocked on the door and just said, 'What the hell are you doing over here?' "

Throughout the years, McColeman became a regular sounding board for Brame about everything from his desired threesome with Linda Watson to his contentious divorce with Crystal. Whether he wanted to or not (and oftentimes he did not), McColeman was often sought out by Brame. It's no surprise that, in the time period of March and April 2003, McColeman was with Brame nearly every step of the way. "I was just there as somebody that had been caught up in the whole Brame thing. That last month, you know, my life had kind of been turned upside down. My weekends and every night on the telephone and my family was put on hold in trying to help Dave get his stuff together."

Brame was calling McColeman "at least every other day" with Crystal updates. Like a lot of others, McColeman noticed that Brame had wild mood swings, from slamming Crystal one moment to saying he'd do anything to get back with her the next. McColeman stood by his friend and often helped him with the mundane chores of setting up his new apartment in Gold Pointe. "I helped him put a bunch of furniture together for his kids over there," McColeman recalls. "I mean, he wasn't real handy and it made me feel good to help him because I'm not very handy either. Compared to him, I was like Bob Vila. He had gotten a bunch of stuff from IKEA that was in about a million parts. It was two beds and two dressers and two night tables. He rented the apartment as of April first but didn't move in right away. He wanted to stay in the house as long as possible."

McColeman was aware that Brame didn't seem to

have any friends outside the department—"No one to do things with on the weekends or anything." So it wasn't so surprising on Easter Sunday morning to receive a call from the chief, who was alone in his new apartment. "He called me and he was very distraught and he said that the dresser he'd been waiting for for his son David had come in." Brame wanted to know if McColeman could come out and work on it.

"Well, Dave, it's Easter, you know."

"Uh, okay, what are you doing?"

"Having an Easter egg hunt at my house with my son, you know."

There was silence on the other end so McColeman filled it in. "Then we're going to do a deal with the family."

Chief Brame was not dismayed or embarrassed to be calling or taking McColeman away from his family on this holiday. Just as when Jeanette Blackwell had told him she was driving her daughter to the emergency room, Brame showed little interest in anything other than his own problems. He was fraying at the edges. "What time is that going to be over?" he asked.

"I don't know. Three o'clock?"

"Okay, well, can you come over at three?"

McColeman was exasperated but knew the situation. "Okay, I'll be over at three."

When he arrived at the apartment, Brame's eyes were red and he made little attempt to hide his crying. In fact, he was blubbering right in front of an embarrassed McColeman. "It was the first time he had been crying since I had been around him. He was feeling real bad because it was Easter and he didn't have his kids and all," McColeman said later.

Brame had a lot of odd meetings with subordinates around this time in his life but this had to be the oddest. For two hours, Brame poured his heart out to McColeman about the troubles in his own family.

Brame began by telling McColeman that the bad feelings between his mother and Crystal went back a long way and had come to a head in 1999 when he was promoted to assistant chief. This is the way Brame told it:

"My mother and Crystal, there was a falling out and it all came to a head at the ceremony when I was promoted to assistant chief. My mom was there with my family and Crystal and at the end my mom said, 'I want to take a picture of the Brames.' Now she meant me and my dad and my brother but Crystal didn't know that and she stepped into the picture and my mom said, 'Just the boys this time.' Crystal got really angry. She thought my mother was out to get her so she walked over to her family and started bitching to them. So I knew she was angry but then all hell broke out when we got outside. Crystal was trying to get between me and my mother while we were walking and they were kind of pushing on each other and my brother finally got between them and said, 'Come on, this isn't the place for this.' "

At that point, Brame's stories got even weirder, McColeman later told investigators from the Washington State Patrol. Brame spun out a story about a relative who, years earlier, said he visited Crystal and began kissing her in the Brame home when David was at work. According to what McColeman told investigators, Brame said he had heard the story from both the relative and Crystal and believed it to be true. McColeman said Brame was clearly shattered by the betrayal.

When Brame finished the story, he asked McColeman what he thought. "I don't know," McColeman said. "It all sounds pretty fucking weird."

"Right," Brame said. "I'm thinking if he'll admit that much, what else happened, you know? And I want to get to the bottom of it. I want this guy to file a declaration with the court because Crystal is portraying herself as Miss Innocent and here's direct proof that she's not. He doesn't want to do it. He says he just wanted me to know because of his new religion and all. I don't know, Barry, it's all so fucked up. I don't know what to think anymore."

At that point, Brame started crying again and McColeman tried to comfort him. It was not the type of Easter he imagined when he woke up that morning. At that point he lucked out, because Brame's mother, Beverly, and his sister, Jane Brazell, showed up with a couple of kids and McColeman told them he had to be getting home.

"Brame ignored them and walked me out to my car, which was very unusual for him. And he just told me, 'I'll never forget what a friend you've been to me.'"

Brame was probably trying to thank McColeman in his own way, but the irony is that McColeman had been around Brame's manipulating ways so long that he wasn't sure if Brame's thanks came from the heart or if he was just basically thanking him for helping him put the kids' furniture together. "That was Dave, you know. That was the way he thought. He thought it was unusual that anybody would do anything without an ulterior motive. That's just the way he operated."

Monday, April 21

On the drive over to Tacoma from his home on Fox Island, Bill Meeks went over and over in his mind the events that had led up to this day—he was getting what he wanted, he was going to be appointed assistant chief. When he'd first met David Brame, he knew he was special. He was a guy with vision, unbelievably smart for a cop—check that, he was unbelievably smart for anyone in any profession. Meeks believed in Brame and now he'd be at his side as they reshaped the Tacoma police department and tried to eliminate the ugly cliques that had formed.

But Meeks couldn't ignore the information Brame had dumped in his lap the night of April 7. David Brame at a nudist colony! It was absurd! Brame was one of the straightest guys he knew. This is the same guy who would move a beer away from him before a photograph was taken because he didn't want anyone to think he drank. Beer, for Christsakes! And here he was cavorting around at a nudist colony in California. Meeks wondered what the good citizens of Tacoma would think if they found out their chief had gone to a nudist colony. He hoped Brame could ride out the storm if *that* became public knowledge.

By eight a.m., Meeks was in Brame's office.

"All right, are you ready for this?" Brame asked him.

"If it's good for you, it's good for me."

"All right then. Congratulations, Assistant Chief Meeks," he said, shaking his hand. "I'll have Jeanette put out the personnel order."

The two of them then went into the chief's meeting. Brame seemed different that day to Meeks, who watched his friend take command. He's on top of his game, Meeks thought. Maybe getting him out of that house was the right move. He seems to be turning it around.

Maybe the breakup was sinking in. Brame, Meeks decided, seemed more together than he had in ages. Maybe, just maybe, everything was going to be all right. But there was one thing nagging at him—what else had Brame wanted to tell him? Whatever it was, he hadn't offered to share it yet.

Meeks didn't know it but David Brame was not over Crystal. Far from it. In fact, he missed his family life more than ever. At 8:28 that night, he called Crystal and left this message on the answering machine:

"Hi, Crystal and Haley and David. This is Daddy, so you guys give me a call. I'm here at home and so page me if it doesn't work right. I think it will work. I just wanted to call you and tell you guys that I love you and that I miss you guys. I look forward to hearing from you, just wanted to say good night to you guys. Daddy loves you with all of his heart. You guys take care, have a nice day tomorrow. I love you. Bye-bye."

Crystal wasn't home because she was over at her sister's home. The Judson and Ahrens families were celebrating the birthday of the "good" Dave—Dave Ahrens, Crystal's brother-in-law. There was a lot to celebrate, and celebrate they did at the Ahrenses' new home, also in a gated community in Gig Harbor just a few miles from the Judson home in Canterwood. Dave was turning thirty-four, the same age as Crystal, but he teased her because in a few days, she'd again be older. Her birthday was April 24 and she was going to turn thirty-five.

Tuesday, April 22

At 2:11 A.M., John Hathaway's work on his column was done and he sent it off to almost three hundred people, many of them Tacoma insiders, including Police Chief David Brame, Mayor Bill Baarsma, members of the city council and the media. Even he didn't know it then, but he was lighting the fuse to a powder keg.

Hathaway's regular readers woke up to a column headlined TACOMA CONFIDENTIAL. It has become a classic and a must-read for scholars of Tacoma history, because it is the first published reference to the divorce of David and Crystal Brame. Although the city's newspapers far outmanned Hathaway in personnel and had regular reporters on court and police beats, not a single mainstream reporter beat this over-the-hill onetime fashion reporter to the biggest story to hit Tacoma in decades.

Here's the column in its entirety; it begins as just another oddball Hathaway posting, but it concludes with a truth that would become all too painful to residents of Tacoma.

OVER the opening strains of "Tacoma my kind of town is," a MONTAGE: a mixture of headlines, television coverage and live action. Downtown Booming! Post Iraq War Optimism! Tacoma: America's No. 1 Wired City! But most prominent among them: ESTRANGED WIFE BUSTS CHIEF OF POLICE! T.V. reporters document crime scenes. Police cars, sirens blaring, race through Tacoma's pothole strewn streets. Where will it end?

CITY MANGER: (V.O.) Ladies and gentlemen, I give you the future of Tacoma! David A. Brame your new Police Chief.

MAYOR: We're selling an image, gentlemen. A Beautiful waterfront. Affordable housing. Trouble-free transportation. And the best police department in the world to keep it all running smoothly.

INTERIOR: Office of Tacoma Confidential. Lurid page one headlines cover the wall where Paul Malone types. The essence of sleaze, Malone is the publisher-photographer-writer of Tacoma Confidential, keeper of inside dirt supreme. As he continues . . .

MALONE (V.O.): Remember, dear readers, you heard it here first, off the record, on the Q.T. and very Confidential.

While Tacoma Police Chief Dave Brame frolics amongst the glitz and glamour of "Sin City", Las Vegas, Nevada, at TPD's expense, his estranged wife is trying to put her life back together. Back together from what you might ask dear readers.

What started out as an amicable divorce proceeding, filed in King County on February 24th, has turned out to be the biggest scandal this "Sin City" has seen since Commissioner Kerr got caught with his pants down on K Street better than 50 years ago. According to filings and depositions, that have been raining down on the court faster than bombs on Baghdad, there are accusations of requested sexual favors, group encounters of threesomes and foursomes, a loaded service weapon left within the children's reach and death threats.

In light of further details to come will Tacoma's East Side fair haired boy invoke "The Infamous Areola Blue Code" or stand up in court like a man and allow his estranged wife and children get on with their lives. That dear readers is the question.

FADE TO T.V. TACOMA STUDIOS: Taping of "Behind the Shield" with the Chief's badge looking somewhat tarnished.

The writing is tongue in cheek but the content dead serious.

Early that morning, Brame's friend Bill Meeks woke up to news that there was an anthrax scare at a local post office.

"Holy shit," he said, watching the early morning news.

Meeks took his new duties as assistant chief seriously; he knew he should be on the scene, especially since Brame was going out of town to Las Vegas that morning to a police conference. He hustled to the scene but it turned out to be nothing. In minutes, he was back at his desk in the County-City Building, and he saw Brame walk into his own office. He was dressed casually in a pair of jeans. Meeks followed.

"Hey, what are you doing here? I thought you had a plane to catch."

"Yeah, I'm getting a lift from Langford. He's meeting me here."

"Oh, right. So how's it going? You feeling better? You looked good at the meeting yesterday."

Brame had started talking about the trip when his computer let him know he'd just received some e-mail.

It was from Gwen Kopetzky, secretary to City Manager Ray Corpuz. She had forwarded the page from John Hathaway's Web site.

"What's this?" Brame asked, and started reading.

Meeks read along. "Ah, it's nothing."

Brame grew pale. "I don't know."

"Don't worry about it. Go on your trip and have a good time."

But Brame was clearly worried. This was the first public mention of his divorce and he knew more was sure to come. The sharks were circling.

"What am I gonna do?"

"You're gonna go to the seminar and do your job," Meeks said. "Not doing your job is what's gonna get you fired. Not this."

"Right, good advice. Thanks."

At 8:06 A.M., a melancholy Brame called home yet again, desperately reaching out for contact with the family he once had under his control. These days, it seemed he could never find them in, so he left the first of three messages that day.

"Hi, Crystal, Haley and David, I just wanted to call and say hi to the kids before they went to school and tell 'em I love 'em and have a good day. Haley and David and all you guys, have a good day, and would you please give me a page if you get this so I can call you. Love you guys, have a good day. Bye."

While waiting for his lift to the airport, Brame walked over to see Ray Corpuz, no doubt to discuss John Hathaway's column. On the way out, Brame stopped at Gwen Kopetzky's desk. She and Brame had hardly spoken since she'd begun to suspect months before that he was trying to entice her into more than a friendly chat. Still, she was sympathetic to his problems and was surprised how distraught he looked.

"You've lost a lot of weight," she told him.

"As you know, I have a lot on my mind."

"I'm sorry you're having problems."

"Thank you, Gwen. I got your e-mail."

"Just wanted you to know what was out there."

"I appreciate that. You know, he doesn't have the whole story. Crystal attacked me on more than one occasion. I love her but she has a violent temper. She even left bruises on my arm and scratches on my neck and I have photos to prove it. I gave that to the court. It will all come out but I wanted you to know I'm not the terrible guy Crystal's trying to paint me to be."

"You have to do what you have to do. You're lucky you have those photos. They should help."

"I hope so," Brame said, taking a moment to think. "You know, this will be my second divorce. I was married once before."

"I didn't know that."

"It wasn't so great. My ex had several affairs while we were married. It was pretty rough."

"I'm sorry."

"Yeah, but the funny thing is that I prefer that over the way Crystal is. She just hates me. She won't even let me touch her. I came up behind her while she was doing the dishes one day and rubbed her neck and she just turned and walked away. It's rough. I wish I had someone who would show some affection, who would reach out and hold me once in a while, you know?"

Uh-oh, Kopetzky thought, here we go again. David Brame again was making her uncomfortable, like he wanted her to say she'd come over to his house to give him a shoulder rub or something. She decided she had to cut the conversation short.

"Well, who knows, maybe you two will work out your differences. I'll pray for you and Crystal too."

"Thanks. I'm confused. The truth is, I still love her

and I don't want to lose her but I've fallen so far from the Christian path."

"Well, I'll pray especially for you then."

"Thank you."

It was the last time Kopetzky ever spoke to David Brame.

Brame was disconsolate. Now his marital troubles were on the Internet for anyone to read.

It was bad timing, but he had to go to the seminar in Las Vegas. At least he wasn't going alone and it might even be fun. He was going with a small group of other Tacoma police officers, including Detective Barry McColeman and Public Information Officer Jim Mattheis. Brame usually enjoyed visiting Vegas. For a guy who often thought about threesomes and nudist colonies, the Sin City aspect of Las Vegas was right up his alley. And it wasn't only the laissez-faire atmosphere of the city. There were memories of happier times as well. Just a year earlier, he and Crystal had celebrated their eleventh wedding anniversary at the Bellagio Hotel. It seemed like a very long time ago.

This time Brame didn't feel like going but, as usual, he took Meeks' advice. At eleven a.m., he was flying to Vegas on Alaska Airlines Flight 6520. He knew he wouldn't be able to concentrate but he had to try. He was there for a three-day labor seminar on collective bargaining, the Fair Standards Labor Act, and how police officers could be held liable for mistakes they made on the job.

Brame's plane landed in Las Vegas at one thirty p.m. and he was soon checked into his room at the Flamingo Hotel. It didn't take long for his thoughts to turn once again to Crystal and his children. He had already called his assistant, Jeanette Blackwell, but Crystal had not called him back so he called them.

Tuesday, 2:59 P.M.

"Hi, Crystal and David and Haley, I'm at a number you can call me. It's area code 702 XXX-XXXX, room XXXX. Call me on the cell phone or page me and my pager should work. I miss you guys and wanna hear from you. Love you guys. Bye-bye."

Back in Tacoma, John Hathaway's Internet scoop was being e-mailed all over town, especially among those in the police department and city government. Reporters from the Tacoma *News Tribune* and *Seattle Post-Intelligencer* began making repeated phone calls to Jim Mattheis, the department's public information officer, who was in Vegas with Brame. *Tribune* editor David Zeeck later claimed his paper had been sitting on the divorce papers for two weeks even though one of his reporters was chomping at the bit to run a story. In retrospect, it seems like a questionable decision. Surely 95 percent of the other newspapers in the country would have run with the story. These were publicly filed divorce papers, not some over-the-transom tip from an anonymous source. To confirm they were legitimate would take little more than a phone call to the lawyers involved. Some people in Tacoma later speculated that the *Tribune*—the only paper in town—moved so slowly because it had a stake in David Brame's career. The paper had previously named him one of the twenty people to watch in the South Sound and it had been a supporter in editorials.

In Las Vegas, the little group that included Detective Barry McColeman, Assistant Chiefs Richard McCrea and Don Ramsdell and Officer Pat Frantz, a top Police Union official, made a deal with each other that they'd take turns wet-nursing their chief of police. Each one would listen to him for a couple of hours before bailing out to have some fun.

McColeman explained, "We'd all been doing time

with him at work, taking turns listening to his problems, and we didn't want him ruining our trip to Vegas."

The detective said he told Brame point-blank that his constant "bullshit" about his divorce was getting very old, very quickly. "I told him I'd spend a couple of hours talking to him about his personal stuff, but snap out of it already. You're the chief of police. Get your shit together. Start running the department. We've all been divorced, so get with the program."

McColeman knew that Brame had great respect for Will Atchison, a Portland attorney who'd been the regular Police Union lawyer for a long time. As soon as he checked in, McColeman sought out Atchison's personal assistant and told her what was going on with Brame and the divorce. Atchison was leading the seminar set to begin the next day, but McColeman begged the assistant to carve out time so Atchison could talk with Brame who, at this point, was driving all the other cops on the trip nuts. "Dave and him were friends, as much as he had friends. He really respected Will's opinion."

During the week, Atchison came through and pulled Brame aside for a couple of pep talks. "Dave was really up after talking to him," McColeman said. "He said he could bounce back. He thought the worst time of his life was when he was going through the divorce. Now he's the happiest he's ever been."

Atchison told Brame to accept that he'd lose money during his divorce. There was no way around it. It seemed everyone knew what a premium Brame put on money. But Atchison told him to give it up. "You're going to lose some money and you've got to get over it," Atchison said. "It's just the way it is. It's a fact of life."

Brame seemed to accept what Atchison was saying but some part of him clearly couldn't accept living without Crystal and the kids full-time. He continued to leave messages but they apparently never called him back either Tuesday or Wednesday.

Thursday, April 24

Debbie Phillips remembers the last day she ever talked to Crystal Brame. It was on Crystal's thirty-fifth birthday, April 24. As she had done some 227 times since first going to the Oasis Tanning Salon on March 1, 2001, Crystal showed up for her appointment with gusto. "She came bounding down the walkway and through the door with her pink lipstick and a bright yellow shirt on," Debbie remembers. "She loved the color yellow. It was her favorite.

"She was just so happy about everything. It was the first birthday as a grown woman that she was going to celebrate without David and she was looking forward to it. She was going to do everything she wanted to do, not what David wanted her to do."

Debbie told her, "You look great, Crystal."

"Thanks, it's my birthday, don't you know?"

"Oh sweetie, happy birthday."

They hugged and then Debbie asked about her plans. "My mom and dad have a party planned over at their house. It's just a family thing but I can't wait. I'm getting my favorite cake, German chocolate."

"It sounds great. You deserve it, you know. How's what's-his-name?"

Crystal waved her hand. "Oh, he's out of town but I should be receiving that restraining order this week."

"Good. You just make sure you're never alone with him. Make sure your parents are there when you switch the kids. He has them this weekend, right?"

"Yep. Don't worry. We always make the exchange on my parents' house."

"When are you moving back to your house?"

"Soon. We're just cleaning it up. You should see the way he left it. All dirty and everything. Nothing was cleaned. Honestly, he's such a pig."

"Men. Did I ever tell you about what a slob my ex is?"

"Only all the time, but tell me again. Oh, listen to this. You'll never believe what he left for me on the dining room table."

"What?"

"The obit page of the newspaper."

A chill shot through Debbie. "Crystal . . ."

"And there was something else. A fortune cookie that said, 'Expect a surprise.' "

"Crystal," Debbie warned, "don't ever be alone with him. I mean it."

In Las Vegas, Crystal was on David Brame's mind. He remembered all too well that it was her thirty-fifth birthday and he knew that she'd be celebrating without him.

A lot of people lose themselves in the glitter and manufactured glamour of Las Vegas. On some level, that's what it's all about—forgetting your troubles and drab life back home and playing the role of a high roller for a couple of days. Eat, drink, gamble and be happy. But Brame couldn't forget anything back home. Almost as soon as he woke up, he was on the phone to Crystal once again: It was seven forty-five a.m. when he left this message, having missed her yet again:

"Hi, Crystal, it's David, good morning. I thought I would call and leave you a message. I gotta get out . . . but I wanted to take the time to wish you a happy thirty-fifth birthday. That's an important birthday and right now I wanted to tell you that it's the right thing to do, it's the nice thing to do, so I wanted to do that, so happy thirty-fifth to you and I hope you have a great day. And I'll be pickin' up the kids tomorrow night, I guess it's over at your mom and dad's so maybe we can hook up, but you have a great day today and again, happy thirty-fifth. See you, Crystal. Love you guys. Goodbye."

Jim Mattheis has the unruffled manner of someone who's heard it all before. He had the perfect disposition to be the Tacoma PD's public information officer and he was about to earn a year's pay in about a month's time. Ruth Teichroeb, a reporter from the *Seattle Post-Intelligencer,* called Mattheis for a comment; the *PI* was running with the story of the Brame divorce the next day. They wanted to interview Brame and were giving him the courtesy of letting him know before the story went to press.

At nine a.m. that Thursday, while they were still in Las Vegas, Mattheis told Brame what was going on and asked him to call Teichroeb. Brame spoke to the reporter, defending himself against Crystal's allegations just as he had in his court papers. The bottom line, he told the reporter, was that Crystal always was the aggressor, and furthermore, he had informed his former chief, Ken Monner, in 1996 when the abuse got so bad that he'd gone to the Gig Harbor police station. Holed up in his room, feeling the walls closing in on his life, Brame made thirty-eight calls during the next twelve hours. There's no official record of what was said but it's believed that Corpuz told Brame just what he told Ruth Teichroeb for the next day's story. "He's doing a great job," Corpuz told Teichroeb for publication. "I'm not interested in exploring David's personal life at this time."

Tacoma mayor Bill Baarsma, Brame's old college professor, echoed Corpuz: "He's been an outstanding chief. Unless there is a complaint filed with the city manager as to his performance, I'm not prepared to comment."

Brame checked in with his assistant, Jeanette Blackwell.

"I have a message here from John Hathaway. He wants you to call him," she said.

"What did he say?"

"He said he has some information about Palm Springs and that he wanted to talk to you about it."

Palm Springs. The words hit David Brame hard. It was a not-so-subtle reference to the nudist colony; Hathaway was letting Brame know that he knew all about it. Now Brame was really worried. He was facing his worst fears and public humiliation.

"Oh no, he's got some good information there. This is bad. This is bad, Jeanette."

Brame needed to talk about this latest problem and he spilled his guts to Blackwell, telling her what a great time he and Crystal had had at the Desert Shadows Inn Resort. He told her that, as far as he was concerned, it was a very freeing way to live and he wished everyone could understand what it was like. But of course Brame knew better. He knew that once it got mentioned in Hathaway's column or the newspaper, it was bound to become something tawdry.

Brame called a lot of people that day but no matter what they said, he couldn't shake his feeling of doom. He spotted McColeman soon after and was more than eager to comment to him. "It's over, Barry. I'm going to have to step down. I'm not going to be able to weather this."

"Oh, come on, man, you're exaggerating. It'll be all right. Have you talked to Ray?"

"Yeah, him and a couple of others on the city council."

"And?"

"They let me know that they'll support me on this thing but I don't know."

"What did Ray say specifically?"

"His position is that it's a civil matter. He told me not to worry about it. Said I was doing a great job."

"Well, there you go."

"I don't know," Brame mumbled, walking away by himself.

Back in Gig Harbor, Crystal Brame was celebrating her birthday. That afternoon, at Canterwood, Crystal ran into Mike Whaley, a local gardener who had serviced the Brames' lawn at their home on Eagle Creek Lane. Mike greeted her and was impressed with how vibrant and upbeat she looked. Crystal hadn't seen him in a while and immediately launched into her version of the divorce, the version she was now telling virtually anyone she came across. As usual, she regaled Mike Whaley with the most personal of details, including the fact that she had applied for a restraining order against her husband that she thought would be issued shortly.

It was a lot to process and not the sort of conversation one has lightly or with a casual acquaintance, but that's exactly what Mike Whaley was to Crystal. He barely knew what to say. "We were wondering why no one ever returned our calls about turning on the sprinkler system at your house. Now I guess I know what happened."

"Yeah," she said. "David left the place a mess. I might need some help cleaning it up."

"I could help you out if you need something," Mike said.

"Great. Let me give you my new cell phone number."

She wrote it down and he promised to call the next week. Later, he told everyone how beautiful Crystal looked that day despite all her troubles.

At six p.m., Crystal celebrated with the most important people in her life: her children, Haley and David Jr.; her parents, Lane and Patty; her sister, Julie; and brother-in-law, Dave Ahrens. Crystal was wearing the same yellow blouse Debbie Phillips had spotted her in earlier that day. Surrounded by those she loved, Crystal was beaming. "She looked so happy," Dave Ahrens said. "She looked ten years younger."

As promised, Patty Judson presented Crystal with a German chocolate cake and then went overboard with presents: a Ralph Lauren shirt, a bottle of perfume, French language computer software to help her brush up on her favorite language, three expensive decorative pillows—one of which said BIENVENUE while another one read, MY OTHER HOUSE IS IN FRANCE—a red crystal wall sconce, a decorating book by Carolyne Roehm, and a black-and-white pillow because Crystal had a plan to do her bedroom in all black and white. Even Patty Judson admits, "We spoiled her because it was her first birthday in a long time where she felt free." Indeed, Crystal enjoyed being spoiled; after all, she had asked for almost every present she received from her generous family. Finally, the saying on her kitchen magnet was coming true: I WANT EVERYTHING AND I WANT IT DELIVERED.

In Las Vegas, the seminar had ended and the police contingent from Tacoma was ready to cut loose and have some fun. There was only one problem, and his name was Chief Brame; he had become an anchor, bringing them down with his incessant divorce talk. They simply did not want to hear it anymore. They were all in their big van going out on the town and Brame told them he wanted to stop at the Bellagio, the only casino he really gambled in. He had a favorite slot machine there and he wouldn't gamble anywhere else. He also was planning to play some special numbers at keno: 4, 24, 68—the date of Crystal's birthday. Always a mama's boy, Brame was playing with some of Mama's money; she had given him $500 to play some numbers for her and himself.

The other cops did not share Brame's enthusiasm for the Bellagio. In fact, they had plans to go to the Hard Rock Café to take in shock jock Howard Stern's extravaganza. But no one tried to get Brame to change his plans. McColeman described what happened when the van got to the Bellagio: "We pull up in front. Door opens. Dave gets out. We all look at each other. It's like, 'Okay, whose turn is it to babysit him?' Nobody says anything. Door closes. We drive off. Nobody gets out with him. Everyone was just kind of tired of it."

Eventually they felt bad and called him, but he said he was turning in early because he had to get up early to fly back to Tacoma. He had to run some errands and then pick up his kids on Friday. But he wasn't really going to bed so early. He was desperate to reach Crystal and called her four times between 8:38 and 9:44 P.M. He finally got through.

How did their conversation go? Patty says she listened in and was shocked by what she heard:

They argued about the children and Brame said, "You were the mother of those children."

"I *am* the mother of those children," Crystal replied.

"No, you *were* the mother of the children," Brame said.

"I *am* the mother of the children," Crystal said emphatically.

"You are not listening to me: *you were the mother of those children,*" Brame said.

But Patty's version is just about the opposite conversation from what Brame reported when he ran into Jim Mattheis and Barry McColeman that evening in the hotel.

"He was up, as high as he's been in the last month," McColeman said. "He tells me that his phone conversation with Crystal went really well. There was even talk of reconciliation. That's what Dave kind of felt. Crystal gave him a little bit of hope. He could really talk to her. He asked her if they could work things out amicably. He told her he had not had any affairs, that the stuff in her divorce filing was just not true. He told me that Crystal had used the word 'amicable' a few times. He was really feeling good, feeling better about stuff. He was positive, like maybe things were going to get a little better."

Crystal, meanwhile, told her mother that halfway through the conversation, she decided to just placate David and tell him whatever he wanted to hear.

38

Friday, April 25

The next morning, Brame awoke at 6:11 A.M. and immediately called Jeanette Blackwell. She read him the online version of the story now rocking Tacoma. The *Seattle Post-Intelligencer* story had run on the front page under the headline TACOMA POLICE CHIEF'S WIFE SAYS HE POINTED A GUN AT HER.

Overall, the story was evenhanded and not overly sensational. Even the subhead was: DAVID BRAME DENIES ALLEGATIONS, SAYS IT WAS SHE WHO ABUSED HIM. It included Brame's denials, his defense and supportive quotes from Ray Corpuz and Bill Baarsma.

But it was still on the front page and it was damaging.

Brame furiously punched the numbers on his phone, calling everyone he could think of. One of those was Tacoma police officer Norman Conaway. Conaway was seriously ill with kidney problems and would die before the year was out; he was an important person in Brame's life because, back in 1996, Brame had called Conaway when he was at the Gig Harbor police, emotionally wrought from his fight with Crystal. It was Conaway who helped convince Brame not to file an official report. Instead, Brame gave his handwritten witness statement to

Conaway for safekeeping. He wanted to be sure Conaway still had those notes. Conaway was feeling poorly, Brame knew, so he left a message for Conaway's wife Tracy and asked her to call him back as quickly as possible.

Brame took off from Las Vegas at eight thirty a.m., and he knew he was flying right into the teeth of a media firestorm. Reporters from Tacoma and Seattle newspapers and television stations were girding themselves for his return and jamming the phone lines to the Tacoma PD, the Gig Harbor PD and the Pierce County sheriff's office. Mitch Barker, the Gig Harbor police chief, called Brame and told him that he had answered reporters' questions about that 1996 incident. Detective Ed Troyer, the public information officer for the sheriff's office, called Brame to tell him much the same thing. It was professional courtesy. The two men did not know each other well, and Brame shocked Troyer with what the detective felt was an unusual question.

"Are you a praying man?" Brame asked.

"What?"

"We need some prayers to straighten this out."

Assistant Chief Catherine Woodard, who had been left to run the show while Brame was in Vegas and Meeks was on a golfing trip to Arizona, tried her best to keep the reporters at bay. She confided in an e-mail to Meeks that "we're trying to put a positive spin on it for DAB."

Across town, another woman read the front-page story in the *Seattle PI* and shook with a mixture of rage and fear. Sally Masters (not her real name), then forty-five years old, had worked with Brame at a court-sponsored youth program.

All these years—since 1988—Sally had kept her distance from Brame but now, with this news coming out about his divorce and the threats against his wife, Sally

was afraid Brame finally would come after her because
of what she knew. Not knowing where to turn, Sally
picked up the phone and called *Seattle PI* reporter Ruth
Teichroeb. Sally's boyfriend at the time thought she was
paranoid, but Teichroeb was very interested in Sally's
story and wanted to meet her in person. They agreed to
meet the next day but that night, Sally began to have
second thoughts. She went to her boyfriend's home,
packed some clothes and left. She'd be damned if she
was going to be a sitting duck at home where Brame
could find her.

By noon, Brame's plane had landed at Sea-Tac Airport midway between Seattle and Tacoma and, by prear-
rangement, Tacoma police lieutenant Bob Sheehan met
him. Sheehan works in the facilities department for the
TPD and had a lot of projects on the drawing board,
including one for a state-of-the-art police headquarters.
Sheehan was always trying to get time alone with Chief
Brame because he needed him to make decisions so,
when he was asked prior to the trip to pick Brame up
at the airport upon his return, Sheehan jumped at the
chance.

"Any chance I get, I wanted to get to him," Sheehan
explained. "I thought this would be the perfect time."

Sheehan knew about Brame's divorce, of course. In
fact, the anonymous letter to Internal Affairs had been
directed to his attention; he knew all about the scene at
the Judson house when Assistant Chief Catherine
Woodard showed up there. Still, he was hoping the trip
to Vegas would "get his [Brame's] head straight." He
never anticipated that the divorce story would hit the
front pages the same day he was due to pick him up.
Far from having his head on straight, Brame was more
confused than ever. "I was disappointed because he was
not refreshed and relaxed as I had expected," Sheehan

said. "In fact, he was a bit agitated about the fact that he was in the newspaper."

Sheehan was supposed to take Brame to his car he'd left parked at the County-City Building, and then Brame was scheduled to pick up his children at the Judsons' for the first time since the incident involving Assistant Chief Catherine Woodard.

But it was clear to Sheehan that Brame had a lot more on his mind than picking up his kids. He started talking about his divorce and the newspaper story and then dropped a bombshell on Sheehan.

"I'm worried, Bob, because there are other things out there about me."

"Like what? What could be so bad?"

"Well," Brame said, taking a deep breath, "there were some indiscretions with other couples at this resort we went to."

"What kind of resort?"

"It's a nudist colony basically but, you know, we met some other couples there and . . ."

"So what d'ya do? Walk around nude?"

"Yeah, that, but we never really made the contact with the other couple. Crystal did spend a lot of time with them."

"So nothing happened with you and them?"

"No."

"If that's all you did, don't worry about it. It's not the end of the world. It's, you know, something you can explain. People do a lot of things in their personal lives that others don't agree with but it's tough. There's nothing anybody can do about that."

The talk made Sheehan uncomfortable and he wanted to settle Brame down. He even got off the freeway and asked Brame if he wanted to get some lunch, but Brame said he wasn't interested. He was on one track—his divorce—and Sheehan couldn't pull him off in another

direction. Eventually, Sheehan had had enough and he
let Brame know it.

"You're screwing up the police department right
now," he told Brame bluntly. "You're making bad
decisions."

"What do you mean?"

"I mean the decisions you're making are bad."

And then, as bad luck would have it, Sheehan inadvertently drove by Crystal's attorney's office. "I think I saw
my wife's car there," Brame said.

"So?"

"Well, drive in there."

Sheehan was adamant about not doing that. "No, forget it."

But Brame was so agitated that Sheehan turned
around and drove by the parking lot. As it turned out,
Brame couldn't tell if it was Crystal's car or not.

Sheehan was disgusted with Brame and drove quickly
toward the County-City Building but, on the way, Brame
called Jeanette to see if the media were waiting for him.
They were. He asked Sheehan to drive to the upper
level of the adjoining parking lot where his car was so
the media would not spot him. On the way, Brame called
Corpuz, and Sheehan heard parts of the conversation. It
revolved around the media and what the Tacoma *News
Tribune* was planning to put in the next day's paper.
Sheehan pulled into the parking lot and dropped Brame
off at his car without the media spotting them.

"He said goodbye to me and I thought—it was kind
of strange in a way. I will never forget that. It's the last
time I saw him," Sheehan remembered.

The moment he left Brame, Sheehan went one step
further. He was angry about his boss's behavior so he
called Ray Corpuz and asked, "What's going on with
this guy?"

Sheehan didn't wait for an answer but babbled on, too
upset to stop now. "You've been babying this guy too

much. I think he needs someone to tell him to get off his ass and do the job he was hired to do. I'm gonna get involved and I'm gonna get on his ass and start being more forceful with him."

"That's fine," Corpuz said. "Someone needs to do that."

"Well, I guess I'm gonna be that person. If he can't do the job, then we'll get somebody else to do the job."

Sheehan let Corpuz know that he was talking about Woodard. "She needs to get out of his personal life and get into doing her job, and someone needs to tell her that."

Always a cool character, Corpuz simply replied, "She's already been told that."

"Good."

Crystal, meanwhile, was even more agitated than usual because of the news story. She sent a letter to her attorney, highlighting a whole series of issues she had with David Brame, most of them involving the couple's bank accounts.

Her letter contained one especially ominous footnote, a fat paragraph Crystal starred to show its importance:

"One very important issue remaining [sic] the IMMEDIATE issuance of the restraining order. I would like this filed with the court today. I have been informed that the Tacoma News Tribune is running a story on this divorce . . . I feel this is extremely important that you are aware of this. I strongly fear for my personal safety and I am strongly requesting that the restraining order be put in place today . . . my concern is when [David] returns from his Las Vegas trip he will come after me. I am pleading with you to please put the restraining order in place immediately for my personal protection."

Investigators for the Washington State Patrol later wrote that this statement was "one of the most disturbing and prescient statements we have ever come across in our collective professional experience."

That afternoon, one of the top editors at the *News Tribune* was indeed thinking about the story that was going to run the following day. At last, after being scooped by John Hathaway and the *Seattle PI,* the *News Tribune* had seen fit to consider the Brame divorce a news story.

While newsroom reporters were busting their butts— and at least one had been pleading with senior management for weeks to run something on the Brame divorce—David Seago, the *News Tribune*'s editorial page editor, sent David Brame an e-mail. Seago later admitted that he wished like hell he could have pulled it back and he apologized to his reporters. Nonetheless, the e-mail shows Seago's state of mind the day before all hell broke loose.

From: David Seago
To: David Brame
Subject: just in case
    Dave,
    We're doing an editorial on your marital troubles Saturday. I think it will be more responsible than the PI story. As you probably know, we were sitting on it because the newsroom didn't think it was substantial enough to run. I don't believe you will have any quarrel with our editorial line but if you have anything you want to discuss with me, let me know. I think we're OK with what we have so far.
    Dave Seago

David Brame called Seago that afternoon and denied once more that he had ever threatened or abused Crystal. To Seago, Brame "seemed in complete control of his emotions. He did not sound like a man who thought his career or his life was over."

By three p.m., some Tacoma city officials were feeling queasy about the story in the *PI* and bracing for the follow-up stories in the Tacoma *News Tribune* and the area's television stations. City Human Resources Director Phil Knudsen walked into the officer of his associate, Assistant Director Mary Brown. They had already discussed the story in the *Seattle PI,* and both thought the allegations were at least serious enough for the city to step in and perhaps offer Chief Brame some time off. If he refused, perhaps they should put him on administrative leave. When Mary Brown saw the look on Phil Knudsen's face, she knew he was serious about pursuing the possibility of "admin leave."

"Let's go down and talk to Elizabeth Pauli about this Brame thing. We have to at least talk about this," Knudsen said, referring to the chief assistant city attorney.

Mary Brown disliked Brame intensely and always had, even before the stories of his divorce began to spread. "Do I really have to go?"

"Yes, you do."

They went to see Pauli and she invited Chief City Attorney Robin Jenkinson to the meeting. They all sat down except Pauli, who paced back and forth the entire meeting. Brown and Knudsen have one version of what happened at that meeting, and Jenkinson and Pauli have another. Neither side agrees on exactly what was said; in fact, all they *do* agree on is that they adamantly disagree with one another.

This is Mary Brown's version of events. She said they began by stating the obvious—that this article, damaging to the Tacoma chief of police, was in the newspaper—and then Mary Brown went further, raising the April 11 visit that Assistant Chief Catherine Woodard had made to the Judson home: "I think that was inappropriate as well because, as a subordinate, it puts her in a very bad position and a supervisor shouldn't have even asked her to do that to begin with."

"I've talked to Catherine about that and it's not a problem," said Jenkinson. "She explained that the divorce lawyers had given her permission to be there so I don't think it's an issue."

Brown persisted. "You know, I think it is a problem. I don't think supervisors should be asking subordinates to be going with them on personal business. It just isn't appropriate and it shouldn't happen."

Jenkinson repeated what she'd already said: "I've talked to Catherine and it's not an issue. As far as the information in the paper, this is a civil matter, nothing has been proven and a lot of things are said in divorce proceedings."

At that point, Knudsen butted in. "We should consider putting him on leave."

"It's a civil matter," Jenkinson said, repeating her previous statement "like a mantra," according to Brown.

Knudsen turned to Brown and, under his breath, said to her, "If this was any other cop, we would be putting him on leave and taking his badge and his gun."

Brown and Knudsen conceded that divorce papers were often filled with nasty allegations, not all of them true. But the Human Resources people thought this was different and much more serious because, in this case, a top city official was being accused of threatening his wife with a department-issued weapon. (At that point in Tacoma, there were no regulations in place for dealing with an officer accused of domestic violence. That has since changed.) According to Brown, Robinson and Pauli said nothing.

"We just felt like we had run into a stone wall. We both agreed it was the strangest meeting that we had ever had with the two of them because normally we have a very free-flowing discussion and this time, it was just like, 'We're not talking.' "

Knudsen and Brown went back to their offices but Brown was steamed. She and Brame were veterans of many a hotly contested labor negotiation between the Police Union and the city when he was a union vice president. "I am the first one to say I did not have a positive working relationship with David Brame. Never did, didn't like him from the first time I met him and never changed my opinion of him. The first time I met him the hair stood up on the back of my neck. I mean, there was something about this guy that I went, wooh, you know. I'd never had such a visceral reaction to anyone like that before.

"I felt like Brame was getting special treatment again. He was being protected and it was getting a little old. He was never held accountable for anything he did."

That afternoon, Chief Brame went back home to his Gold Pointe apartment. At five p.m., Tracy Conaway returned the call he had made to her that morning. Brame began babbling on and on about Crystal and the divorce and all that was happening to him. It was too much private information and Conaway stopped him.

"Dave, this is something you should share with your close friends and your attorney. It does no good to tell me all this."

"I know, I know, Tracy, but a person can only take so much. I don't know where to turn anymore."

The conversation upset Conaway. She'd never heard Brame, normally a stoic, talk with such emotion, and she began to wonder if she'd done the right thing. She herself was an officer on the Tacoma police force. Maybe she owed more to Brame than to rush him off the phone. Conaway was so concerned about Brame's mental state that she paged Catherine Woodard, who returned the page promptly.

"What's up?"

"Listen, something's wrong with the chief. I just spoke with him and . . . I never heard him talk that way before. Is he okay?"

"You mean he wanted to talk about his divorce?"

"And how. That's *all* he wanted to talk about. I rushed him off the phone but now I'm feeling guilty. There's something wrong with him."

"He's been like that all week. We know. He just got back from some seminars in Vegas and everyone was saying the same thing. All he wanted to do was stay in his room and talk about Crystal. The guys were pretty pissed off at him. They said he ruined their trip."

"Listen, I'm leaving on a vacation tomorrow with Norm and I want you to call us if anything bad happens. I just don't have a good feeling."

"Go. Enjoy yourself. Nothing is going to happen. He's under a lot of stress but Corpuz told him his job is safe. He'll be okay. A lot of people get divorced. I should know, right?"

They both laughed and hung up, but Conaway said she never felt right about Brame. There was stress and then there was *stress*.

Having read the newspaper story in the *Seattle PI* David Brame's sister, Jane Brazell, rushed over to his new apartment to lend her support. "He was sad but he wasn't angry or anything like that," she said.

Despite all the events swirling around him, Brame was intent on one thing: his weekend with the kids was about to begin and nothing was going to stop him from going over to the Judson home that Friday night to pick them up. Remembering what happened on the last visit with Woodard, this time he asked Jane if she'd like to accompany him. After all, she was family and he'd have a witness. He felt he needed it now that everything had become public and he didn't want another scene like the last time he'd made the exchange. Jane agreed to go and he called Crystal.

"Hi, I'll be over for the kids around six and I'm bringing Jane with me."

"No, you're not. I'll call my lawyer, David. Don't you dare."

"Crystal, Jane is my sister."

"Don't bring anyone here."

"I'll see you at six."

After he hung up, Brame turned to Jane. "Don't be surprised if the sheriff's deputies are there when we get there."

"This I've got to see."

At six p.m. Brame, with Jane, pulled up to the Canterwood guardhouse and announced his presence. He was told to wait right there. Soon, Lane and Patty pulled up in their car followed by Crystal and the kids in her car. The exchange was made at the gatehouse without any of the ugliness that had occurred last time. It was a beautiful spring night as Lane, Patty and Crystal watched Brame's car disappear around a curve with Haley and David Jr. inside.

That evening, Crystal called her therapist, Dr. Max Knauss, and left a message on his answering machine. Clearly, the public stories about the Brames' divorce papers had her on edge. She left Knauss a short message: "I'm afraid for my life, now more than ever."

David Brame was not without his supporters, one of whom was his former chief, Ray Fjetland, who called him at home to try to cheer him up.

"Hi, Dave, how you doing?" Fjetland asked. "You're in some challenging times but I know you can work through it. The sun will come up tomorrow, trust me. Remember, put your trust in Jesus Christ. This is where your strength is, it's within you. I'm going to a prayer group Monday night. Would you let me take your name just to let the Holy Spirit be with you and to give you guidance?"

"Sure, Ray, I'd appreciate that."

"It isn't always about keeping your job. It's about doing your job, Dave."

Brame was mostly quiet during the conversation and Fjetland later said he was unsure how upset Brame was. He told Brame not to worry about the newspaper stories, that they were just going to be lining some birdcages in a few days.

"You're the police chief and you're always gonna be."

And with that, Fjetland rang off.

At ten forty-five p.m., David Brame made one last phone call of his own, dialing Jeanette Blackwell's number. As always, he leaned on her for emotional, not just professional, support.

"So I picked up my kids today and brought them to my new apartment," he told his assistant.

Jeanette was tired of the late-night phone calls but, as always, she was understanding. "How did it go?"

"Pretty good, I think. At first Haley was a little cold towards me but I think that's just her mother's and grandparents' influence. The longer she spent with me, the more she warmed up. After dinner, we were wrestling and running around."

"That's great, and how's David doing?"

"He's so cute, he's great. You should have heard him when I was putting him to bed. We were cuddling and he said, 'Daddy, I love you. I want to stay with you forever.' "

"Wow, that must have made you feel good."

"Yeah, you know, I let them blow off a lot of steam and run around the apartment. They can never do that at their grandparents'. They're so uptight, just like Crystal, Little Miss Perfect. Even at my house, the kids couldn't touch anything when we were living together."

"That's important. Kids need to blow off some steam. Let 'em jump around on the beds, run around the house. All that stuff is important."

"Yeah, I guess you're right."

"What are you doing now?"

"I was watching my wedding video again."

"You've got to stop doing that. It's just painful, is all it is."

"I know, I know. Not as painful as the newspaper is gonna be tomorrow. The *Trib*'s running a story about my divorce."

"Forget that. Don't read the paper. It won't change anything anyway. Just play with your kids and think about them this weekend. Enjoy 'em. That's all you can do. Forget what other people are saying."

"Yeah, good advice. I don't know, Jeanette, I'm kind of disorganized here. I don't even know what I'm gonna give them for breakfast. Crystal always took care of all that."

"Don't sweat. Just throw out some bowls, milk and cereal. Kids don't need a complicated breakfast. Keep it simple, especially now. I'm sure they're just glad to be with you, have their daddy."

They talked until midnight, until Jeanette said she was tired.

"Okay," Brame said. "Thanks for listening. Good night."

"Good night and remember what I said. Concentrate on your kids, not your problems. Ignore the newspaper stories."

"Okay, good night."

39

Saturday, April 26

Early the next morning, David Brame ignored Jeanette Blackwell's advice and scanned the front-page headlines in the Tacoma *News Tribune*. The major news story of the day was about a top cop getting in trouble with the law, but it had nothing to do with David Brame. This time it was former Pierce County sheriff Mark French's turn on the griddle. As part of an international investigation into a Russian-based child pornography Web site, French's computer was seized from his forty-seven-foot houseboat at the Tacoma Yacht•Club in Point Defiance.

Brame told friends that, initially, he was relieved to see that the Tacoma *News Tribune* had still not seen fit to give the chief's divorce front-page play. Inside, however, it was a different story. On the front page of the metro section, the *TNT* finally ran the story under the headline CITY WILL NOT INVESTIGATE POLICE CHIEF; ABUSE ALLEGATIONS RAISED IN DIVORCE CASE.

The story was carefully written and was almost an indictment of the previous day's story in the *Seattle PI* as well as the subsequent media attention. Reading between the lines, the story in the *TNT* had an air of superiority to it, almost as though the pursuit of tawdry divorce news was something the other guys did. "Friday," the story by Stacey Mulick read, "the couple's allegations against each other were publicized by a Seattle newspaper, television and radio stations [sic]."

Even the lead was a negative: "Tacoma city officials will not investigate allegations of abuse raised in Tacoma Police Chief David A. Brame's now public divorce."

Again, there were supportive quotes from City Manager Ray Corpuz and Mayor Bill Baarsma, with Corpuz proclaiming that he was not "interested" in investigating any civil proceedings. Corpuz went on to say, "There haven't been any discussions or complaints from within the department." But of course that wasn't true. By saying that, he was dismissing the April 15 letter from a group of Tacoma police officers calling for an investigation into Chief Brame's and Assistant Chief Catherine Woodard's conduct at the Judson house. Apparently, Corpuz felt it wasn't a legitimate complaint because it was anonymous.

The story was one thing but, as Brame thumbed through the newspaper, he found his name surface again, this time on the editorial page. The editorial board of the newspaper, always separate from the news division, was much tougher on the chief. Basically, the board said the charges made by Crystal in the divorce papers—that Brame allegedly threatened her life with a city-issued gun—had to be investigated. CITY MANAGER CAN'T IGNORE BRAME CASE was the headline.

But the toughest line took Ray Corpuz to the woodshed: "Brame's boss, City Manager Ray Corpuz, says the dispute is a civil matter; he sees no reason to get involved. Corpuz is wrong . . . Mrs. Brame's accusation hangs in the air. The city manager and the citizens of Tacoma can't ignore it. Investigate."

It was everything Brame feared. His dirty laundry was all over the newspaper and an investigation was being called for. Brame knew in his heart what that investigation would reveal because John Hathaway had already given him a hint of what was to come. Whether it had anything to do with Crystal's charges or not, the fact that Chief Brame and Crystal had visited a nudist resort, not once but three times, would surely surface—if not in the newspaper, then on Hathaway's Web site. Either way, anyone could read about episodes in his life that he would prefer to keep quiet, if not secret.

But not even Hathaway—the self-professed man who knew too much—knew everything. There were other secrets about David Brame's life yet to be revealed, and they were more troubling than anything that had been in the newspaper thus far. Even if she hadn't surfaced yet, Brame knew that Sally Masters was out there reading all these stories; it had been a long time since they'd seen each other but that didn't matter. If she went to the newspaper, he was a goner. And he would definitely be a goner if Detective Linda Watson opened her mouth about the way Brame had linked the promise of promotion with his desire for a threesome.

The clouds were all black, at least as far as David Brame was concerned. He called Ray Corpuz to see exactly where he stood; he wanted to hear it directly from the horse's mouth.

"Ray, I just read the paper. This is bad. My career's over."

Corpuz had some of less-than-stellar qualities as a leader of men but he *was* loyal, sometimes to a fault. He did his best to keep Brame's spirits up.

"David, listen to me. I know you're upset but this is all a personal matter as far as I'm concerned. You're not gonna get fired. Just hang in there. These things have a way of blowing over and this will too. Just come in to work on Monday and we'll deal with it then. Don't worry so much and stop reading the papers. It will all work out."

Brame was not mollified. Next, he called Jim Mattheis, the department's PIO. "Tell me when my career is over."

"It's not that bad, they're asking for an investigation," Mattheis said.

Brame knew Mattheis was probably just trying to make him feel good. "You know, Jim, I don't know how much more of this I can take."

Then Brame sighed and told Mattheis he had to get David Jr. over to his karate lesson at the Gig Harbor Karate Academy, the same place Crystal was due to take an all-day class in personal security the following day. At nine thirty a.m., Chief Brame dropped his son off at the karate school. Bill Kortenbach, head instructor and founder of the personal safety course, noticed Brame and remembered all the stories Crystal had told him. Kortenbach was especially attuned to Brame's presence but admitted later that he noticed nothing unusual about him.

Crystal was wired that Saturday morning. Her divorce was all over the newspaper and television and she had told her parents and friends that she was more worried than ever before. There were endless conversations with her parents and her sister as she stomped around the house gobbling down her favorite snack—Diet Coke and red licorice sticks called Red Vines, her substitute for breakfast. By eight a.m., she and her parents were driving in separate cars over to the house on Eagle Creek Lane. Now that David Brame had moved out, she was ready to retake her home. On the way over, Crystal and her parents stopped and bought some stuffed animals and toys to make the house special for the children.

When they got there, they continued to comment on what poor condition David Brame had left the house in. Lane in particular was fond of saying that Brame had left the place "trashed." He had previously taken a vid-

eotape of the premises after Brame moved out. Lane
also asked neighbor Tony Shepard to come over so he
could see for himself. In a later statement to cops, Shepard said that although the house was not in pristine condition, it certainly wasn't "trashed."

But it wasn't just the condition of the house that had
Lane and Crystal worried. Their paranoia was in high
gear. They were convinced that, because he was a cop,
David had the wherewithal to wiretap the phones and
plant bugs around the house. They wanted to be absolutely sure that everything was "clean" before Crystal
moved back in. Crystal had previously enlisted the aid
of Edward Lewis of LPI Services. At a cost of $45 an
hour, Lewis had made four visits to the Eagle Creek
Lane house since David had moved out. He checked
everything and told Crystal and the Judsons that the
house did not seem to have any listening devices in it.
He advised them to have the locks changed but Crystal
still wasn't satisfied so, on the morning of April 26,
Lewis was back.

As he had before, Lewis taped the calls that had been
left on Crystal's answering machine, all the while listening to a soliloquy from Crystal about the things David
had done to her and how she was in fear of her life. It
seemed nothing that Lewis did satisfied Crystal and her
parents. They asked for more and more assurances that
no one was listening to their conversations, and Lewis
had no choice but to suggest more and more expensive
ways of inspecting and monitoring the house.

In his notes on his visits, Lewis remarked that what
he was hearing with his own ears did not match up with
what Crystal was telling him. For instance, Crystal and
her parents had told Lewis many times that David
Brame would never call her by name or tell her he loved
her or wish her a happy birthday. But that was not what
Lewis was hearing on the messages left at the house. In

fact, it was the opposite: "On these recordings, he stated he loved her and the kids many times."

After Lewis left on the morning of the twenty-sixth, Crystal spent her time puttering around the house, cleaning some crystal glasses and generally straightening up. Then it came time for her to leave. She was due at Mary Bridge Hospital at ten a.m. for a class, required by the state for all divorcing parents, on how to talk to your children during and after a divorce. Crystal had rarely, if ever, been completely alone since leaving David Brame; her mother, Patty, was a constant presence. But this time, Crystal balked at her mother's insistence that she accompany her daughter.

"Mom, it's a four-hour class. I don't want you sitting there bored the whole time."

"I don't mind. I want to go."

"No," said Crystal. "I have to be on my own sooner or later. You stay with Dad. I'm going to go on my own. It'll be fine. I'm sure it's just a bunch of other women."

Patty reluctantly agreed and Crystal took off.

David Brame, meanwhile, was having the sort of Saturday morning parents all over America have, particularly those who are divorced. He was running his kids here and there and, after David Jr. got out of his Little Dragons karate class, Brame headed back over the bridge to his new apartment in Tacoma, where he made the kids lunch. His sister stopped by. "It was just about as normal as it could be. He was sad but he wasn't angry, just kind of down," Jane said.

Over at Mary Bridge Hospital, social worker Rich MacLeod didn't quite know what to make of this nervous little woman taking his required class that day. Crystal Brame had burst into his class and more or less taken it over. There were nine others in the room taking the course but you'd hardly know it; Crystal held court.

"I'm the woman in the newspaper," she said.

"I'm sorry," MacLeod said, "but I don't know what you're talking about."

"I'm divorcing my husband. He's David Brame, the Tacoma police chief. He pointed a gun at me and said, 'Accidents happen.'"

Crystal being Crystal, she kept on talking about virtually every aspect of her relationship with Brame. The other class members could only gape in surprise as Crystal went into elaborate detail about how Brame weighed her every day, how he checked the odometer to monitor her whereabouts, how he kept close tabs on every penny she spent. Then she began talking about taking classes at the University of Washington and how she wanted to start a new life.

The class was becoming the Crystal Brame Show until MacLeod felt compelled to stop her; after all, there were other men and women in the class with similar stories of abusive spouses. They had their own problems and Crystal was sucking all the air and time out of the class. MacLeod suggested they talk at two p.m. when class ended; if she liked, they could talk one-on-one.

After lunch, David Brame packed up Haley and David Jr. and headed back over the Tacoma Narrows Bridge toward Gig Harbor. He left a dark suit on his bed, some Bible verses on the nightstand and, for some reason, stuck his .45 Glock pistol in a holster on his waistband beneath his sweater. He didn't ordinarily carry his gun when off duty but, like many cops, sometimes he did. There didn't seem to be any pattern to it and there didn't seem to be any reason why he felt compelled to take it this day. There were no plans to meet Crystal and there is no evidence he even had any idea where she was that morning.

It was his first weekend in his new apartment with his children. The rooms had turned out just as Brame had hoped, neat and well thought out. But Brame had not had time to buy all the little things that children enjoy— candy, coloring books, special shampoo and soaps. So after lunch, he was back running errands to get some of these things and headed back to where he knew all the stores—back to the place he'd lived for nearly ten years—Gig Harbor.

David Brame's first stop was the Great Car Care Center in Gig Harbor, something the children always enjoyed. They were in and out in ten minutes. It was 2:27 P.M.

Next stop was Bartell Drugs on Olympic Drive. David Brame bought lightbulbs, children's bath toys, coloring books, some Laffy Taffy candy in cherry and banana, a Hershey's milk chocolate bar and a 3 Musketeers king-sized bar. It was largely junk food, but that's what divorced fathers do with their kids on their visitation days. David Brame wanted his kids to like him and he had every intention of buying them whatever they wanted. He was just following the advice of everyone he'd been talking to who told him to stop focusing on the divorce and just have fun with his kids when he was with them.

When David Brame pulled his car out of the drugstore parking lot, it was 2:47 P.M.

Back at Mary Bridge Hospital, the divorce class ended and Crystal took Rich MacLeod up on his offer to go over her personal story at more length. They talked for nearly an hour, until Crystal felt all talked out. "This is a dangerous situation and you have to talk to your attorney," MacLeod told her.

"I have been. He knows all about it," Crystal said, gathering her things, including a pamphlet entitled *What Children of Divorce Really Need.*

"Take care and remember—no matter how much you

might want to confront him, stay away from your husband."

"I will. I'm just heading home to clean up the mess he left in the house."

MacLeod watched her leave; it was two forty-five p.m.

David Jr. wanted a product called Crazy Foam, a children's bath soap, but so far no one had it. His father had promised he'd try to get it, so they headed over to the Fred Meyer supermarket. They bought another bagful of goodies—chocolate Jell-O Pudding, vanilla Jell-O Pudding, X-Treme Jell-O, Swiss Miss chocolate pudding, strawberry Nesquik, chocolate Nesquik and a loaf of bread—but the store did not carry the one item David Jr. really wanted, Crazy Foam. They all decided to keep looking. It had become an adventure. When they left the Fred Meyer parking lot, it was 3:02 P.M.

Unbeknownst to David Brame, Crystal was driving in the same direction. She had a tanning appointment at the Oasis Tanning Salon and was chatting away on her cell phone with her mother, telling her all about the class she'd just attended.

Suddenly, not far from the Harbor Plaza mall, Crystal stopped short.

"I think I see David's car," she told her mother.

"Do you see the children?"

"I'm not sure."

At that point, Lane heard the conversation from his end back in his house at Canterwood. "Tell her to get the hell out of there," he told Patty.

Patty began to relay her husband's sentiment, but Crystal interrupted her mother. "I gotta go, I gotta go."

The police theorize that Crystal got off the phone quickly because she was in the wrong lane of traffic and wanted to catch up with David. Why? That's something no one knows.

The call between Crystal and Patty ended at 3:07 P.M.

*   *   *

David Brame was headed to the Rite Aid drugstore in his continued search for Crazy Foam, meaning he had to turn right. Crystal was going to a tanning appointment; she should have turned left. Although their cars were close to each other, they should have headed in opposite directions at the last second. But for whatever reason—perhaps she just wanted to make sure the children were with him or maybe, as Crystal's parents say, she just wanted to get some medicine for a cough she had—the reality is that Crystal spotted David Brame's car and, despite telling everyone how fearful she was, she nonetheless followed him into the parking lot at the Harbor Plaza mall. It is the type of mall replicated all over America: along with some local shops, there's a Starbucks, an Ace Hardware store, a Hollywood Video and a Rite Aid.

It could be Anywhere, USA, but it's where Crystal and David Brame wound up at the same time and place that Saturday, April 26. They even parked in the same lane, about six car lengths apart on opposite sides.

By now, David Brame had spotted Crystal's car. As soon as he parked, he told his children, "I see your mother. Stay in the car. I want to talk to her."

He walked toward the entrance to the parking lot where Crystal's black Toyota Camry was parked. Those next few minutes remain a mystery. No one knows exactly what happened or what was said, but eventually David Brame was in the front driver's seat of Crystal's car with his feet outside the car. The door was open and Crystal was leaning in; their heads were very close to one another. Crystal placed her cell phone on the roof of her car.

Rod Baker, an information specialist at a hospital in the nearby town of Bremerton, was leaving Schuck's Auto store right around 3:10 P.M. For some reason, he said, he parked his car in a different spot than normal, one that gave him a clear sight line to the tragedy about to unfold. Baker was just about to get into his car when he heard a sound he'd never heard before.

"I heard a high-pitched voice," he says. "It didn't even sound like a sound that a human would make. It sounded like an animal."

Baker, who was approximately thirty yards from Crystal's Toyota, says he saw Crystal leaning into the car, her face just inches from Brame's. Brame was sitting sideways in the driver's seat of her car with his feet outside on the asphalt. Baker watched for a few seconds until he heard her say, "Oh no . . . don't."

In the next moment, Baker heard two quick gunshots, one right after the other with no more than a split second between them. He watched the sickening image of Crystal falling to the ground. "It was so strange," he says. "She just collapsed, like there were no bones in her body, just meat. I've never seen anyone fall like that. She fell just like a rag doll."

Baker ran back inside Schuck's. "Call 911, there's been a shooting in the parking lot."

For a few seconds everyone looked at him like he was nuts—until he explained the situation further. The first 911 call came from Schuck's at 3:11 P.M.

Then Baker went back outside and circled around toward the car. He wasn't sure if whoever did the shooting was still alive and intending to shoot again.

Another witness, a woman named Karen Deeds, was sitting in her car facing Crystal's black Toyota. She had her window open and was looking straight ahead but, just at the precise moment the shots were fired, a motor home crossed Deed's line of sight. That's when Deeds heard the gunshots. As the motor home cleared her sight line, Deeds saw Crystal fall to the ground. Deeds told police that the shots were about two seconds apart, and she too saw Crystal fall *after* the second shot.

Deeds then told police she heard a little girl yell, "Oh no" and saw her run in the direction of the car. She watched bystanders help the girl and a little boy who stood next to her. Figuring everything was being done that could be done, she drove her car out of the parking lot.

Just moments earlier, Steve Sutton and his wife, Barbara, were coming out of Rite Aid walking in the direction of Crystal's car when they heard a car alarm go off. It was coming from David Brame's red Toyota Camry, which was parked near the Suttons' car. As they looked over to see what was going on, they spotted a young girl and a boy—Haley and David Jr.—leaving the car where the alarm was sounding. At nearly the same time, they heard two pops. "I immediately recognized them as gunshots," Steve said.

Sutton and his wife followed the children as they ran to their mother's car. All of them stopped in their tracks when they saw the woman struggling on the ground in a pool of her own blood.

"She was trying to get up and people were patting her on the back, trying to get her to stay down. It was a terrible sight," Rod Baker said.

By now, Baker had circled back to the car and spotted David Brame's .45 caliber Glock pistol lying between his feet outside the car. He looked inside the car and saw Brame sprawled back toward the front passenger seat. There was blood all over his head and the car's interior. Baker carefully picked up the gun and put it on the grassy median near the cars. He told another witness to keep an eye on it and not to let anyone else touch it.

Witnesses would later say that the worst thing they saw that day was the sight of Haley and David Jr. looking down at their mother as she struggled for life on the unforgiving asphalt. Haley was beside herself with grief, telling one and all, "My daddy's hurt my mom. Help her. Help her. My dad's mean to my mom."

Barbara Sutton and another witness, Kris Monro, looked in the car and saw that the male passenger appeared to have shot himself in the head. They knew instinctively that the man was the children's father, and they gathered up the children and tried to divert their attention from the unimaginable scene playing out in front of them in the most mundane of surroundings.

Ray Lanier, a paramedic, drove into the Harbor Plaza mall parking lot seconds after the shots were fired. Suddenly, an ordinary trip to Rite Aid turned into a life-and-death situation. Lanier saw people running in all directions but mainly toward a black Toyota where a number of people had gathered. He pulled over quickly and jumped out of his car. Lanier had no equipment with him, but people all around were calling 911 on their cell phones and he knew it was just a matter of minutes before he would have help.

Lanier went to Crystal first. The blood on and around her head was so thick that he could not tell where the exit and entry wounds were, but he heard someone say she'd been shot and he took notice of brain tissue in the blood that was pooling around her. The only thing to do was to clear her air passageway so she could continue to breathe. "I lifted her head from the blood pool and asked a lady to bring something to place over the blood," he said. "She gave me a blue towel. I placed it on the victim's face and rotated her slightly toward her left side and asked the woman to hold her in that position while I went to check on the man in the car."

Lanier opened the passenger-side door of the Camry to get to David Brame. He obviously had a head wound and, as Lanier cradled his head to see where the blood was coming from, "I felt multiple fragments of skull move." He could tell that the bullet had gone in Brame's right temple and had come out the left side of his head. He noted the brain matter all over the car and figured David Brame would not be alive much longer.

Lanier cradled Brame's head until the fire department arrived. He told them a "bag mask" was needed and backed away to let them do their jobs. As he did, he felt something that was stuck to his right shoe. "It was some type of certificate with a gold seal affixed, a woman's name typed on it, and it mentioned something about divorce," he said.

It was the proof that Crystal had completed the mandatory course on children of divorce. Lanier didn't know what to do with the certificate but thought it might be part of the evidence. "I gave it to an officer at the scene."

Lanier's wife LeEtta Cole, like most of the women on the scene, was drawn to the two small children crying miserably. Barbara Sutton and Kris Monro were already trying to walk them away and get their attention on something beside, the horrible sight in front of them. If there is such a thing as every child's nightmare, this was it. Both parents were bleeding profusely from head wounds and it looked as though neither would survive. Cole listened with horror to the words spoken by Haley: "My daddy is a policeman and he's very mean to Mommy. I think my daddy has killed her. Please help my mommy. They're in a divorce."

Cole's heart was ready to break.

It was at that moment that Jennifer Nicole Lovin, a nineteen-year-old worker from Hollywood Video, walked into the scene. Lovin wants to be a nurse, so when someone ran into her store and said they'd heard gunshots, she naturally left the store to see if she could help. But the scene outside was beyond anything she had ever imagined. A woman had already placed a towel under Crystal's head and a man who said he was a paramedic was working on the man in the car.

The only ones left to help were the children, who were by now surrounded by adults. She heard what Haley had to say and knew that it was not doing either child any good to stay there and watch their parents struggle for life.

"We should get these kids out of here," she told the women around Haley and David. "I work in Hollywood Video. We can take them in there and get them out of here."

In a split second, they were all heading into the store. Haley latched on to Jennifer and held her hand. Jennifer talked calmly to Haley and listened as she spoke of the divorce and other acts of violence by the father against the mother.

Once in the store, Lovin and others got Haley to calm down long enough to give them the phone number of someone to call. Haley remembered her grandparents' number.

Back at Canterwood, Patty Judson had been dialing Crystal's cell phone number ever since she had hung up and told her mother, "I gotta go." Patty dialed the number over and over but it just went to voice mail time and again.

Finally, at 3:25 P.M., someone from Hollywood Video called her back. "There's been a serious incident," the man said, telling her where to go to pick up her grandchildren. He would not say anything more.

Patty began to cry. As she and Lane headed out, they called Julie and Dave Ahrens, told them what was happening and asked them to join them at Hollywood Video.

The children could not stop crying, both trying to tell their grandparents what they had seen. "Haley told me that she saw her dad hurt her mom and she saw blood on her mom," said Pierce County deputy Todd Donato. "David said he saw blood coming out of his mom's mouth."

As gently as he could, Deputy Donato stopped them in order to minimize the trauma they'd been through. They were witnesses to the mayhem and he didn't want their memories clouded by questions from those who were not there. Donato thought, rightfully, that only a skilled professional could help draw the children out about what they had witnessed and help them somehow deal with it.

Everyone in the store was trying to calm them down. Lane and Patty knew that it was time to get out of there. The police had briefed them. Crystal was seriously hurt and paramedics were taking her to St. Joseph's Hospital. Their son-in-law was being taken to the same emergency room. Deputy Donato told the Judsons, the Ahrenses and the children that he would take them to St. Joseph's immediately.

As they were leaving the store and entering the parking lot Oona Copperhill, a photographer who works for the *Peninsula Gateway,* the local Gig Harbor newspaper, snapped a photo of the four of them. The raw grief and emotion etched on Lane's face and Julie's shock as her hands cover her mouth will be preserved forever.

A police officer walked up to the Judsons and Ahrenses in the parking lot. He had a single question: "Do you know who could have done this?"

All four adults answered in unison, "David Brame."

BOOK III

THE AFTERMATH

Trying to Make Sense of It

Because of the information provided by Haley and David Brame Jr., people and police in that Gig Harbor parking lot knew almost immediately who the victims were. The man and woman at the heart of the troubled divorce the public had been reading about and seeing on television—Chief David Brame and his estranged wife, Crystal—were now lying right in front of them with gunshot wounds to their heads. The news spread rapidly across the Tacoma metropolitan area and soon, all over the United States. Although police departments around the country have been plagued by officer-related domestic abuse for years, there has never been another case quite so flamboyantly grotesque—a case in which the police chief of a fairly large American city had shot his wife and then himself in front of their two young children.

Detective Ed Troyer, the public information officer for the Pierce County sheriff's office, was at home when he got a page. "I get pages for plane crashes, fatalities. You name it, I get pages. But this was something I couldn't believe when I saw it. I looked at it and it said, 'Chief Brame just shot his wife and then himself. Call radio.' That's all it said, didn't go into detail or anything. And I literally had to hit my buttons again and look at it to make sure I was reading it right 'cause I couldn't believe it.

"At first, I thought maybe the page was really a bad joke. But then, very quickly, I remembered the articles of the past couple days and the conversation I had with Brame the day before where he asked me to pray for him. It just took a couple of seconds for me to convince myself that, yes, this really did happen."

Troyer put on his black jumpsuit with the word SHER- IFF printed in large letters on the back and sped to the scene with one thought on his mind: "This is going to be a big story, the kind you're gonna read about for a long time."

Gig Harbor detective Dave Crocker, who has a baby face and an easy, likable manner, was hanging around the house with his wife and children that day "just doin' stuff you do around the house on a Saturday." Crocker, a native of Chicago, had specifically chosen to join the Gig Harbor police department years earlier after falling in love with the area. He enjoyed police work but he knew he'd investigate very few big crimes in Gig Harbor. "It's a family place, one of the most beautiful spots I've ever seen."

He was one of only two detectives on the force and had never covered a homicide. In fact, there had been only one other homicide in the previous sixty years that Gig Harbor had been incorporated, and that was back in the 1990s when a man killed his mother. Crocker, who had been promoted to detective only two weeks prior to the shootings, spent most of his time on duty tooling around on a bicycle making sure everyone kept the town as peaceful as its well-deserved reputation. The last thing he expected on a beautiful Saturday afternoon was to be leading a possible murder-suicide investigation in Gig Harbor, of all places.

His quiet Saturday at home ended with a call from the dispatcher.

"What do you have?" he asked.

"You're needed down at Point Fosdick Drive where Chief Brame has just shot himself and shot his wife."

Crocker, who had never met Chief Brame but knew of his solid reputation, was floored. He jumped in his truck and raced to the scene; the only other detective on the force was out on his boat in a sailboat race and was unavailable until later. Driving there, Crocker could scarcely believe what he was hearing. "I was shocked. I mean you just don't have these kinds of things happen in this little town. I was literally shocked and as I was driving there—a newly appointed detective with the police department—I'm thinking, 'What do I know of anything that I can do to contribute to this investigation?' I wasn't expecting that when I got there I'd be assigned as the lead investigator."

But that's exactly what happened. Crocker had plenty of help and worked closely at the scene with Detective Ed Troyer and others from the Pierce County sheriff's department. From the beginning, they made sure that officers from the Tacoma police department were not directly involved because they were too close to the man at the center of the investigation. Crocker admits to being "overwhelmed" but he did what he had been trained to do: he gathered the first officers responding to the scene, found out what happened and started interviewing witnesses. All the nearby stores were canvassed and security videotapes were seized but nothing came of it; none had picked up those final few minutes.

Crocker began the investigative process. He called Verizon and secured the cell phone records of both Brames. A search warrant was obtained for Brame's new

Gold Pointe apartment, while the Judsons gave the police permission to search the family home on Eagle Creek Lane. Chief Brame's laptop computer was seized.

Crocker felt a hint of relief in knowing that, in many ways, this was an "easy" investigation. "There was no question of who had done it. It was a disaster and a tragedy but it could have been so much worse," he said, noting that the children were, at least physically, unharmed.

Over in Tacoma's North End, Jim Mattheis picked up Ray Corpuz and took off for Gig Harbor. Both of their pagers and cell phones were going haywire with calls from everyone from reporters to city council members.

"Why would he do this?" Corpuz asked Mattheis as he drove.

Mattheis couldn't believe the comment. What the hell was Ray Corpuz talking about? Did Brame have to take out a billboard that read "Help!"? For weeks, Chief Brame had been telling everyone from his assistant to his assistant chiefs how lonely and hopeless he felt, and yet the city manager was now tacitly acknowledging that he had paid no attention to any of it. Not only did Lieutenant Bob Sheehan and Assistant Chief Catherine Woodard tell him in no uncertain terms about what was going on—he could read about it for himself in both of the area's major newspapers. He had even told Woodard that he'd warned Brame to focus on his job. Mattheis said nothing; he just kept driving toward Gig Harbor.

Catherine Woodard had spent the better part of her Saturday running household errands. She had visited a tanning parlor called the Pink Coconut in preparation for a family trip to Florida, went to a Top Foods grocery store and then the dry cleaners. By early afternoon, Woodard and her daughter Elizabeth went to Nordstrom's at the Tacoma Mall where they bought bathing suits.

At two forty-five p.m., she and her husband, Bill, a retired assistant chief with the Tacoma police department, were at the Pavco Flight Center at the Tacoma Narrows Airport. The Woodards were interested in getting their pilot's licenses and were taking flying lessons. Just after three p.m., they were scheduled to go up in a Cessna 172 and were completing a preflight inspection report. Woodard had just climbed into the rear seat of the Cessna when she received a phone call from her daughter Elizabeth.

"Mom, you're supposed to call Sargeant Barry Parris at the office right away. He said it's important."

"Okay, did he say what it was about?"

"No, but he said it's urgent."

She climbed down and called Parris. "What's up?"

"There's been a shooting in Gig Harbor. It's the chief. He just shot his wife and himself in some parking lot."

"What?"

"I know, I know, but it's true. I have confirmation. Corpuz is on his way and he wants you out there."

"How badly are they hurt?"

"Bad. They were taken to St. Joe's but the word is they might not make it."

"Holy shit."

"I know, it's unbelievable."

"Okay, I'll get there as soon as I can."

Woodard returned to the plane to tell her husband. Woodard thought back to her conversation with Tracy Conaway. Tracy had been right; something bad *had* happened to David Brame. But as Woodard drove over to the parking lot, she kept asking herself how anyone could have predicted something like this.

By some weird quirk of fate, Sally Masters pulled into the parking lot just thirty minutes after the shooting. She had come to pick up a bottle of wine for that night's dinner with her boyfriend, Chris. She saw the police tape and ambulances and crowds but had no idea what was going on because she always listens to music in her car, never the news stations.

She parked in front of a liquor store and went in. The place was buzzing with excitement; everyone was looking out the windows.

"What's going on out there?"

"You didn't hear?"

"No."

"The Tacoma police chief just shot himself and his wife in the head."

Sally froze. "You mean Brame?"

"Yeah, some trouble with their divorce or something. There was something in the paper this morning. Guess he didn't take it too well."

"Guess not," someone else said.

Sally began shaking.

"Hey, are you okay?"

"Yeah, yeah. Where's your vodka?"

She pulled a bottle of Absolut off the shelf, paid for it and ran out of the store.

More than a thousand miles away, Assistant Chief Bill Meeks was getting ready to tee off on the eighth hole at a golf course in Tucson, Arizona. The weather was picture-perfect and they'd been enjoying a terrific golfing afternoon. The cell phone of his buddy and fellow Tacoma police officer Tony Abuan rang and Meeks heard him say, "Oh no."

Meeks stared at him, thinking, Brame's blown his fuckin' brains out.

Abuan put the phone away. "You'll never believe it," he told Meeks.

"Brame killed himself, didn't he?"

"He's not dead yet, but he shot Crystal too."

Meeks refused to believe it. "No way, that's not the Dave I knew. It can't be."

The men raced back to the house. Meeks punched at his cell phone the whole way until he finally got through to Catherine Woodard.

"Is it true?" he asked simply.

"Yes."

Assistant Human Resources Director Mary Brown was at her daughter Lori's house helping her prepare for her kids' baptisms. Brown was still ranting and raving about what had happened the day before, when she and her boss Jim Knudsen had been rebuffed when they suggested David Brame be put on administrative leave. At that point, she knew nothing of the tragedy that was unfolding a few miles away.

Then the phone rang; it was Brown's friend Jody Guilliardi, one of David Brame's secretaries.

Mary Brown listened to what was being said, hung up the phone and then broke down and began sobbing.

"That son of a bitch just shot himself and his wife in front of their two little kids."

"Why are you crying?" Lori asked. "You hated him."

"Because we should have done something. We sat down. We talked about it. And we didn't do anything. It sucks."

"Mom, it's not your fault."

"It's all of our fault. We should have stopped that son of a bitch. We had our chance and now it's too late."

David Seago, the editorial page editor of the *News Tribune,* began second-guessing himself the moment he heard the news. He thought about the conversation he had had with Brame the day before the shooting. It had been Seago's job to break some very bad news to Brame, telling him that indeed the newspaper was going to publish Crystal's allegations against him. Despite that, Brame was calm. As Seago later wrote, "I had no inkling he was capable of such murderous rage and self-destruction. Questions kept running through my mind after I learned the terrible news: Who knew? Who could have known? Did anyone outside the couple's closest relatives have any idea how frayed the Brames' marriage had become or that Brame was capable of such violence? Count me among the many Tacomans who are stunned and disbelieving."

Back in Tacoma, David Brame's parents, Gene and Beverly Brame, were just coming home from a funeral at about three p.m. on the afternoon of April 26. A woman who had babysat for their children, including David, had died and, after paying their respects, they headed for an afternoon of leisure and gambling at a local Native American gambling parlor, the Emerald Queen Resort, just three blocks from their home on East Thirty-fourth Street.

"I had such a feeling of peace coming back from that funeral. I don't know why," Beverly Brame said.

Gene and Beverly separated in the casino, each going their own way to gamble. At around three thirty, one of the women who works at the hotel walked up to Beverly. The woman could not stop crying.

"What's the matter?" Beverly asked.

The woman could not get a word out but just kept looking at Beverly and bawling her eyes out. A feeling of dread spread throughout Beverly's body; she feared the worst.

"Is my son dead?" Beverly asked. "I want to hold my son."

Because of all the things David had told her over the years, Beverly says she immediately thought Crystal had killed him.

Just about the same time, several Tacoma police officers arrived at the casino. They had been trying to get in touch with the Brames to give them the news and had called their daughter, Jane, who told the officers where her parents might be.

The officers asked the casino manager to make an announcement for Gene Brame to come to the front door.

"I heard my name being announced on the PA system," Gene says. "Then I saw Beverly crying and the officers and they took us outside to the parking lot and told us what had happened."

The officers told the Brames they would take them to St. Joseph's Hospital to see their son.

As she was being transported to the hospital Crystal Brame was still conscious, although she was not talking. But incredibly she had enough of her wits about her to reach into her mouth and, to the amazement of the medical personnel, pull a bullet out and hand it to the EMT working on her. None of them had ever seen such a badly wounded victim do such a thing.

Crystal soon was transported by helicopter to Harborview Medical Center in Seattle. There was hope she might recover even though her head wound was very serious. Doctors at St. Joseph's had stabilized her and now she was being transported to the area's major trauma center. Her parents, her sister and brother-in-law and her two children followed along in various police cars.

Meanwhile, at St. Joseph's, Pierce County sheriff Paul Pastor came out to the parking lot to talk to the assembled press and tell them what he knew. At precisely 5:43 P.M., Pastor told them, David Brame, the forty-four-year-old native son and hometown favorite—the man who seemed destined to be police chief—died of his self-inflicted gunshot wound to the right temple.

Brame left the hospital like any other crime victim, his hands bagged to preserve evidence.

*   *   *

Even before getting word that David Brame was dead, City Manager Ray Corpuz had already made Catherine Woodard the acting chief of the Tacoma police department. She was the first woman to ever hold the post. There was no doubt she was qualified, but it soon became clear that she had a number of issues, not the least of which were the rampant rumors running through the department that she and David Brame had been lovers. The rumors were fueled by Woodard's lending Brame help when he needed it most. She had been at his new apartment a number of times, she had called Crystal and essentially spied on her for Brame and, worst of all for her, she had been present on April 11 at the Judsons' house for the ugly confrontation that developed between David and Crystal and her parents.

Woodard met the rumors head-on. She showed up for the turnouts on each shift, essentially the roll call, and calmly made a statement at each that she was now running the department and they all had a lot of work and healing to do—together.

Concerning her actions on the night of April 11, Woodard said it was her understanding that the lawyers for both Brames had agreed that she should be present. She said she was just helping Chief Brame as she would any friend going through a tough divorce. "People in situations like this do that all the time," she said. "I did that for the chief."

As for allegations that she and Chief Brame were romantically involved and having an affair, Woodard said: "That is simply not true . . . it's BS."

CSI: Tacoma

As police from the Gig harbor police department, Tacoma police department and the Pierce County sheriff's office surveyed the horrific scene in the Harbor Plaza mall parking lot they had a lot of questions, but one was paramount—what had happened in those final few seconds? It looked like a classic case of an estranged husband shooting his wife and then himself in the head, but they couldn't go with theories or what they supposed happened. They needed hard evidence. They needed an experienced forensics investigator.

As it happened, Steven Wilkens, the lead forensics investigator for the Pierce County sheriff's office, was on call that weekend and was driving around in a county car outfitted with specialized equipment. It was good luck all around because Wilkens, forty-seven, is an experienced forensics investigator. He's worked for the Pierce County sheriff's office for thirteen years after working as a small-town cop in Missouri. He left there to go into forensics, eventually training in San Diego, Dallas and Miami with one of the giants in the field, Toby Wolfson. Wilkens is well-versed in shooting-scene reconstruction and books thirty-five to fifty murder investigations every year in and around Tacoma.

On April 26, 2003, Wilkens' wife had gotten off work at two p.m. and he had picked her up for a lunch date in the nearby town of Lakewood. They had just finished eating when Wilkens got a page that he was needed over in Gig Harbor. That was odd, he thought. He never did any work in Gig Harbor; in fact, the Pierce County sheriff's office did not even have a contract with the town because there were never any homicides there. Wilkens called dispatch directly and was told there had been a shooting in a parking lot.

He got there at four p.m. and noticed that there were a lot of civilians—"lookie-loos," he calls them—who were watching every move the police made. The size of the crowd was unusual for a crime scene.

"All I knew was that there had been a shooting but when I got there I immediately found out it was Brame and his wife," Wilkens said. "The chief of the Gig Harbor police, Mitch Barker, came over to me and said, 'This is yours.'

"There was a frenzy out there. The bodies were already gone and both had shown signs of life. I did a walk-through to get my bearings to determine the location of the evidence and what I'd need. I wanted somebody's total station team."

Wilkens explains that a total station team is a mobile unit with computerized equipment that can survey the scene and take exact measurements and a video overview so that a precise sketch can be made. For one reason or another, the Washington State Patrol wound up sending its total station team to work with Wilkens.

"The deputies had done a great job securing the scene. More than a third of the parking lot was cordoned off."

Wilkens located the gun on the parking island where witness Rod Baker had moved it; the forensic investigator told a deputy to "stand on it" and make sure no one else touched the weapon or moved it.

Then Wilkens examined the scene inside the car where his real work would be done. He immediately came up with the answer to one riddle: why was David Brame sitting in the front seat of Crystal's car with his feet out on the pavement? The answer, Wilkens says, is simple. David Brame was a much bigger person than Crystal, and he literally could not sit in her car with his feet inside because she had pushed the seat up so close to the steering wheel; there was just no room, so Brame turned and sat at an odd angle with his feet on the pavement outside the car. But even Wilkens had no idea how or why Brame came to be sitting in Crystal's car to begin with.

It was up to Wilkens to come up with a scenario, based on the physical evidence, of what happened in those last few moments. The key was finding the "point of convergence." He explains that as "the point where all the blood spatter patterns come together on a plane so you can do an analysis of the angle of impact. That gives you the point of origin of where the blood came from."

In layman's terms, Wilkens' job was to figure out, from the blood patterns, how the shooting took place or how the bullets were fired and the angle at which the gun was held. The car was, of course, a mess. There were "transfer stains" of blood smeared all over steering wheel and door panels that had occurred as paramedics pulled David Brame out of the car. Wilkens spent nine hours at the scene and eventually he would return to the car after looking at the clothing to come up with a scenario that made sense; his work would involve using manikins and Styrofoam heads placed where the blood spatter and pooling told him Crystal's and David Brame's heads had been.

But after doing all that, he had a problem. "The only

real bloodstains were for *his* shooting," Wilkens said. He could tell from the blood spatter where David Brame's head was when he apparently shot himself but, at least initially, he couldn't tell where Crystal's head had been. "With her head, the only thing we could put together was from the blood stains on his clothing," he said.

Given that, "her head was probably close to his lap. He was probably holding her by the hair. The only way her head would have been in that position is if he was holding her there."

Crystal was shot behind her left ear, which initially seemed like an odd angle to Wilkens. Consider: if you're sitting in a car seat and facing the driver's side door with your feet outside the car on the ground, are you really going to hold a gun *to the side* of someone's head? Or, if you're intent on doing what you're doing, would you just shoot the person straight on in the face or body?

The only way the angles made sense to Wilkens was if David Brame was holding Crystal by the hair and pulling her down toward his lap. "She was trying to pull herself out and when he shot her, he let go of her and she fell to the ground," he said. "The only way the puzzle fits is for her head to be down in that position. It's the only logical conclusion. If she was just standing there to stop him, it would have been frontal. Her head had to be down."

Toward the end of our conversation, I asked Wilkens what he thought about the evidence that shows Crystal followed David into the parking lot that day. "Right," he said. "Who was stalking who?"

Despite that, Wilkens' report became the last word on the subject of what had occurred in the car. One cop even told me that David Brame had "executed" Crystal, pulling her head down and cold-bloodedly putting a bullet behind her left ear. It became the story of the shooting, the one everyone told to make the angles make sense.

Wilkens said he knew David Brame personally and had never seen any sign that he would snap the way he apparently did. Just a short time before the shooting, David Brame had given a eulogy at a funeral for another investigator who had died of cancer. "He did an excellent job. He was great there."

Wilkens said he could not make sense of Brame's actions that April 26 except to say, "There was no sane individual out there that day. What you had here was two people not dealing with reality anymore. Both of them. The stress was very high."

But that, he said, was his personal opinion and not part of the official report.

The Children

Late on the afternoon of April 26, over in Spanaway, Cornelia Thomas was getting her children ready for the babysitter. A light-skinned African American woman with an attractive, open face, Thomas loves children, both her own and those she works with at Mary Bridge Hospital where she is a forensic child interviewer. It has to be one of the most heartrending jobs around, talking to innocent children about the most horrible events they have ever witnessed, events that will probably haunt their psyches for the rest of their lives. The horrors committed against children ran the gamut to pretty much anything imaginable. She has talked to them about sex abuse and yes, even about the murder of their own parents. The worst case Thomas can recall is one where a young boy watched his mother's boyfriend repeatedly stab her in front of himself and his younger sister. The boyfriend had locked the trailer door so there was no way to escape, but the boy managed to crawl out a small window and run to a bar where he told the roomful of men to call police. "My daddy is stabbing my mommy. He's killing her." The woman lived, thanks to her son.

Thomas had interviewed that boy right after he witnessed the stabbing and she later testified at the trial. That was her job, to preserve the memories of children who had seen horrors without embellishing them or helping them along.

On the evening of April 26, she had a date planned with her husband and was just waiting for the babysitter when her phone rang. It was bad news. The date would have to wait and so would her husband. There had been a shooting involving children and their parents. The police were not sure what the kids had seen but they needed Thomas to drive to Harborview Medical Center in Seattle to interview the children.

By nine p.m., Cornelia Thomas was in a children's playroom inside the burn unit of the Harborview Medical Center. Authorities had been careful not to ask the Brame children too much about what they had seen. They did not want to disturb the children and they also did not want to muddy the waters for the investigations that were sure to follow. Neither child had been told that their father was already dead or the severity of the injuries to their mother. "They got us in there right away because kids will shut down if they have to wait too long," Thomas said. "They can also add to what they saw and fantasize about it, so it's better to interview them right away."

After meeting the children and having a brief discussion, Thomas came away with several impressions. "They were in a dissociative state. David, for instance, was playing like it was any other day. He was riding around the room in a toy car. Haley was not crying but she was sullen, quiet. They understood the seriousness of what had happened but they were overwhelmed by it."

Both children were tired but because he was younger, it was determined that David Brame Jr. would be interviewed first. "He was trying to figure it out for himself,"

Thomas said. "It's hard to say if he heard the shooting or saw it. I don't know. If they did see it, it was clearly overshadowed by seeing their mom on the ground."

Detective Mike Portman of the Pierce County sheriff's office and Joe Lombino, the Judson family attorney, were in the room to observe but were not allowed to interrupt or ask any questions of their own.

Thomas began slowly with easy questions. She asked David how old he was.

"I'm five."

"Oh, you are?"

"And I'm gonna be six and seven and eight and nine."

"You sure are."

But the little boy had a lot on his mind and it showed. After telling Thomas his birthday was November 4, he said, "And my dad shooted my mom . . . she was laying on the floor with her eyes closed and there was blood coming out of her and he, me and Haley outside were cryin'. My dad, and my dad was like this [David closed his eyes and leaned his head back] and Mom punched him."

Since he wanted to talk about the shooting, Thomas questioned him further. "Did you see your dad shoot your mom? Or did you just hear that?"

As always with little children, there was confusion.

"No, it wasn't today."

"Why don't you tell me about that from the beginning to the end."

"He shooted at her today, he brung his gun."

"Did you see the gun?"

"Yeah. And it shooted my mom into flat dead. Then they called an emergency. And that woman was tryin' to take care of me. And there was a fire truck tryin' to save my mom and my dad."

After a confusing exchange, Thomas again asked David Jr. the question of the hour.

"Now, did you actually see your dad shoot your mom?"

"Yeah, and she went over and punched my dad [demonstrating a punch underneath the chin]. And it wasn't good. It, it ruined my dad to be alive but now he's dead. He got, my dad, my mom just run up and punched him. And he shoot the gun."

There were more questions about the condition of both parents.

"Where did your dad put the gun on your mom and shoot?"

"Right in the mouth and she fell on the ground. Her, her eyes were closed like this [closing his eyes]. Out her mouth there was blood coming out, out of her toes and out of her back and out of her brain. Me and Haley were so scared."

At times David Jr. answered Thomas' questions completely and head-on, but other times, he was all over the place and it's difficult to know what he did actually see. He seemed to be mixing up present and past events, but it was clear he'd seen his mother struggle on the ground after being shot.

"She was bleeding and she bleed blood out of her mouth and she was on the cement and there was blood comin' out of her mouth . . . and I touched my mom."

Thomas tried to get him to talk about the past and what the situation was like inside the Brame house as he was growing up.

"Have you ever seen your dad hit your mom?"

"No, he didn't hit her."

Soon the interview was over. It had lasted only twenty minutes and David needed to get some sleep.

Cornelia Thomas' interview with Haley was next. It was hoped that because Haley was older, she would provide more detail and perhaps answer some of the questions everyone had.

After going over the ground rules of what was truth and what was a lie, Thomas dove into the heart of the matter. "I want you to tell me what happened earlier today and I want you to use your own words and take your time."

But just like some of David's answers, Haley's were at odds with the physical evidence at the scene and didn't seem to make sense.

"[My dad] saw my mom and then he went like this to her [Haley demonstrated a push or shove back into the car] and he kinda pushed her into the car and then I didn't see him with a gun but he, I know he shot her 'cause I could see blood all over her and blood all over him. And after that happened, like, three ladies came over and they helped me and I went into the store and they helped me for a little bit and then I told them my mom's phone number. I mean my grandma's phone number and my grandma and grandpa and my aunt and uncle came."

But there was no way David Brame could have pushed Crystal into the car because witnesses saw her outside the car, standing and talking to David Brame, her face close to his. There is no evidence he ever pushed her into the car. Thomas kept going, trying to pinpoint what happened to bring Crystal and David Brame together in that parking lot.

"Was your mom's car parked when your dad saw it or was she driving?"

"No, she was parked."

"Was she inside the car, outside the car?"

"Inside."

"So what's the first thing your dad does when he spots your mom's car?"

"He pushed her over [Haley demonstrated a push] on the seat where the steering wheel is and he shot her. And then I think he pulled her over and then, over to the ground, and then I think, well, then he had blood on him for some reason, I don't know why he had blood on him."

Despite being older, Haley's answers made even less sense than David Jr's. Just hours after the shooting, it seems that Haley—an impressionable child—was picking up information from adults and using it as her own story. The fact remains that the shooting could not have happened the way she says it does; she also cannot bring herself to say that her father shot himself.

Thomas moved into another area, asking Haley about what it was like to grow up in that house.

"He's been really mean to my mom, really mean."

"Tell me what you mean by 'mean'."

"I don't know what threaten means 'cause he's like, one time he said that he wanted to snap her head off." (It's unclear what incident Haley was referring to or if she misheard adults talking about a verbal confrontation, not a physical one.)

"And you heard him say that?"

"I think I did, it was years ago."

Again, Haley seems to be influenced by all the talk around her during the divorce proceedings. Crystal had been talking with her parents a lot about the divorce. It's likely Haley was sitting there listening to the adults talk. We also know from David Brame's notes that he believed Crystal was manipulating Haley to pry information out of her estranged husband.

All in all, it's hard to know what Haley actually saw and what she heard the grownups talk about. Consider this exchange with Thomas:

"Haley, have you ever seen your dad point a gun at your mom any other time?"

"No, only once years ago."

"Have you ever heard him threaten her or say he was gonna kill her any other time?"

"Yeah, I've heard her say that."

"What has he said?"

"He said, like, I'm gonna kill you or I'm gonna snap your head or neck off, whatever it was, head or neck, I can't remember."

Virtually everything Haley said in the interview are statements that can be taken from the divorce proceedings, things the adults in her home had been discussing nonstop for a couple of months. Whenever Thomas questioned Haley closely about what she actually saw, she says she can't remember.

By 10:25 P.M., the interviews with the children were over, both of them frustrating and unclear. The mystery of those last few moments leading up to the shooting remained.

Crystal Brame, meanwhile, was hanging on to life, and her immediate family, including Haley and David Jr., remained in the hospital, hoping against hope for a recovery.

The Secrets Begin to Leak Out

In the days following the murder-suicide, City Manager Ray Corpuz, the Tacoma police department and the city government found themselves at the center of a firestorm. Everyone, from the average Joe to the local and national media, wanted answers. How had this happened and who knew what when? How does a man who was so unstable that he would shoot his wife and kill himself in front of their two young children become chief of police? There were no immediate answers and, in fact, as David Brame's darkest secrets began to leak out, there were only more questions.

Reporters were on the hunt looking for everything and anything they could learn about David and Crystal Brame. The national press was interested as well. Back at my desk in New York, I was asked to look into the story by my boss Susan Zirinsky, the executive producer of the broadcast. I began making calls and realized that I would have to get on the next plane to Tacoma. I wasn't alone. When I arrived, I watched a local television reporter for KIRO, the CBS affiliate in Seattle, tell viewers that producers from *60 Minutes, Primetime Live,*

20/20, Dateline NBC, and of course *48 Hours* were in town.

The first person I had arranged to meet was John Hathaway. I had called him from New York and we'd agreed to meet for dinner at Stanley & Seafort's, one of the better restaurants in Tacoma and coincidentally just down the street from Hathaway's apartment. It has good food and an even better view of the Tacoma Dome and all of downtown.

I wasn't prepared for the Hathaway experience. John and his wife, Carolyn, had arrived at the restaurant before me. They were facing the view and all I could see were their backs. Hathaway, of course, had on one of his trademark fedoras and Carolyn was wearing a knit cap. It's fair to say they stood out among the crowd of after-work diners, couples out on dates and birthday celebrants. I took a deep breath and introduced myself.

"Can I get you a drink?" I asked.

"We're way ahead of you," Hathaway said, raising his glass of scotch to my good health.

This guy is all right, I thought. We began to discuss the Brame affair and Hathaway told me that the Rosetta Stone of information was the Brame divorce file—that was key to beginning to understand what all the fuss was about. I got a copy from the CBS affiliate in Seattle and, like every other reporter covering the story, I began to pore over it, calling those who had filed declarations with the court. Initially, neighbors of the Brames' on Eagle Creek Lane came forward to tell what they knew of the couple, but they soon made a pact to speak no more to the press. My job was to get them to talk, especially the principals: Lane and Patty Judson, Dave and Julie Ahrens, Ray Corpuz, Catherine Woodard, Chief Brame's friends on the force and Crystal's friends in town.

After ringing doorbells and calling neighbors, I did find someone who was willing to talk—Marty Conmy, the salesman who lived in the same cul-de-sac as the Brames. Conmy refused to join his neighbors' demand for silence. "I thought the last conversation I had with Crystal happened for a reason," he said. "I think she wanted me to tell what I know."

Conmy told the story of running into Crystal and Patty Judson after David Brame had moved out and the women were checking over the house before Crystal formally moved back in. Like most of the neighbors, Conmy and his wife had never had many dealings with the Brames aside from a few odd incidents like the time Crystal panicked after David Jr. knocked over a lamp and left a nick in the wall. Conmy admitted he always thought David Brame was a bit of an oddball and that Crystal came off as a nervous wreck. Now he understood why.

Conmy could not forget his last interaction with Crystal. "We were not friendly at all, just neighbors who waved hello to one another from time to time," he said. "She always seemed to be in a rush."

But a week before the shooting, Conmy spotted Crystal and Patty leaving their house and walked over to tell Crystal that he was sorry about her divorce. "I could barely believe that this was the same person. Before, she was always hunched over, but now she was standing tall, and while before she was very nervous and quiet, now she looked me in the eye and told me things I can scarcely believe."

Meanwhile the local newspaper, the Tacoma *News Tribune,* finally had awakened from its yearlong slumber. As slow as the paper had been in getting off the mark, it was moving equally fast now. To give credit where it's due, the Tacoma *News Tribune* staff deserves kudos for breaking story after story once the shooting occurred. Its reporters attacked the Brame tragedy with gusto. "This was in our backyard," said Sean Robinson, one of the star reporters who wound up leading the paper's coverage. "Everyone had their sources, everyone knew someone."

Robinson is a burly reporter's reporter for the *News Tribune* who prides himself on his writing style and intellect but affects the "working-class stiff" persona common to print reporters all over the country. Ties are bad; scruffy is good. Robinson has the look down. He was off Fridays and Saturdays at that time and was the one reporter in the newsroom not asked to come in that first day to work the story. The editors figured they had to save someone and Robinson was the guy. "I was bummed but they told me to rest up, that there would be plenty for me to do the next day," he said.

And there was. "We always have these 'to do' notes when we come in. This was the biggest 'to do' list I'd ever seen."

Among the marching orders Robinson received there were two names, women who knew a lot about David Brame and perhaps could comment better than anyone about his character. One was his ex-wife Betty Brame and the other was Sally Masters (both names have been changed).

Within hours, Robinson was on the doorstep of the house where Brame's first wife lived. Betty Brame had eventually married her next-door neighbor and had a child with him. She'd even moved to Oregon, but now she was divorced once more and back in Tacoma. Unfortunately for Robinson, it did him no good. To this day, Betty Brame has never given an interview about her eight-year marriage to David Brame, not to Robinson, not to anyone. Rumors had it that he was just as controlling with her as he was with Crystal but aside from the lists Crystal found in the house she shared with David, there is nothing to back that up. Whatever her reasons, she's not said a word.

Frustrated by Betty Brame, Sean Robinson turned his attention to Sally Masters. Sally had run into David

Brame years before and the interaction was so traumatic for her that she had kept her eye on him ever since, marveling at his rise to power. She had already called Ruth Teichroeb from the *Seattle PI* but so far had refused to meet with her to tell the reporter what she knew about Brame's past. Now she was on the run, hiding out in motels because she feared that cops and reporters would come looking for her.

But David Brame's enemies within the department were happy to provide grist for the mill. Finally, they felt that all the dirt they'd been collecting on Brame would get a full hearing. The first hint of what they had came in the sidebar story about Brame's career that very first day. The story mentioned that Brame had secured many commendations during his twenty-two years on the force but then, buried deep within the story, came this paragraph:

> His career also included an Internal Affairs investigation in the late 1980s after a complaint was lodged against him. Ray Fjetland, who was chief at the time, has declined to explain the complaint but said it was unfounded.

This paragraph alluding to that old Internal Affairs investigation without telling readers what it was about, was the first time the public had ever been made aware that Brame was once the subject of such an investigation. Most readers probably glossed over that tiny fact.

Brame's enemies within the department went to reporters and told them the gist of the investigation, but there were still no first-person sources willing to go on the record. The *Tribune* had to be careful; this was a very serious allegation. In the meantime, the newspaper quoted Ray Corpuz, who said he had discussed the mysterious investigation with former chief Ray Fjetland

"and was told it concluded the investigation was unfounded." But the lid was slowly lifting off Brame's private Pandora's Box.

In the same article, Corpuz went on to say that he had talked to Brame about his marriage problems and had been assured by Brame that "he was in control of his emotions." But Corpuz admitted that he had never read Brame's personnel file before appointing him chief. It was a damning admission that would come back to haunt him.

Meanwhile, the chief's old enemies in the Tacoma police department pointed reporters to a 1999 lawsuit filed against David Brame, Ray Corpuz and the city of Tacoma. At the time, Tacoma police lieutenant Joe Kirby had sued the department and the city for favoritism, claiming a good old boy network was promoting whomever they wanted despite union rules. It was a $10 million lawsuit that had a lot of ugly things to say about then-Assistant Chief Brame and City Manager Ray Corpuz. The depositions in the lawsuit spelled out in detail what had happened when Internal Affairs investigators hauled David Brame in back in 1988. In fact, the lawsuit contained a deposition from one of those investigators who said he thought the charges filed against David Brame were true even though they were "not sustained."

It should have been an easy matter to get hold of that lawsuit but there was a big problem. Assistant City Attorney Shelley Kerslake had succeeded in getting the Kirby lawsuit dismissed. Then, Kerslake went a step further; she moved to have its entire contents sealed. A judge had agreed, so the lawsuit was off-limits to curious reporters. It appeared that David Brame or his allies had covered his tracks very neatly.

That did not, however, stop Brame's enemies from pointing reporters in yet another direction. The key, they said, was a woman named Sally Masters. Why? Because

Sally Masters had come forward in 1988 to allege that she'd been raped by a Tacoma police officer she thought she knew as a friend. The officer was David Brame.

The race was on to find Sally Masters and get her to talk.

In the Eye of the Hurricane

Sally Masters is a thin, intense woman with long, curly
blond hair worn in the seventies style made popular by
Farrah Fawcett circa *Charlie's Angels*. Sally stands about
five feet two inches and her biceps have the kind of
definition some women would die for; she is clearly
strong and an outdoors type, although that is not to say
she is unfeminine. In fact, she is quite attractive and has
the type of body that turns heads even at forty-five years
of age. But what you notice most about Masters is her
nervous manner. Her crystal blue eyes often dart around
the room while you're talking, as if she's never comfortable talking to you or even standing still in one place
too long.

Thanks to whispers that were growing to shouts, many
reporters had her name and knew the broad outlines of
her involvement with David Brame. Sally quickly became known as "the woman allegedly raped by David
Brame," and every reporter was after her. For her part,
Sally had been laying low since Ruth Teichroeb wrote
the first story about the Brame divorce papers on April
25. She had kept on the move, at first in fear of David
Brame and the cops, later in fear of the press. Some-

times she stayed with her boyfriend Chris, other times with her mother in the nearby town of Puyallup or in motels between Tacoma and Seattle.

But reporters and television producers can be persistent, and the media soon learned that Masters had at least three addresses. Two of them were houses she owned but never lived in. She leased them to college students for the rental income. Masters lived in the third house, a small eight-hundred-square-foot cottage type of house. One night, when she went home for a change of clothes, Masters was cornered in the tiny apartment by a television news crew. While they knocked on the door and peered in the windows, Sally had no choice but to hide in the shadows for hours until they finally left. She was very afraid that someone from the police department, a supporter of David Brame's, might hunt her down if she came forward. Besides, no one had believed her fifteen years earlier when she had come forward, so why would they believe her now?

As I set out to produce the David and Crystal Brame story for *48 Hours,* it became clear to me that Sally Masters was one of the keys to securing the story. Rather than chase Sally down, I elected to go through her lawyer, Jack Connelly, who agreed to set up a meeting.

Sally and I hit it off immediately. We met at her lawyer's office and by the end of the meeting, I liked her and believed her and could tell she trusted me. I agreed to keep her in shadows for the television interview and promised we would not describe her in any way she was uncomfortable with. I even suggested that she wear a baseball cap to hide her hairstyle, which was fairly distinctive even in silhouette. But she wasn't sure. She wanted to think about it, and of course I agreed. Sally already had a "deer in the headlights" look; pushing her for a commitment might mean pushing her away.

Sean Robinson, meanwhile, who contacted Masters before I did, had more immediate concerns. He needed

Sally to tell her story to him quickly before Sally swung back to Ruth Teichroeb at the *Seattle PI*. Sally had met and liked David Zeeck, Robinson's editor at the Tacoma *News Tribune,* but she was not ready to go public.

That did not, however, stop Robinson and Zeeck from going ahead with the rape story, because they had other sources only too willing to tell them what had happened between David Brame and Sally Masters. On Wednesday, April 28, Robinson and Zeeck coauthored a front-page story, headlined BRAME: WHO KNEW WHAT, WHEN?

For the first time, Tacomans were being told that their former police chief had a rape allegation in his background, an allegation that had been investigated by the Internal Affairs department of the Tacoma police. The reporters lacked Sally Masters's first-person account, but they did have the overall outline of the story.

Masters and Brame had met when they worked together in the late eighties. One night, they went out after work and everything went very badly. Sally claimed that she had been raped; Brame told everyone the sex was consensual. But at the heart of the *Tribune* story were three members of the Tacoma police department: two of the original Internal Affairs investigators and Police Officer Reggie Roberts, who had been a childhood friend of Brame's. All three revealed for the first time that *they* had always believed Sally had been raped by Brame. Roberts, a friend of both Sally's and Brame's, went a step further. Roberts said that he had confronted Brame at the time the alleged rape had occurred and that Brame admitted the rape to him.

But if that was true, why had the Internal Affairs investigators not suggested some sort of punishment for Brame who, by the way, was never arrested for the alleged assault? Well, the investigators said, there were problems with the case. Sally had waited fifteen months to come forward, by which time there was no physical evidence and, in addition, Brame, when questioned by

Internal Affairs investigators, *denied* telling Roberts that he'd raped the woman. All the investigators had left was a case of "he said, she said." Brame had behaved so oddly in the formal interviews, however, that the investigators concluded Sally Masters was telling the truth. "But we did not put our opinions in the final report," investigator Dave Olsen said. "We had to go with the facts and the facts were inconclusive."

In the final report sent to then-Police Chief Ray Fjetland, they found the report of the alleged rape "not sustained." It was gray language but damning nonetheless. "Officers hate that one," one of the investigators told the *News Tribune.* "They want to hear 'unfounded' or 'exonerated.'"

The rape story hit Tacoma hard. Now the Brame case was going beyond even the horror it originally was. The police chief was dead, his wife was clinging to life and now it was revealed that David Brame—always the favorite for the chief's job—had been investigated for a rape in 1988, a rape City Manager Ray Corpuz said he knew nothing about. Among the questions now being asked: why had none of these damning details come to light *before* Corpuz chose Brame to become police chief?

That's not an easy question to answer. Corpuz had already admitted he had never read David Brame's personnel file but that hardly mattered, since the report of the rape was not in Brame's personnel file. But there was more to the story. In fact, a worried Brame had sought Corpuz out *before* he was appointed chief to let Corpuz know that Brame's enemies in the department might spread a story that he had had a sexual allegation lodged against him years before. At that point, Brame again said it was a case of consensual sex, and Corpuz decided to let the matter drop. Former chief Fjetland, who had been in charge when the complaint was lodged by Sally Masters, later said that Corpuz had never called him to ask about the Internal Affairs investigation. But even if he had, Fjetland considered the matter unfounded; he remembered it as a case of rough sex between consenting adults. Verbatim, here's how Fjetland described the alleged rape to investigators: "It had, uh, been a friendly, uh, encounter over a date, uh, or a relationship, as I recall. Um, she said that, uh, in the course of them kissing and, uh, basically embracing, uh, he assaulted her by carrying the, the, um, um, the petting to, um, sexual consummation, rape, uh, sex against her will."

If it doesn't sound too convincing, there's probably a reason. Investigator Dave Olsen says there is just no way Fjetland can say he didn't recall the alleged rape. Olsen wrote in an e-mail:

> Chief Fjetland has claimed he wasn't told that the case involved rape and the threat of a firearm. The rape complaint was the most serious allegation of criminal misconduct by an officer that I recall during my twenty-eight years with the department. I believe that it was the most serious allegation of misconduct to cross Fjetland's desk during his tenure with the police department. He was provided with all available information at the time and I recall he seemed informed about the case during the conversations I had with him.

But Fjetland stuck to his story, saying he just didn't know the allegation was that serious. The former chief says that because Brame was a young officer with no previous trouble, he was inclined to refer him for psychological counseling to help him control his anger problem. There is no record of whether Brame received that counseling or not. In any case, Fjetland was so convinced Brame had reformed himself that he promoted him not once but twice *after* the investigation—to sergeant and lieutenant.

With all these revelations being made public, it appeared to some that the leaders of Tacoma were corrupt, stupid or both. The headline in the *Seattle PI* said it all: TACOMA IN TURMOIL.

Crystal Hangs On . . .
And in Tacoma, Life Goes On

In the Gig Harbor parking lot where the double shooting occurred, a shrine of sorts had sprung up. Those saddened by what happened in their little community or those just curious to see the actual murder scene began leaving flowers, notes and even balloons in the parking space where Crystal Brame once writhed on the pavement. There was one chance for Tacoma and Gig Harbor to recover from this tragedy, and that was if Crystal could somehow survive.

An interdenominational ceremony was held in the parking lot to bless the spot and essentially chase away any bad spirits. Ministers beseeched God in heaven to watch over Crystal. Signs and notes went up all over Tacoma praying for her recovery. At the shooting site, a sign read, WE LOVE YOU CRYSTAL, YOU GO GIRL.

At Harborview Medical Center in Seattle, Lane and Patty Judson had not left their daughter's side. They, the children and Julie and Dave Ahrens lived round the clock in the critical care unit watched over by a kind-hearted Seattle police officer and nurses who tended to the children, trying to make the best of an awful situation.

At the same time, funeral arrangements were set for David Brame, now Public Enemy Number one in Tacoma. He would be buried on Saturday at the By His Word Christian Center in Tacoma. The children had been told their father was dead but Crystal's parents would not let them attend the funeral. The Judsons' understandable bitterness toward David Brame was unyielding and even went beyond him; they were especially angry with Beverly Brame because of Crystal's allegations that the woman had once spanked young David. Beverly never denied swatting David Jr. but said it was no more than a tap and one tap at that.

All eyes were on Crystal. And for part of the week, it appeared all the prayers were being answered. On Wednesday, the same day it was revealed that David Brame had an alleged rape on his résumé, Crystal's condition was upgraded from critical to serious. She had partially opened one eye and lifted a finger. On Thursday, she squeezed Patty's hand and that of her lawyer upon request. It was a very positive sign. Doctors were guarded but said a patient's ability to respond by request was a good sign. Crystal was taken off her respirator and began breathing on her own. It was still hard for the Judsons and Julie and Dave Ahrens to look at what had been done to Crystal, but their spirits and those of many people in Tacoma and Gig Harbor lifted just a bit.

Gene and Beverly Brame, who had had nothing to do with the actions of their son, were understandably crushed by his death, Crystal's injuries and all that was being said about David's past. They were reeling, but they did have their supporters.

The day after Bill Meeks returned from Arizona he and fellow assistant Chief Don Ramsdell made it a point to visit the Brames. Gene was a former detective and, aside from the kinship of the blue uniform, Meeks had known the Brames for a long time.

"I drove over there and the moment I got out of my car, I saw Gene and Beverly up on their patio. I rushed over to them and hugged them for a long time and all of us were crying like babies, believe me," Meeks said. "There were just a lot of emotions."

Some Tacoma police officers, including Meeks, felt their sadness turning to anger for what David Brame had done to their department. The public suspected a lot of officers knew or should have known how unstable Brame was because he worked with them every day; everyone was looking for someone else to blame.

"He's left us an awfully big mess to clean up," said Detective Jim Mattheis, the beleaguered police department spokesman.

Anger was also being directed at the media—especially Internet reporter and local bartender John Hathaway—for airing the Brames' dirty laundry in the first place. Patrick Frantz, the president of the union that represents police officers, fired off an e-mail to Hathaway that read in part, "If you want to throw stones, you had better live in a bulletproof glass house."

Hathaway and his wife, Carolyn Cohen, were stunned. They interpreted the e-mail as a death threat because Frantz was once a member of the local SWAT team and remained an armed police officer. "I sat up all night with my wife, who had stomach problems," Hathaway told the *Tribune*. "She is scared to death."

The e-mail was especially nasty because in it Frantz, who had been a Brame loyalist, also threatened to air dirty laundry against Brame's enemies. Frantz believed one of them, most notably Lieutenant Joe Kirby, had leaked the publicly available divorce papers to Hathaway.

Kirby contacted his lawyer, who wrote a letter to the city attorney:

> *Lt. Kirby is off today and does not feel safe in returning to work until he sees his counselor and*

*officer Frantz is relieved of his firearm and placed
on administrative leave pending an investigation of
this perceived threat.*

Acting Police Chief Catherine Woodard acted quickly,
referring the matter to the Pierce County sheriff's office
to ask them to determine whether a criminal investigation was warranted. In the Alice-in-Wonderland world
that Tacoma had tumbled into, a police officer was saying he was too afraid to report to work because of a
perceived written threat by a Police Union official. It
was unreal.

"It's not okay when you do stuff like this," Woodard
said. "We are going to deal with things appropriately
and swiftly."

There was so much anger to go around that the media
was even criticizing one another. More than a few people had noticed how slowly the Tacoma *News Tribune*
had moved on the story. Days after the shooting, *Tribune* editor David Seago wrote a column apologizing for
his overly friendly e-mail to David Brame. What's more,
Seago admitted that Brame had also told the editor
about a woman who had accused him of date rape a few
years before. Despite that, Seago did nothing to derail
Brame's bid for the top job. Seago admitted he had
made a mistake.

Columnist Robert L. Jamieson Jr. of the *Seattle Post-
Intelligencer* took Seago and the *News Tribune* to the
woodshed in a blistering column:

> Anger is reserved, too, for The News Tribune,
> the Tacoma newspaper suddenly in hot pursuit of
> this story. The paper knew of a "serious" allega-
> tion in Brame's past but didn't investigate deeper.
> The paper knew about Crystal Brame's many accu-
> sations, including that her husband waved a loaded

gun at her. But The News Tribune wrote what it knew only *on* [his emphasis] the day two gunshots sounded.

So the nerve of the paper to write a huffy editorial this weekend: "The Brame scandal, however, is only partially about crimes. The greater part of it appears to involve administrative negligence, cover-ups, the politics of the police department and perhaps cowardice or folly in high places."

How about the folly of the Tacoma paper, which heard the rumblings and shrugged? Talk about a public disservice. More lapdog than watchdog.

The Other Woman

A few days after the shooting, Detective Linda Watson was sitting in her cubicle trying to understand the previous six months, how a man she had once looked up to could disintegrate so quickly. At least so far, she was the forgotten woman in the whole scandal and that was fine with her. She was hoping against hope that it would stay that way.

David Brame had threatened not to promote her unless she agreed to participate in a threesome with him and his wife but at least as far as Watson knew, that secret had died with Brame. She doubted Crystal, if she survived, would want to revisit that ugly chapter in both their lives. But Watson was still worried. Brame had told her that Crystal had named her in the divorce papers, and she had no reason to doubt his word. She knew the media was all over everything associated with Brame and sometimes wondered why they were not already at her front door. She still did not know that Brame had been lying and that she had never been named in Crystal's divorce papers.

She feared that the media was closing in and about to ask her what were bound to be sordid questions about

David Brame's obsession with her. Her emotions were welling to the surface. She tried not to but spent some time at her desk crying or tearing up; people noticed, especially Catherine Woodard. The acting chief had called a special meeting of detectives and, just as she had with the patrol officers, she stood up squarely to the group and stated flat out that she—Woodard—had never had an affair with David Brame. The meeting ended, detectives returned to their desks and soon, Linda Watson got the word that her supervisor, Detective Mark Langford, wanted to speak with her.

"Please sit down, Detective," Langford said. "It's a tough time for the department, for all of us, and I just wanted to know how you're handling all of this. Are you doing okay?"

"I'm doing okay but, you know, it's tough."

Despite her best efforts, Watson's eyes began to tear up. She was thinking about the storm that might show up on her doorstep any moment if reporters got hold of her name from the divorce papers.

"I wanted to make sure you know that we have an employee assistance program to deal with any problems or emotions you might be having. There's always someone there, a counselor or a therapist you can talk to."

Watson shook her head. "I'm aware of the program and, you know, if I feel like I need it, I'll talk to them but right now, I'm okay."

"Good, all right then."

Watson got up to leave but stopped. "Why did you call me in here? Is this something you're doing for everybody?"

"Catherine asked that I talk to you. Someone had seen you crying and she, you know, just wanted to make sure that you're okay or at least as okay as you can be."

"I wasn't crying."

"Perhaps she was mistaken—I'm just glad you're all right."

"Thank you."

But it wasn't going to be as simple as that, and deep down Watson knew it. The next day, she again was at her desk when a good friend, Detective John Bair, poked his head around the corner of their shared cubicle.

"Hey."

"Hey."

"Listen, Linda, I've been hearing some rumors about you."

"Like what?"

"What about you and David Brame? Is it true?"

"Is what true?"

"Were you guys having an affair?"

"Absolutely not," Watson said. "Absolutely not."

"Okay then, that's good. I didn't think so but I had heard it and I just wanted to come to you myself and find out from the horse's mouth."

Bair went back to his desk, but Watson was very unsettled by the conversation and her encounter the day before with Detective Langford. Her rumored affair with David Brame was now being spread throughout the department and people at the highest levels had heard it. She had to do something; she thought it through for an hour and then went to talk to Bair.

"John, this whole thing is so ugly. That's a pretty serious rumor you heard and I need to know where it's coming from. I've had other people coming up to me asking about it. Where did you hear it? I have to address this before it really gets out of hand."

"I'll tell you what I know," Bair said. "I think it's coming from a secretary in the chief's office."

"Thanks."

Watson went back to her desk and called Woodard's office; she was going to meet this thing head-on.

"This is Detective Watson. Is the chief available to talk to me? It's important."

"I'll get back to you."

That afternoon, Woodard called Watson down to her office. When Watson walked in, the acting chief stood up and embraced her.

"I'm so sorry for all this. How are you holding up?"

"Fine. I'm sorry to take up your time. I know there's a lot going on but I had one of the other detectives, John Bair, come up to me this morning and ask if I had had an affair with David Brame and I just really need you to understand . . ."

At that point, Woodard held up her hand. "Linda, I know about you and David and Crystal and the threesome."

Watson sat stunned. She'd only told her family and boyfriend the details. Little did she know that David Brame's desire for her was an open secret known by Woodard, McColeman, Jeanette Blackwell, Assistant Chief Rich McCrea and even Assistant City Attorney Shelley Kerslake.

But Watson had no way of knowing that. When Woodard told her that she knew, Watson was glad she didn't have to explain the whole thing all over again. "I'm so relieved. I'm glad someone knows what the truth is. I never knew what to do when Brame suggested a threesome; he made it clear to me that my promotion was in jeopardy if I didn't go along with it, but I never did what he wanted. I just sort of ignored him until he went away."

"And you were promoted anyway."

"Right. I don't know, maybe he thought it would make me think more of him, but he gave me the promotion. I don't know why. I never had anything to do with him sexually, romantically or in any way."

Woodard sighed. "He told me all about it," she said. "We had three conversations. First, he told me he was trying to arrange a threesome, then he told me it was someone within the department and finally he told me your name. I'm sorry, Linda. He was crazy; we all know that now. He even told me that he and Crystal fantasized about the whole thing. I was appalled that it was someone within the department but he always said it was consensual, that you were interested and that Crystal was the problem. He said she did not want to go along and that he was going to work on her."

"It was absolutely not consensual. You don't know what a hell he made out of my life, always calling and having Crystal call. I couldn't stand it, but I didn't know what to do or where to go."

"I'm really sorry, Linda. I wish I would have gone to you and talked to you about it but I was afraid that you might view me as the other woman. I've told you that David and I were not lovers but at that point, I didn't know what you would think."

Watson wasn't quite sure what Woodard was talking about, but she wanted to make her point. "The thing that bothers me most, especially now, is that David made Crystal think we were having an affair because I didn't want to participate in a threesome. I think he told her that I didn't like her or didn't think she was cute or whatever. He was another horny guy, that's all."

Again, Woodard put up her hand. "I know, it's a mess. I talked to Crystal about this whole thing and she was crazy about it. She even told her eight-year-old daughter that Daddy was having an affair with another woman. I mean, really."

"Are you kidding me?"

"I wish I was. I don't think any of us really knew David Brame—or rather the real David Brame."

"I'm concerned for my reputation. I had nothing to do with this guy and now everybody's talking about this affair. What can I do? I mean, there's no way I can work here if people think that about me."

"Do you feel harassed? Has anyone else talked to you about this?"

"Barry McColeman. The other day, after the suicide, he came to me and said if I needed to talk, he'd be there for me. Barry said he knew about my supposed relationship with Brame. I told him there was no relationship but I'm not sure anyone believes me."

"I believe you," Woodard said.

"What can I do about this?"

"Look, I have to talk to the human resources people about this and I'll get back to you right away, okay?"

The next day, Woodard called Watson and told her she was obligated to file a report with the city. And that's how, even after his death, David Brame was hit with a sexual harassment complaint that, without naming Watson, outlined how the chief had tried to entice a female subordinate into having a threesome with himself and his wife or risk losing a promotion. The story ran on the front page and was yet another black mark on the quickly eroding reputation of the man once considered Tacoma's favorite son.

No one dared asked the question: what next?

The Sex Rumors

If there was one skeleton in his closet that David Brame especially feared, it was his sexual addiction. No one knew how far-reaching it was except Brame himself. But when you begin to pick up the pieces of David Brame's life, the issue of sex crops up again and again. There was the alleged rape of Sally Masters, his repeated visits to nudist resorts, his attempt to form threesomes and foursomes with couples from those nudist resorts, his attempts to "date" underlings while still married to Crystal, his sexual harassment of Linda Watson and finally the sexual demands he placed on Crystal.

It's no wonder then that, in the aftermath of Brame's death, the rumors about the raunchy sex surrounding Brame and the Tacoma police department were rampant. Some were true, some were fictitious, but none of them seemed to have anything to do with the tragic shooting in Gig Harbor. Still, investigators were required to run everything down.

The heart of the investigation was centered on a swingers' club called New Horizons in nearby Lynwood, Washington. New Horizons bills itself as "the Pacific Northwest's finest swingers' resort." Not shy about what it offers, the club advertises that it was founded more than twenty years ago as an "adult social club" that's been called "the most beautiful club of its kind in the United States and perhaps the world." The club's Web site is filled with sophomoric double entendres like this come-on for a July Fourth party: "Come create your own fireworks with us" and ads that beseech members not to miss "Gigolo Weekend."

The club spokesman at one time was a former Tacoma police officer, and there were rumors that many other Tacoma cops were also members.

The club is not illegal and all members are over twenty-one; consensual swinging, after all, is not against the law. In the end, investigators came to the conclusion that the Brames were not members and there was no proof that they ever set foot in the club.

But the rumors did not end with the New Horizons club. Investigators had heard of sex parties involving top brass from the Tacoma police department and had to run them down. After all, David Brame wanted to engage Linda Watson in a threesome with Crystal. Had he done the same to other attractive women on the force? Had being attractive become a prerequisite for getting promoted?

Catherine Woodard was grilled about this by investigators but denied any knowledge. All she knew about was a party years earlier that got a little out of hand, where a police captain had jumped into a fountain in his underwear. She also told investigators that she had heard rumors that Ray Corpuz was sleeping with a top city official and that they'd been discovered taking a naked hot soak in his Jacuzzi in the middle of the afternoon by Corpuz' daughter. Was it true? Did it matter? Investigators decided it didn't and let that episode drop, although both Corpuz and the woman were inadvertently named in the investigators' summary of the case.

Under the intense questioning Woodard, who has

been married twice, admitted to a ten-year affair with another police officer. In fact, Woodard's randy side was public and well-known. One police official was forced to counsel Woodard on her behavior after he spotted a cop with his hand up Woodard's skirt in an office where others could see them. That male officer later married another woman on the force and Woodard admitted she and the other woman had "words" over their mutual love interest. Other cops told investigators the encounter actually had been a fistfight.

As for David Brame, Woodard vehemently denied they were having an affair but, because Brame talked about his preferences to everyone, Woodard knew an awful lot about his sexual likes and dislikes. She knew, for instance, that Brame desired Watson because she was well-endowed and had long legs. "I'm not his type," Woodard told investigators. "He liked dark-haired females with big boobs, which I'm not."

The investigators were left shaking their heads over what was clearly unprofessional behavior throughout the department. The police chief had been trying to arrange threesomes with underlings, another high-ranking Tacoma officer was a member of a swingers' club and the new acting chief admitted to a ten-year affair. "The TPD was a sexual hothouse but it had nothing to do with Brame shooting Crystal," one said.

More Secrets

Acting Chief Catherine Woodard and her assistant chiefs Bill Meeks, Don Ramsdell and Rich McCrea were trying to get the department back to normal and focus at least some attention to the job and away from David Brame. Even his official photograph was taken off the wall in a vain attempt to put some distance between Brame and the department he now seemed to haunt. Each day brought forth a new revelation, one more damning than the next.

By Wednesday, Woodard and her assistant chiefs were in a private meeting when Woodard's assistant, Jeanette Blackwell, came in with a strange look on her face. She had a piece of paper in her hand and a look of shock on her face.

"Look at what I found," she told them, sliding the paper onto the table.

It was a one-page recommendation sheet based on a psychological interview given on September 20, 1981. More specifically, it was David Brame's recommendation sheet filled out by a psychologist following an in-depth interview. Applicants then and now are required to pass

the psychological report before joining the Tacoma police department. The news was not good.

> *As a result of the examination,*
> I do ____   I do not __X__
> *Recommend the candidate for employment as a*
> *police officer with the Tacoma Police Department.*
> • Steven H. Sutherland, Ph.D., clinical psy-
> chologist.

Woodard and the assistant chiefs looked at each other.
What the hell was going on? Was there no end to this
mess? This piece of paper, never before seen by those
present, revealed the latest outrage in simple detail:
Brame had failed the psychological examination required to join the department—failed, and yet he'd been
hired anyway. He should never even have been a cop,
never mind the chief of police. It was an astounding
revelation.

"Where did this come from?" Woodard demanded.

"It was in a file," Blackwell said.

"Shit," Meeks mumbled under his breath. "This is all
we need. The media's gonna have a field day."

Woodard took a deep breath. "Well, we have to release it. Any other surprises in there?"

"Not yet," Blackwell said.

The moment the meeting broke up, each of the assistant chiefs crept up to Blackwell one by one. They each
wanted to look at their own files to make sure they'd
passed their own psychological exams. They all had.

For his part, Steven Sutherland, the psychologist who
chose not to recommend David Brame as a police officer
back in 1981, did not remember anything about the
young man who had become the most infamous police
chief in Tacoma's history.

David Zeeck of the *Tribune* was angry. The newspaper had requested David Brame's personnel file when he was named a finalist for the chief's job and a number of pages that suddenly were circulating had not been in the original packet of material. The obvious question was, why? It appeared that someone was covering up for David Brame and had been for a long time. Consider:

- There was no reference to the Internal Affairs investigation of the rape allegation in Brame's personnel file.
- The Internal Affairs report itself apparently had been destroyed and it looked like Brame may have had a hand in that. While he was a vice president of the union, he convinced the city to go along with a union plan to destroy unfounded Internal Affairs records three years after they'd been compiled. His own alleged rape report apparently had been destroyed thanks to that provision and no copy of it has ever surfaced.
- The new, now public and damning psychological report had been left out of the original records released to the newspaper.

Making matters worse were the comments of Ray Corpuz. Presented with the psychological report, he told the *News Tribune*: "I didn't see this. I saw this for the first time in the last few minutes." Compounding Corpuz' growing credibility problems was the fact that he was such a poor public speaker. He may have been a mover and shaker behind the scenes but his public image is lackluster in the extreme. Aside from his tendency to mumble and stumble over words, Corpuz, just before the Brame scandal broke, had injured his ankle while jogging and had to suffer through the greatest crisis of his thirteen years in office on crutches. It made him look that much more ineffectual.

*   *   *

The newspaper and David Brame's critics, both within the department and without, wanted answers. According to procedure in place at the time, if an officer candidate failed his psychological exam, he had a right to ask for another one.

Again, records were checked and rechecked and again, something else surfaced that had been kept hidden until now. There was a second psychological report given by a Dr. James H. Shaw and it wasn't pretty. "It appears Mr. Brame is a marginal police officer applicant and the prognosis for his developing into an above average officer is judged poor at this time," Shaw wrote in the November 17, 1981, report. "While this examiner would not recommend Mr. Brame be hired as a police officer, he does not display either the pathology or the history which would result in his rejection."

It was hardly a resounding call to hire David Brame but he had passed, barely. Still, according to procedure at the time, if two psychological reports were given and they disagreed with one another, a third report should have been given. No one could explain why there was no third test in the files but, apparently even without one, Brame was hired to be a Tacoma police recruit.

Along with the new psychological reports, Tacoma police released a separate twenty-three-page file that included the report of a police officer, Sergeant J. Richburg, who had checked the personal references Brame had given the police department back in 1981. Even Sergeant Richburg, who apparently had no psychological training whatsoever, raised a number of red flags when he began speaking to those who knew Brame well. Based on those interviews, he wrote that "[Brame] is a very quiet individual who speaks only when it is of interest to him. His introvert-type of personality and lack of life's experiences makes it very doubtful that he will survive probation."

Sergeant Richburg recommended Brame be hired "with reservations." Richburg took special note of an interview he'd conducted with a man named Dave Davidson, a friend of Brame's older brother. Davidson told Richburg that Brame was a quiet person who did not say hello or acknowledge Davidson's presence at the Brame family home. Richburg wrote, "Davidson said, to his knowledge, David Brame does not socialize with anyone his age. Davidson felt David Brame hinged [sic] on antisocial behavior."

Remember, Sergeant Richburg interviewed Davidson at David Brame's request; he was one of Brame's references!!

Trained psychologists and experienced police officers, after interviewing the young David Brame or seeing him in social situations, all felt he should not be made a police officer. It was yet another in a long series of damning revelations coming out during what was quickly becoming "Hell Week" for the Tacoma police department and city government.

Incredibly, there was more. Mary Brown, Tacoma's assistant director of human resources, told the *News Tribune* that she went to Ray Corpuz to report that Brame's own references were "troublesome." This became an important point because Corpuz had said previously that he had never read Brame's file but instead relied on a report from his human resources people. But one of those human resources people—Mary Brown—wrote to Corpuz *during* the selection process to warn him that "from a professional human resources standpoint, the references provided by David Brame were troublesome."

Why? Because Brame:

- Omitted as references the three police chiefs he had served under most recently.
- Inaccurately listed as a "supervisor" the

Pierce County sheriff who had no supervising authority over him.

- Listed as "peers" people he supervised.
- Listed as a reference the spouse of a former assistant chief who still reported to him.
- Did not list as references his current chief or fellow assistant chiefs. Later, all three declined to respond to any questions about Brame's candidacy as Tacoma's chief.

Human resources workers reported that they were unable to get some of the most high-profile people in Tacoma—people listed as references by Brame—to return their calls. The list included the Pierce County sheriff, former Tacoma police chief Ray Fjetland, and Bill Woodard, a retired assistant chief, who is married to Catherine Woodard.

In a "confidential executive summary" prepared for Corpuz, Cynthia Winder, who conducted the background checks for the Human Resources department, reported that "unsolicited pro and con contacts . . . ran the gamut from strongly supportive to strongly negative." In an ominous paragraph that would later ring all too prescient, Winder wrote, "While not specifically citing what it was, three references indicated there might be something in his past, either personally or professionally, that if made public would embarrass him or the city."

Mary Brown further claimed she had walked Corpuz through each paragraph to make him aware of all the red flags in Brame's personnel record. It was getting harder and harder for Corpuz to claim that he had no way of knowing David Brame might act out violently. He sure seemed to have had plenty of warnings that Brame might not be the right man for the job—and ignored them all.

*   *   *

So why *was* David Brame hired onto the force? John Hathaway had a simple answer: the Blue Code. "Just like in New York or a lot of other places, if your father is a police officer, you get hired no questions asked."

It was a simple answer, perhaps too simple. Gene Brame, David's father, had retired in 1979, well before David had even applied to be on the job. What's more, he had never risen above the rank of detective and didn't seem to have the juice to get his son hired after those two psychological examinations reports.

Ray Corpuz, who was now feeling the heat from all sides, called for a thorough investigation. The vultures were no longer circling; they had landed, and the focus now turned to Corpuz' own history and his cozy relationship with the police department.

49

Family Problems

In 1997, Tacoma police were called to the modest home of Ray Corpuz and his wife, Lynda. Patrol Officer Reggie Roberts was one of the first officers on the scene, and he says that he thought it was a fairly "routine" burglary. But as it turned out, nothing was routine about this burglary, and it would reverberate throughout the Tacoma police department for years to come, eventually becoming a footnote to the Brame scandal.

As soon as he learned where the burglary occurred, then-Police Chief Phillip Areola ordered some of his men to leave another crime scene and join him at Corpuz' house. He, at least, was taking this seriously. Nevertheless, no one was ever caught for the break-in, and the hothouse rumors inside the department were that Ray Corpuz' son Dito, who been arrested more than once, was responsible for the break-in. That too was never proven.

But another member of the Corpuz family would get in deep trouble for the burglary—Ray's wife, Lynda. She filed a report with the Safeco Insurance Company, claiming $23,000 worth of items had been stolen. Safeco paid off the claim, but company investigators were very suspicious and the more they looked into the signed affidavits by Lynda and Ray Corpuz, the more convinced they became that this was out-and-out insurance fraud. For instance, Lynda Corpuz listed as missing some valuable Native American masks she had purchased for thousands of dollars. It turned out that the masks were made by Lynda's brother, who is not Native American, and who later admitted to investigators that he had not charged his sister for the masks.

Safeco investigators brought their findings to the Tacoma police department but fully anticipated the matter might be referred to the sheriff's office because of an inherent conflict of interest—Ray Corpuz could not be investigated by the Tacoma police department because he had appointed the chief. But Safeco reported the matter to the Tacoma cops anyway so as to go through all the proper channels. One of the police officers to get wind of the investigation was David Brame, then captain of detectives. He and others informed then-Chief Phil Areola about the investigation—and this is where things get complicated. Areola should have just passed the case on to the Pierce County sheriff's office but, before he did that, he tipped off Ray Corpuz that he and his wife were under criminal investigation for insurance fraud. That was a big no-no. In fact, some thought Areola was interfering in a criminal prosecution and could have been charged. He was in fact investigated but no charges were brought.

Lynda, however, eventually worked out a deal with prosecutors where she reimbursed Safeco $30,000 and accepted responsibility.

Given a slightly different set of circumstances, Ray Corpuz—whose signature was on the insurance papers— could have been investigated himself but, fortunately for him, his wife took the fall. It was a small incident, but

Ray Corpuz no doubt realized how valuable a cooperative police chief could be. Without the heads-up from Areola, the damage might have been worse.

When stories about the insurance fraud case and David Brame's tangential involvement circulated in published reports after the deaths of David and Crystal, some people in Tacoma, like John Hathaway, theorized that Ray Corpuz had paid Brame back by appointing him chief. Furthermore, there was speculation that this was the reason that Corpuz was so protective of Brame and did not put him on administrative leave despite repeated warnings that he was no longer up to doing the job of chief. That's probably a simplistic notion. More likely, Corpuz wanted a friend as police chief—one who knew the way Tacoma politics worked—and that's why he appointed Brame chief. As to why he didn't intercede after Brame's troubles became clear, that's harder to say.

Whatever the truth, the stories about the Safeco investigation further damaged Ray Corpuz' reputation. The man who had single-handedly brought Tacoma back from the dead was now rarely seen in public. He spent some nights drinking with friends at the El Gaucho steak and cigar bar, just blocks from the city's glittering new downtown.

50

David Brame's Next Victim

Even with only a few days under her belt, Catherine Woodard was reveling in her new job as acting police chief of Tacoma; it was clear she was the right person for the job at precisely the right time. The department needed some serious nurturing and that had always been Woodard's strong suit. She also had met the rumors of her alleged affair with David Brame head-on and denied them in no uncertain terms. With all the damaging secrets about David Brame coming to light, Ray Corpuz had to be thinking that at last he'd made one correct decision.

Tacoma's citizens were reeling and events seemed to be picking up even more speed as the week wore on: David Brame's funeral was still a couple of days away, Crystal Brame continued to improve, and investigations were being requested to determine how and why David Brame became a police officer, never mind the chief of police. Even in death, his reputation continued to take a beating, first by news of the alleged rape of Sally Masters and now by a sexual harassment complaint lodged by Detective Linda Watson.

If Catherine Woodard felt like screaming, no one

would have blamed her. Even her reputation had taken a hit with the public revelation that she had been at the Judson home the night of April 11 and that Crystal had felt so threatened by her appearance that she'd called 911 to file a formal complaint. When the audiotape of that phone call was made public, it felt like Crystal was reaching out from her hospital bed to slap down a rival. Still, Woodard remained on the job. The stress and pressure of what had occurred would have caused a lot of people to crack but through it all, Woodard remained a cool customer. It looked and felt like she would be there as Tacoma recovered from its many wounds.

But then came the morning of May 1 when City Manager Ray Corpuz called Woodard to his office. Corpuz liked Woodard and thought she was doing a good job but a big problem had developed. In a search of David Brame's apartment, police had found Woodard's handwritten notes from the conversation she'd had with Crystal in early April.

Woodard admitted taking the notes but said she'd been ordered to do it by David Brame.

At this point, Corpuz was just as weary as Woodard with the nonstop revelations. "I hate having to make this call but I have to put you on administrative leave pending an investigation," he said.

Woodard was in shock but could only say, "I understand."

Corpuz said there was another problem as well. Police had found a note in Crystal's bag after she was shot. It read:

"Catherine Woodard—Asst. Chief
- Has called my parents' residence to intimidate me.
- Has gone through our home + my personal clothes.

- Knows *every* detail of court papers and divorce.
- Entered Canterwood premises under false pretenses.

Woodard sat and stared at Corpuz. She knew then that her career was over; they were placing her on administrative leave. She got up and calmly walked out. She was given until the following morning to turn in her badge, gun and police ID card.

At the County-City Building, Assistant Chief Bill Meeks was in his office talking to Rich McCrea and Don Ramsdell, the other assistant chiefs, when Jeanette Blackwell walked in.

"Have you heard?"

They all looked up. "What now?" asked Meeks. "Can there possibly be any more?"

"Corpuz just put Woodard on admin leave."

"What?"

"It just happened. She's on her way back here now."

"Holy shit," Meeks said.

They were still talking about it when Woodard came back from her meeting with Corpuz and walked into her office. Meeks, Ramsdell and McCrea were at her side in a split second.

"Is it true?" Meeks asked.

"What?"

"You're on admin leave?"

"How did you hear that?"

Meeks shrugged. "Jeanette told us."

Catherine called Jeanette in and asked her if she had told them. She said she had and Woodard just nodded. "All right then. Yes, it's true."

They began firing questions at her and she told them all she knew, which wasn't much. In a moment, Blackwell came in and told Ramsdell that Corpuz wanted to speak to him. In minutes, he would be made the new acting chief, if only because he was less of a friend of Brame's than Meeks and McCrea.

"I can't wait for this fuckin' week to end," Meeks said to no one in particular.

He had no idea that it was about to get worse.

51

Titlow Junction

Titlow Junction is the name of a railroad crossing on the west end of Tacoma. The train tracks run along the water and face west toward the Tacoma Narrows Bridge. At night, families head down to grab an informal meal at Steamer's, a local restaurant that features beer, fish tacos and a fabulous view of the setting sun. There's also a small beach and walking path down past the train tracks where couples and families can unwind from a day of work by taking in the mellow sunset.

Sally Masters lives less than a mile away and it was there that she first told me her story about David Brame.

Sally Masters first crossed paths with David Brame in 1988 when she was thirty and he was thirty-two. Sally was a former teenage runaway and, at that point, had dedicated her life to working with wayward kids who wound up in the court system. David Brame was a liaison officer, as was a mutual friend of them both, another Tacoma police officer named Reggie Roberts. They and the other cops and social workers got along famously. In fact, David Brame and Reggie Roberts were childhood friends and, if you talk to Reggie today, he remembers

when he and David Brame played on the monkey bars
together as young kids. Roberts, a big African American
with a friendly personality, loves music and has cut a
number of jazz CDs. Sally plays guitar and sings and,
back in the day, she and Reggie used to play in a band
together with a couple of other cops.

David Brame wasn't a part of that band, but he was
a constant presence in the court and Sally came to think
of him as someone special, a good guy. He seemed to
have it all. He was tall, good-looking, had a good job,
and he was not macho, a quality Sally abhorred. She
knew Brame had recently been divorced, but so what?
A lot of her girlfriends were divorced and so was she.

"He was just another guy who worked with us. We
were friendly and we had a good relationship around
work. He asked me one day if I wanted to get together
that evening to go get a bite or something and I said
that would be fine. He asked me for my phone number
and he was a nice guy, so I gave it to him."

Sally says she was going out with Brame to check him
out for a girlfriend. Brame knew Sally had a new Jeep
she was proud of and asked if she wanted to drive out
from her home in Tacoma to his house in Spanaway.
She agreed and, when she arrived, he immediately offered her a tour of the house. She liked that; he seemed
different from a lot of other cops she knew, certainly
more sensitive. As they walked around, Brame seemed
a little stiff and his bedroom seemed as bare as the rest
of the house. The only place he stopped for any length
of time was a separate room where he had his plaques
and trophies from his days as a high school jock. At that
point, her attitude toward him began to change. She
began to think he was too full of himself. He seemed to
sense it because he shifted gears, "Hey, you can see the
rest of the house later. Do you have any idea where
you'd like to go?"

"Not really," she said.

"Well, how about Plush Pippin'?"

"Sure."

Sally drove them some twenty miles back into Tacoma proper in the direction where she had just come from. The conversation in the car stalled and she realized that, socially, David Brame was very awkward. It was one thing to talk to someone at work about work but the real test was getting that person away from the job to see what they had to say. David Brame pretty much had nothing to say other than to talk about his divorce, which was something she didn't particularly want to hear. Still, she felt a little sorry for him and held up the conversation in the car and at the restaurant. The topper came when Brame asked her to split the check for coffee and pie. Hadn't she worked hard enough just keeping the pitiful conversation going? Now she had to pay for it too? She had the money but that wasn't the point— his stock was dropping like a rock.

The atmosphere in the car going back was icy but when they arrived, David Brame invited her to come in.

"It's still early," he said. "Would you like to watch some television?"

Sally felt sorry for him because he seemed so lonely and sad; against her better judgment, she reluctantly agreed to go inside.

While she sat on the couch fiddling with the remote, he excused himself to go to the bathroom. He took a long time and Sally convinced herself that the moment he returned, she was going to politely excuse herself and get the hell out of there. Brame was a loser in her eyes.

At that moment, he came out of the bedroom area and sat on the couch. Before she could say a word, he was trying to kiss her.

"David, no, I don't want that. I'm going."

Then he grabbed her, wrapping his arms around her body. He was nearly a head taller and a hundred pounds heavier.

"David, no, don't do this. I want to leave."

He didn't say anything, letting his actions speak for him instead. He picked her up and began carrying her toward the bedroom. She was kicking and screaming at him, she said, begging him to stop.

It was as though he was in a trance. He threw her down on the bed and pulled her jeans off. Then he grabbed her hair and made sure she was looking at the nightstand. At this point, Sally cries when she tells the story.

"He made sure I saw that he had put a gun there. I didn't see it before when he showed me around the house but it sure as hell was there now. And he jerked my head up by my hair to make sure I saw it."

"Now you're going to do this," he said.

Then he raped her.

Sally just cried and cried while it was happening and continued to cry after he finished. The weird thing, she said, was that David Brame began crying too.

"I'm sorry, I'm sorry. I never did anything like this. I don't know what came over me. I'm a Christian. I'm not supposed to do things like this."

He seemed nearly as upset as she was. Before he could revert to the monster who'd raped her, Sally grabbed her clothes, got in her Jeep and took off for home. Unfortunately for her, she immediately took a long hot shower and didn't go straight to the police who could have done a rape kit.

Instead she kept her secret to herself, but it was eating her up so badly that she finally told some friends. They told her to report it to the police.

"How can I?" she asked. "He *is* the police."

At the time, Sally was a divorced mother with two young kids. She didn't need trouble and she wanted to hold on to her job, which involved working with a lot of cops. She couldn't afford to be unemployed.

She went back to work in the court system but that

involved seeing David Brame and people who knew him. In fact, some people had even heard they had gone "out" and began teasing her about what had happened, totally oblivious to the truth. The only one who noticed that something was wrong was Reggie Roberts.

"You've got to tell me what's going on. You're not yourself. What happened between the two of you?" Reggie asked her.

"David Brame raped me."

"What?"

Sally told Reggie everything.

At the end, Reggie didn't say anything right away, but he was thinking, We've got big trouble here.

As a police officer, Reggie was now in a tough spot. By all counts, he should have filed a report with his superiors but instead he asked Sally, "What do you want me to do?"

"I want to confront him for what he did."

"Okay," Reggie said, not really knowing what he would do.

But within a few days, Reggie contacted Brame and told him that he wanted him to come to his house to talk with Sally, who was very upset. For whatever reason, Brame agreed.

It was tense when the three of them sat down at Reggie's dining room table. He was in uniform; David Brame was not. Sally and Brame sat across from each other.

Her message was plain and to the point: "You raped me."

There was only a moment's hesitation; Reggie could feel himself holding his breath. "I know, I know," Brame said. "I'm sorry."

The room was silent but electric. "Please don't tell anyone," Brame begged. "I'm a good Christian and I'm going to get counseling from my pastor. Please don't tell."

Again, it seemed as though Brame was nearly as upset

with himself as Sally was. Reggie broke in. "I'm going to make sure you do what you say. If you don't, I'm gonna report you."

Later, Reggie told Sally that he was pretty sure David Brame was receiving counseling from the police department's chaplain but couldn't confirm it. Sally was angry; she didn't want Brame to hurt anyone else. She had let a lot of time pass but she finally went to a friend named Walt DePuy, a prosecutor. He agreed to take her case to the Tacoma police department's Internal Affairs bureau but by now, fifteen months had passed since the alleged rape.

Ron Hill and Dave Olsen were the Internal Affairs investigators. It was a tough case because Sally had waited so long. There was no physical evidence that she'd been raped. Reggie Roberts went to the investigators and told them of Brame's admission to him. That was significant, of course, but they told Reggie that it would not be allowed in court because Brame had never been read his rights. The confession was as good as worthless. When it came time for David Brame to face the Internal Affairs investigators, he simply said it was a case of consensual sex and that Sally was angry because he would never call her after that. Brame even told his mother that it was consensual sex; it's possible that the reality of what happened was so shameful that he had convinced himself it was consensual.

But the weird thing is that Hill and Olsen, two hard-nosed police investigators who had no reason to take the word of a civilian over a fellow police officer, chose to believe Sally. Perhaps it was how odd Brame appeared when questioned. Olsen in particular said he would never forget it. "He sat there and rocked back and forth like a child the whole time and kept referring to himself in the third person. He said, 'David Brame is a good Christian. David Brame would never do anything like that.' "

52

The Worst Day

By Saturday, May 3, everyone in Tacoma needed a break. But there would be no letup. Two events were scheduled; the third event, unplanned, would break the city's heart.

The Tacoma city council was set to meet that afternoon to discuss what had now been dubbed the David Brame affair. Everyone on the council and especially Mayor Bill Baarsma and City Manager Ray Corpuz were getting deluged with phone calls and e-mails from citizens pleading for something to be done. Brame's suicide was taking a personal toll on Baarsma. He had known Brame as a young man when the budding police chief had taken one of Baarsma's classes at the University of Puget Sound. Baarsma, who had pushed hard for Brame to get the top job, amazingly was still defending Brame even after the shootings, sometimes with nearly comic results. At one gathering of the press, Baarsma said, "Look, no one knew this was going to happen. David Brame was a native of the area who went to the University of Puget Sound." To which one smart-aleck reporter said, "Yeah, but you could say the exact same thing about Ted Bundy."

But the main target of public wrath was now Ray Corpuz. It was being openly discussed that he might be put on administrative leave himself, pending the results of an outside investigation. The council would stick with him this day but made it clear that Corpuz would have nothing to do with any of the investigations about to unfold.

Before the council met, the funeral of David Brame began at one p.m. at the By His Word Christian Center. The day was gray and windy, perfect for a funeral. Unlike many police funerals, especially one for a man who had held the rank of police chief, David Brame's funeral was a very low-key affair. There was no caravan of police cars from other jurisdictions, no mourners in dress uniforms. Officers were present, but the crowd of only two hundred people was relatively modest. Most heart-breaking of all to the Brame family was the absence of David Brame's two children; they remained at their mother's bedside at the Harborview Medical Center in Seattle.

Gene Brame, David's grieving and upstanding father, came as close as anyone mentioning the unmentionable—the twin shootings in Gig Harbor. "The stress and depression he was feeling after the divorce proceedings became insurmountable and he could no longer endure the problems," Gene Brame said. "His brilliant mind snapped."

No matter who did the killing, everyone felt the pain of David Brame's parents, who remain proud of their son to this day. "I'm not highly educated," Gene Brame told those assembled before him. "But I am his father and I am proud of him."

He even read David's birth announcement, perhaps to remind himself of a much happier time: "David Allen, six pounds, fourteen ounces . . . We have our baby at last. He is a little doll. I know you'll love him when you see him."

David's siblings did their best to remember the good things about their brother. Dan Brame, a Pierce County deputy sheriff, stopped in front of reporters and told them, "I'm not here to defend or deny the tragedy. We know what happened but life goes on and the memory of David goes on."

"Everyone can believe what they wish to believe," said Jane Brazell, David's sister. "But the Brame family knows the truth. He was an angel on earth and now he is an angel in heaven."

Pastor Jann Butler obliquely compared the shooting to a "black dot" and said, "We cannot cast the goodness of a man away because of one little black dot. Because of one little black dot—one act of emotion—we cannot judge this man for all of eternity. That's not what God would have wanted."

After more than two hours of remembrances, the body of David Brame was placed in a hearse and the procession headed to Mountain View Memorial Park in Lakewood. It was just past three thirty p.m.

What no one in Tacoma knew at that point was that Crystal Brame had taken a turn for the worse the night before. She developed a fever and fans were brought in to cool her down; it was exactly what doctors had been worrying about. They were not sure why her temperature had shot up so quickly. It could have been encephalitis or some other metabolic reaction.

Crystal's family, still at the hospital, was alerted to the downturn in Crystal's condition. Haley and David were kept in another room but Crystal's parents, Lane and Patty, and her sister, Julie, and brother-in-law, Dave Ahrens, were by her side. Things went from bad to worse and on Saturday afternoon, just about the time David Brame's funeral procession was heading to his final resting place, doctors let Lane and Patty know that Crystal no longer had any brain activity. The end was at hand.

"Would you like to say goodbye to your daughter?" a doctor quietly asked Lane.

"No," he said, crying. "We're not going to say goodbye. We'll just see her around the corner . . . someday."

With that, Crystal's family left her side for the first time since she'd been shot. Her time of death was placed at 4:40, nearly the precise moment when David Brame's body was being lowered into the ground at Mountain View Memorial Park.

Back in Tacoma, someone called the city clerk with the news; he then handed a folded piece of paper to Mayor Bill Baarsma in the middle of the city council meeting.

Baarsma opened the paper and read it aloud to everyone present. "Crystal Brame has died," he said.

A stunned silence followed; no one seemed sure what to do. Finally, Baarsma himself began crying out loud. He was soon joined in his crying jag by his wife, Carol, and his secretary, Cindy Leingang. Ray Corpuz sat there, not saying a word.

"We're absolutely brokenhearted," Carol Baarsma said. "We all prayed for a miracle that didn't happen."

Councilman Kevin Phelps covered his eyes with his hands while others said prayers aloud. "There was all this optimism as she seemed to get better. This hit the council like a ton of bricks."

It hit a lot of people that way. Sherry Bockwinkel, a local domestic violence advocate, summed up the feelings of many. "When you think it can't get any worse, it does. Crystal was not heard when she was alive and now we'll never get to hear her. It's just beyond grief."

In the Tacoma *News Tribune* newsroom, even jaded reporters found themselves unable to work, at least temporarily. "That was the worst day," one editor said. "Everyone thought she was gonna make it. That, as horrible as it was, at least she'd somehow pull through and live to tell her story. I've never felt worse."

But the reporters and editors knew they had a job to do. The next day's paper was the Sunday edition and there was so much news, it nearly seemed unreal.

When they finally dragged themselves back to Canterwood that night, Lane and Patty found Haley and David Jr.'s psychologists waiting for them. The doctors told everyone not to hide things from the children but to answer their questions as best they could. Patty was impressed with the types of questions the children asked but at one point, it was all too much. David Jr. began crying very hard and the adults could barely console him.

"What's wrong, David?" Patty asked.

"I just want to kiss my mom," he said.

No one knew what to say but after a moment Patty said quietly, "You can kiss her, David."

"How?"

"Just blow her a kiss up to heaven."

Little David did just what his grandmother told him to and then smiled that sweet smile of his. "Grandma, she caught it."

There were four stories on the front page of the *News Tribune* the next day, and three of them were about the Brame case. It was the apex of the story. The main headline read, CRYSTAL BRAME DIES; COUNCIL SUPPORTS CORPUZ. The subhead was, AMAZING PROGRESS BUT THE CHIEF'S BULLET DID FATAL DAMAGE.

There was also a report on Corpuz, who was told he could remain on the job but would be kept out of the investigation.

The other story was the first-person account of Sally Masters' alleged rape at the hands of David Brame. Finally, Tacomans could read her story for themselves.

Sean Robinson wrote a riveting account of their fateful encounter under the headline, IN HER OWN WORDS: "NO, DAVE, I WANT TO LEAVE!"; BRAME ACCUSER SPEAKS OUT.

On the inside of the newspaper, there were other stories as well, including one about a women's group forming to represent the battered wives of police officers.

Finally, there was yet another story about Ray Corpuz that once again highlighted his "barely there" leadership style: CORPUZ SAID UNAWARE OF MOVE TO PULL BADGE.

It was no big surprise to anyone paying attention. Corpuz said he had no idea that his top human resources people wanted to pull David Brame's badge and gun a day before the shootings. Corpuz defended himself by saying the first time he heard of that meeting is when he read about it in the newspaper.

53

Crystal's Final Goodbye

On May 10, 2003, Crystal Brame's white coffin was carried into the Chapel Hill Presbyterian Church in Gig Harbor, and more than six hundred family, friends and the curious gathered to say their final goodbyes to the woman who had come to epitomize the horrors of domestic violence.

Haley and David Brame Jr. entered the church last, led by their grandparents, Lane and Patty Judson, and their aunt and uncle, Julie and Dave Ahrens. Haley, then eight, wore a red dress and a blank look on her face. But David Jr., then five, seemed too young to know what was really going on. The spitting image of his father, he wore a blue sweater and a tie and waved to people he knew in the crowd; he appeared restless and even smiled on occasion. There was nothing wrong with his reactions; he was simply too young to absorb the horror right before his eyes, the loss of his mother.

Pastor Mark Toone seemed unable to even grasp for words, saying, "There is nothing I will say to you today that will not sound like a cliché."

Toone did his best to explain the unexplainable and then addressed Haley and David Jr. by name. "Crystal loved being your mother. She loved being your mother. She loved being your mother."

The eulogies were delivered by two family friends of the Judsons, but nothing came close to packing the emotional punch of a slide show that quickly summarized Crystal's short life. High above the crowd was a screen, and the slides of Crystal's life thankfully buzzed by quickly while the song "From a Distance" blared from the speakers. There was Crystal, the baby in a high chair, face covered with chocolate; Crystal, the little ballerina and ice-skater; the cheerleader, Daffodil Court Princess, aspiring model, mother. And always, in nearly every photo, there was Crystal's loving sister, Julie, who could not stop her tears as she sat and watched from the front pew. So many in the crowd were crying that ushers quietly passed down the aisles and handed out boxes of tissues.

The immediate family escorted Crystal's coffin to the Haven of Rest cemetery; it's just off Highway 16 in Gig Harbor and it's enchanting in its beauty. Crystal's final resting place is on a hillside that overlooks the town's harbor on one side, and off in the distance is towering Mount Rainier. Lane Judson thanked those who were there for coming and led Haley and David Jr. away. There were no more words or tears to share. It was time to go home.

54

Corpuz Delicti

There was a saying in Tacoma that the reason City Manager Ray Corpuz had kept his job for so long was because he knew how to count to five. As long as Corpuz had five votes on the city council, he never had to worry about losing his job. He was not an elected official; he was appointed by the council and he made damn sure he always kept at least five of them happy.

But that was getting harder and harder to do in light of the mushrooming David Brame scandal. The twin funerals had stirred nearly everyone in town to call for action; citizens wanted some immediate answers. After all they'd learned about David Brame since the shooting, the obvious question was asked over and over: how could this guy have been appointed chief with all these red flags all over his personnel file? The newspaper and the citizens were developing a lynch mob mentality; after all, they'd been deceived by David Brame for a long time and everyone was looking for someone to blame.

But so far, Ray Corpuz had managed to survive despite damaging revelations.

That all changed when Assistant City Attorney Shelley Kerslake finally emerged to admit that she knew all about David Brame's alleged rape nearly a year before he became police chief. Kerslake had sought and won the right to waive the usual lawyer-client confidentiality that existed between her and Corpuz. Incredibly, Corpuz gave her permission to say whatever she wanted.

Kerslake had been the city lawyer defending Brame and Corpuz against Lieutenant Joe Kirby's $10 million lawsuit against the city. She had listened as depositions were given outlining the rape allegations against David Brame in great detail. Kerslake, a friend of Brame's who eventually tried to get a job with the police department when Brame later become chief, didn't believe the allegations, and she knew that they had been found to be "not sustained." In her defense, she also was aware that then-Police Chief Ray Fjetland had promoted David Brame, not once but twice, after the rape allegations landed on his desk. Fjetland believed in Brame at the time; why should she question him all these years later? He'd been investigated by Internal Affairs and more or less been cleared of the charges, even though investigator Dave Olsen said under oath that he believed Brame's accuser was telling the truth.

Kerslake successfully fought off Kirby's lawsuit and then—without telling her boss—applied to a judge to have it sealed. Her reasoning was that the charges contained in it were unfounded and unfair. In light of the current scandal, however, her previous actions on behalf of Brame left her wide open to second-guessing and claims that she had participated in a cover-up. It was only after the public outcry following David Brame's death that another judge had the lawsuit unsealed.

The moment Kerslake admitted she knew of the rape charges a year before Brame's appointment as police chief, the next obvious question was, had she told Ray Corpuz?

Initially, she left that question for Corpuz to answer but, of course, he refused to say. "I prefer not to make any comment at this time," he said. "I'm in a situation where I don't want to violate the city council's clear direction for an impartial investigation."

He was sticking to the same story he'd been telling since the shooting: that he had never heard the word "rape" used in connection with the Internal Affairs investigation into David Brame.

In light of that, Kerslake came forward again and contradicted Corpuz on the front page of the *News Tribune*. In fact, she said, she had arranged a meeting between Brame and Corpuz nine months before Brame was appointed chief. She was present when Brame calmly outlined for Corpuz the fact that a woman he had dated once had come forward fifteem months later to say she was date-raped by him. Corpuz asked Brame whether the matter had been thoroughly investigated by Internal Affairs and he said it had. Corpuz then said he would call Ray Fjetland, and the meeting was effectively over.

At this point, the city council and a lot of Tacoma citizens had heard just about enough about Ray Corpuz. Now it was clear he had known all along that David Brame had allegedly raped a woman but had appointed him chief anyway. Corpuz had already said he never read Brame's personnel file and didn't know he'd failed one psychological test and barely passed another before becoming a cop. Finally, he'd more or less ignored one of his own human resources people who told Corpuz that Brame's own personal references did not check out and were considered red flags and "troublesome."

Even if all of that was ignored, there was still the fact that Corpuz had elected not to investigate the April 11 incident at the Judson house that was brought to his attention by a group of anonymous police officers. An investigation into that matter might have raised enough attention to put Brame on administrative leave.

In addition, Corpuz stood by Brame when his divorce papers were made public, saying they were a private matter. By doing so, he sent the message to city attor-

neys that no immediate action would be taken by the
city. When the city's human resources director recommended taking David Brame's gun and badge and putting him on leave the day before the shootings, the city
lawyers rejected that notion and didn't even bother to
tell Corpuz. They knew their boss; he would do nothing
to stop David Brame—and he didn't.

Political animal to the end, Corpuz tried to quiet the
calls for his head by announcing that he was putting
himself on paid administrative leave at a cost to the city
of $700 per day. That was on May 6. Corpuz promised
to return once the Brame investigations had been
wrapped up.

But the endless revelations swung the city council
against Ray Corpuz. By the end of June, Corpuz could
no longer count to five, at least not five in favor of re-
taining him as city manager. On July 1, the Tacoma city
council finally took the action they had to take: they
fired Ray Corpuz. It was an emotional meeting. Many
in Tacoma, and not just Corpuz' allies on the council,
claimed that if it had not been for Ray Corpuz' strong
leadership, downtown Tacoma would still be the sewer
it once was. It wasn't so easy to get rid of the man
credited with transforming Tacoma.

"This is a political coup," said councilmember Sharon
McGavick. "This is an overthrow of the city manager."

"The bigger picture," responded councilmember Rick
Talbert, "is what is important for the city of Tacoma
and its taxpayers."

Corpuz did not appear personally at the public firing
but he did send the council a letter, asking that he be
kept on for another six months. Had the council agreed,
Corpuz would have received a fatter pension but, in the
end, it refused. Corpuz was gone, but the council hardly
punished him; he did not get any severance but he did
retire with an annual lifetime pension of more than
$100,000 per year.

A Different Life

From the moment David Brame pulled the trigger on his Glock .45 automatic, life changed dramatically for Haley and David Brame Jr. They had suffered something nearly unparalleled, something no child should have to live through. Both parents were dead and the children were there to witness the unspeakable ending. They had seen their mother crawl around in her own blood; whether they saw their father sitting in the car with a bullet in his head is known only by the children's counselors, but it's a good bet they did. From the moment news of the tragedy hit the airwaves, everyone wanted to know about the children. How were they doing? Would they ever get over it? Who would raise them now?

I spent some time with both children and can provide a small glimpse into their lives during that stressful time. For the most part, they appeared to be doing fine. I never saw them cry, not even when we visited their mother's grave. If you didn't know what they had lived through, I don't believe you would notice anything different about them.

That is not to say they have not been psychically

changed by what happened to their mother and father. According to Lane and Patty Judson, Haley's low point came on a summer's day in 2003 when she visited her mother's final resting place. The grave marker for Crystal DeEtte Judson is flat amidst the grass of the Haven of Rest Cemetery and it makes no mention of the name Brame. It was there—on one of her first visits after the funeral—that Haley lay down on her mother's plot and sobbed. Little David watched, stunned, until he too began to cry. No need to mention the reaction of Lane and Patty Judson and Julie and Dave Ahrens. Each day, they wondered if they had cried themselves out but then came the following day.

David Jr. was only five years old when the tragedy struck and his family wondered what he had absorbed. They found out one day when they were sitting around a swimming pool with him. David was playing with a little girl about the same age when he blurted out, "Do you have a mommy and a daddy?"

"Of course," said the girl. "Everyone does."

David shook his head. "I don't. I lost mine. My daddy shot my mommy."

The little girl just looked at David. "I don't believe you," she said, and then ran away.

David kept playing as if nothing had happened.

It was, the Judsons say, a heartbreaking moment.

There were other moments just like that but despite their grief, Haley and David Jr. are, after all, just children and by late June, they were doing what children everywhere do: anticipating their summer vacation. Julie and David Ahrens are their legal guardians but everyone, including the children's counselors, thought that it would be best, at least in the immediate aftermath of the tragedy, if the children could live for a while with Lane and Patty. After all, they'd spent a lot of time at Grandma and Grandpa's house and that's where they had been living since February 24, 2003, when Crystal left the house on Eagle Creek Lane.

I was there one morning as Lane and Patty got Haley ready for school. David's preschool had already ended but he too was up bright and early. "We're parents again," Patty said. "It's been a long time but we have plenty of help."

While Patty made sure the children were dressed and had what they needed for the day, Lane prepared crepes for breakfast. He was in the best mood I'd seen him in since the tragedy, smiling and bouncing around the kitchen. "Every morning David comes down and says, 'Grandpa, I'm handsome and I'm ready for crepes,' " Lane chuckled.

There was unabashed joy as Lane spread out his batter, poured in the chocolate syrup and carefully folded the crepes, presenting them with a flourish. Patty stood by, wiping mouths.

Soon it was time for Haley to leave and she gave little David a huge hug. It was sweet to see her concern and obvious love. As always, David was more distracted, looking at the visitors in the house and running off to play his video game. As Haley put her lunch into her backpack, she pulled out a note from the day before.

"Grandma, I almost forgot. I made this for you."

Patty opened an envelope and found a small card made by Haley. "Grandma and Grandpa, Thank you for taking such good care of me and David. Love, Haley."

Patty couldn't hold back her tears.

Days later, the Judsons and the Ahrenses were gracious enough to give me a private tour of the house on Eagle Creek Lane, the house once inhabited by the family of Crystal and David Brame, the house where so much pain had occurred. As soon as Lane opened the garage door, all his memories of the last morning he spent there with Crystal came flooding back. David Brame's red Toyota Camry, the car he had left the children in while he went to see their mother that fateful day, was parked in the garage. Lane could barely look at it. "What are we supposed to do with that?"

On the other side of the garage were the contents of Brame's Gold Pointe apartment. "We were told we had to clean it out. This is his stuff, his personal effects," Lane said. "We don't know what we're going to do with it."

Lane brushed past the boxes and opened the door leading to a laundry room. He pointed out the many cardboard boxes on the shelves. Crystal had carefully and precisely written what was in each box. He kept moving, no doubt seeing ghosts wherever he looked, but in the kitchen he stopped.

"It's just like it was that last day," he said. "You can see all the cleaning supplies here. We were getting ready to clean the place up."

To me, the Brame house didn't seem to need much cleaning. It was neater than many I'd been in. True, the house was missing a fair amount of furniture that David had been allowed to take when he moved out, but otherwise it was in move-in condition. Crystal's favorite photograph of the children still hung on one wall. It is black and white and shows little Haley and David Jr. from the back standing on a beach holding hands. The cream-colored rug was fairly clean and all in all, it was a nice, though fairly typical, suburban house. There were sliding glass doors and a fireplace and the furniture that was left was formal and conservative.

"Crystal was looking forward to decorating the house the way she wanted to," Patty said. "He always bought everything for her and now it was going to be her turn."

Crystal may not have liked the limited edition Thomas Kinkade lithographs but she was aware they might have value and, because they had been gifts from David, she had insisted he leave them when he moved out. "It was the first thing she wanted to take off the wall," Patty said. "She told me, 'Ma, I don't like them.'"

Lane seemed to want to get the tour over as quickly as possible but he paused at the dining room table, choked up by grief. "That was the crystal she was cleaning up," he said. "She was going to finish it when she got home that day but she never got home."

Then he pointed out an obituary page from the *News Tribune* of April 15 that still lay spread out on the table. "That's what he left for her," Lane said, barely able to contain tears that were quickly turning to anger.

"Why is it still here?" I asked.

"Because it might have fingerprints on it. It might be evidence. We want to know the truth. We want to know why he murdered our daughter, because that's what he did. He didn't shoot her—he murdered her!"

Lane's face was red with rage as he no doubt thought—for the one millionth time—about the havoc left by his son-in-law.

It took Lane a few moments to regain his composure but it didn't last long. The only thing left to show on this morbid tour was the master bedroom and the closet where Crystal had taken so much abuse from David, at least according to her family. Lane couldn't go on, so Dave Ahrens completed the tour.

He walked into the closet and pointed out some of Crystal's threadbare sweatshirts. "See what they looked like? She didn't have any money for clothes. Any money she got went to those kids."

He looked around the closet and said, "This is where I saw his guns. He left them right here where there is a step stool that the kids could stand on and get ahold of them. Crystal spent a lot of time in this closet. He locked her in here for hours and she was terrified."

Dave's thoughts wandered away to another time, and then he too went outside to stand with Lane and Patty.

They talked among themselves for a while and then said they had to leave—being back in that house was just too much.

By year's end, the car and the house were sold.

Watching It All Play Out

By September of 2003, the hour I was preparing for
48 Hours was ready to air and it was time for me to
leave Tacoma.

Before I left, I went looking for the two people who
played critical roles in the Brame affair: John Hathaway,
who had busted the town wide open by publishing the
damaging divorce revelations on his Internet site, and
Sally Masters, the woman allegedly raped by David
Brame, who had the courage to come forward after fifteen years to tell the world what kind of man the Tacoma police chief really was. If not for the acts of both
these private citizens, this whole story would be completely different.

I found John Hathaway outside Lincoln Lanes, the
bowling alley where he bartends and holds court five
nights a week. He wanted a cigarette, so we walked outside into the warm summer air.

As always, Hathaway was wearing his trademark fedora. He hadn't shaved in a couple of days, so his usually
stylized mustache was lost in a haze of gray facial hair.
But he still looked like a modern-day Philip Marlowe.

The night air was warm and humid but there was a stubborn breeze trying to keep things cool. A half moon hung dramatically in the sky. The breeze nearly blew out the match Hathaway was holding but he cupped his hand and took a deep drag.

"Ever feel guilty?" I asked.

"Nah, I did what I had to do. I had the divorce papers. They were ironclad. No problem."

A lot of people were upset with Hathaway before, during and after Crystal died, but Hathaway shrugs off all the bad vibes. When he says all he cares about is his city—Tacoma—you believe him.

Hathaway is Tacoma and Tacoma is Hathaway. A little rumpled, a little sad, a little down on their luck but at the bottom, there's a lot of good there—in the city and in Hathaway's soul.

We just stood there, looking up at the moon. I didn't say anything else but Hathaway hears his own questions: "What can I say? It's my town and I care a lot about it. I've got nothing to apologize for. Nothing."

Someday, the woman I call Sally Masters is going to find peace, but it seems like it's going to be a long time coming. She's endured tragedy after tragedy in her life and strange as it sounds, being raped by David Brame was not the worst thing ever to happen to her. Her personal life is a battleground; she's a one-woman Oprah show, and while I'd like to share all her experiences to illustrate what a strong woman she truly is, she told me about them in the strictest confidence. I promised to keep her secrets and I will.

The day after I saw Hathaway for the last time, I sat in Sally's small cottage. We had become friends in the middle of all the craziness. It was somewhere near seven p.m. but it was summer and the sun was still high in the sky. The light streamed in through her small window and a cool breeze blew the curtains toward where she sat strumming her guitar.

"This guitar is out of tune," she said.

"Quit stalling and just play," I teased.

"Shut up."

So I did. She hummed a bit and tuned her guitar and finally began singing a sad song about her life and all she'd been through. I closed my eyes and thought about the time when she felt David Brame was a friend. It truly was a long time ago, a very long time ago. When I opened my eyes again, the room was dark and Sally was staring at me.

"You fell asleep."

"Sorry."

"S'okay." She laughed. "I told you I wasn't any good."

I rubbed my face, tired and suddenly famished.

"I owe you dinner."

"You sure do, LaRosa."

We went outside; our plans for the evening were going to take us one last time to Gig Harbor and over the Tacoma Narrows Bridge. We were going to Anthony's for some salmon.

"Are you feeling brave tonight?" she asked me.

"What did you have in mind?"

She pointed to her new motorcycle. Taking a nighttime ride on a motorcycle over a windswept bridge that had once fallen into the water below definitely would be testing the limits of my courage. I lean toward subways myself, but in a weak moment I had promised Sally I'd take a ride on her hog someday. I was going home the following day, so I was out of tomorrows.

"Let's do it," I said.

She got on first and I sat behind her, holding on for dear life. We headed over the Tacoma Narrows Bridge toward Gig Harbor. It had only been a few months since April 26, but it felt like a lifetime.

Epilogue:
Questions and Fallout

Questions

One year later to the day, at the exact moment of the shooting, I stood in the Harbor Plaza mall parking lot in Gig Harbor with Rod Baker. He is apparently the only one who witnessed the few moments prior to the shooting. Baker saw Crystal arguing with David. As you can imagine, he's haunted to this day. He still remembers hearing the high-pitched sound made by Crystal as "unlike anything a human would make," and then he heard the two shots.

What's most fascinating about Baker's account is that he says he saw Crystal crumple to the ground *after* the second shot. Sound and eyewitness testimony can both be very unreliable, but Baker's theory is that David Brame pulled out his gun and was threatening to kill himself and that Crystal was desperately trying to talk him out of it. Baker believes that, at the exact moment David pulled the trigger, Crystal grabbed hold of the gun to try to stop him. In doing so, Baker believes, Crystal pulled the gun forward and inadvertently caused it to fire at her own head. Glocks fire very easily once your finger is in the trigger position; Baker thinks Brame pulled it once and, in grabbing the gun, Crystal accidentally caused it to fire a second time.

Preposterous? Maybe. Clearly, the police don't put much stock in Baker's theory.

Detective Dave Crocker, the chief investigating officer, told me that he believes David grabbed Crystal by the hair, executed her by shooting her once behind the ear and then killed himself.

But what's troubling is that the two gunshots were in rapid succession. All eight witnesses acknowledge that the two shots were no more than two seconds apart and perhaps quicker than that. One thing is clear: given the immediacy of the two shots to one another, David Brame had no time to think. The decision to shoot had to have been instantaneous, as the police claim, or . . . what if Baker's theory is correct? What if Crystal grabbed the gun in those last fleeting seconds to stop David from shooting himself and, in effect, shot herself in a tragic accident? Might that be why the gun was found outside the car between David's feet—because Crystal was pulling it toward her? We'll never know, because no fingerprints were taken off the gun; Steven Wilkens says it is too hard to get fingerprints off the plastic housing. But what if everything we think we know about this now infamous shooting is slightly askew? Here the word "slightly" carries enormous consequences.

I thought Baker's theory was far-fetched, but there have always been some things about those last few minutes that do not make sense to this day. Consider:

- Crystal told everyone she was deathly afraid of David. Then why, once she spotted David's car—as she told her mother on the cell phone—did she follow him into the parking lot where she had no business? Her tanning appointment was across the way. When David went right, Crystal should have gone left. She did not. She went into the same parking lot as the man she supposedly was deathly afraid of. Her mother later told cops that Crystal had a cold and maybe was going to buy some medicine in the Rite Aid drugstore in that parking lot. Still, she had spotted David's car; couldn't she have found a different drugstore or waited until later? Remember, just a couple of days earlier, Crystal had begged her lawyer to help her get a restraining order against David. And so what if her children were with David? She certainly knew that.

- One thing everyone agrees on: when the shooting broke out, Crystal was standing *outside* her car while David was seated inside. Why was she still standing there? Why, if she was so afraid of him, didn't she run into a store when she saw him walking toward her? Why stop to argue with a man you're afraid of, especially since the children were not in that car but safely tucked away in David's car?

- If forensic investigators really believe David Brame pulled Crystal down by the hair, why did they not check whether there were strands of her hair in his hand? When I interviewed him about the case more than a year later, Wilkens said he had put in his report his theory that David Brame had pulled Crystal by the hair and held her head in that position when he shot her. I told him there was no mention of the hair-pulling in his report. He checked it, said he couldn't remember why it was not placed in the report, but repeated that it was the only scenario that made sense. His hands were bagged at the hospital after he died.

- Glock automatics are prone to going off at inopportune times, as almost any police jurisdiction in the country can attest. Why? Because of a unique design that has the safety on the trigger. In fact, cops have so often fired their own Glocks inadvertently that cops refer to "Glock leg," which is what happens when you are holstering your gun and it accidentally fires a bullet into your leg. Even forensic investigator Steven Wilkens, who has been around guns all his life, says, "Glocks are dangerous in my opinion. I see accidental shootings all the time."

- If David Brame were sitting in the driver's seat and intended to shoot Crystal, why would he shoot her in the *side* of the head? Why hold the gun at such an awkward angle? Why not just shoot directly into her face or body?

- Baker found the Glock between David's feet *outside* the car. Experienced police investigators say that there's no telling where the gun will wind up in a situation like this but, if the police scenario is the correct one—if David Brame executed Crystal and then immediately put the gun to his right temple and shot himself with his right hand—wouldn't it make sense for the gun to be *inside* the car somewhere on the passenger side?

Rod Baker may be completely wrong about what he saw and heard. Still, one cannot ignore the inconsistencies in those final few moments. There is no videotape of those final few seconds, no way of knowing what actually happened in the final few moments that changed Tacoma—and many people's lives—forever.

The Fallout

There were three major investigations into the David Brame affair, but no criminal charges were brought against anyone. There was, however, plenty of fallout affecting those directly and in some cases indirectly involved in the Brame affair.

- David Brame's reputation. Since his death, his entire life has been combed over by investigators desperate to learn the truth. One key report on Brame's hiring and career conducted by the Washington Association of Sheriffs and Police Chiefs concluded that Brame's hiring and promotions at the Tacoma police department were all done properly. But that same report also was very critical of the police department's Internal Affairs unit for its failure to refer the rape allegation against Brame to an outside police agency. Of course, had that been done—had the rape allegation not been swept under the carpet—Brame might have been fired and/or convicted and most likely would never have been considered for the chief's job. A few weeks after this supposedly exhaustive report was concluded, a custodian cleaning out an old filing cabinet found a file on David Brame that contained the missing psychological report everyone had been searching for. It explained—once and for all— why Brame was hired despite failing one exam and barely passing another one. No one could understand why a third exam had not been given and the answer was that it *had been given*. That psychologist had passed Brame and recommended him for the force. At last, one mystery about Brame's career was solved.

- Lane and Patty Judson. Lane and Patty Judson have always wanted the entire truth to come out about their son-in-law and who knew what and when. As such, the estate of Crystal Brame filed a wrongful-death lawsuit against the city of Tacoma as well as former City Manager Ray Corpuz, Mayor Bill Baarsma and Catherine Woodard. In September, 2005, the city agreed to pay Crystal's estate $12 million and to rename the county's new family justice center in her memory. The settlement included a stipulation that Corpuz, Baarsma and Woodard would still be deposed even though the wrongful death lawsuits against them were dismissed.

- Julie and Dave Ahrens and Haley and David Jr. Crystal's sister and brother-in-law became the legal guardians of Haley and David Jr. On March 7, 2004, their guardianship became very real when Haley and David Jr. finally moved in with the Ahrenses from the Judson home where they had been living since the tragedy. The Ahrenses, who have no children of their own, became instant parents. After a year in which the children were featured in newspapers, magazines and on television, the Ahrenses have moved to shield them from the glare of publicity. On the one-year anniversary of the shooting, reporter Sean Robinson in the Tacoma *News Tribune* wrote of a calendar made by David Jr. hanging on a kitchen cabinet in the Ahrens home. In addition to David's drawing of a sailboat, Haley had written on the day of April 26, "Mom got shot." Both children continue to receive counseling and sleep over at their grandparents' house as many times as they can. Haley is taking ballet lessons and David has entered kindergarten. The children no longer use the last name Brame, preferring to call themselves Haley and David Judson. To that, Beverly Brame said, "Once a Brame, always a Brame."

- Gene and Beverly Brame. Since the shooting, the parents of David Brame have not been allowed to see their grandchildren. Just months after the shooting, the children's temporary guardian, Tonya Pemberton, said that the children should eventually be reunited with their paternal grandparents. "I am recommending that both minors be reintegrated into both sides of the family," Pemberton told the court. However, Haley and David Jr.'s psychologist has said that the children are afraid of their grandmother Beverly Brame. The Judsons and Ahrenses harbor very bitter feelings against Beverly Brame because Crystal accused her of once spanking David Jr.; Beverly denies she spanked David Jr. but admits she gave him one light swat on his rear end. After repeatedly being denied visitation, the Brames filed a petition with the court demanding that they be allowed to have some visitation with their grandchildren. The Brames remain deeply troubled by the stories that have surfaced about their son, of whom they are still proud. "There has never before in the annals of law and justice been a crime built on such lies and false allegations," Gene said. As far as they are concerned, Crystal pushed David over the edge. "I hope his tormentors are happy now," Beverly Brame wrote in a letter to the newspaper. They are a gentle elderly couple bewildered by what has

happened to them in their old age; both have
had serious health problems in the last year.

- Ray Corpuz. Tacoma's former city manager,
the man credited with restoring Tacoma, had
a hard fall after he was fired from his job in
July 2003. It's true that he was retired from
public life with an annual pension of $101,392,
but that only tells part of the story. On the
night of February 18, 2004, a Pierce County
sheriff's deputy in the Tacoma suburb of University Place spotted Corpuz' Mercedes-Benz
with two flat tires weaving in and out of traffic.
The deputy said Corpuz' car drove past three
patrol cars that had their lights flashing during
a traffic stop. The sheriff's office said that Corpuz nearly hit two deputies. He was arrested
and charged on suspicion of drunk driving. Police believed that Corpuz looked and smelled
like he was intoxicated, but he refused a
blood-alcohol test. At a court appearance in
June 2004, a humiliated Corpuz stood by while
his lawyer, Ken Fornabai, told the court that
Corpuz had medicated himself with alcohol
because he was suffering from depression and
isolation. Fornabai said Corpuz had been
"boiled in oil" by the media in the aftermath
of the Brame affair and "lost his life's
work . . . the stress got to him. No support
group, no wife [they have separated], no
friends. People who he worked with for years
shunned him. A good man who did nothing
wrong was put in the position of a leper." In
exchange for deferred prosecution on a drunk
driving charge, Corpuz agreed to two years of
intensive treatment and three more years of
probation. In addition, his driver's license was

suspended for one year and he was forbidden
to use alcohol. Because court papers were
sealed, it was not clear if his treatment would
be for alcohol abuse or for a mental illness
such as depression. However, Corpuz' life did
take a positive turn in mid-2005 when he was
appointed the new city manager of Seaside,
California.

- Catherine Woodard. After being put on paid
  administrative leave in May 2003, then-Acting
  Police Chief Catherine Woodard never again
  returned to active police duty. Several months
  later, she applied to retire on a medical disability leave for a bad back and her request
  was granted. Having served nearly twenty-five
  years in the Tacoma police department, she
  was granted a tax-free annual disability payment of $65,540 for the rest of her life. To this
  day, she traces all her troubles to being in the
  wrong place at the wrong time. As she delivered the final report on the David Brame affair, Washington state attorney Christine
  Gregoire criticized Woodard for having "extraordinarily poor judgment." A later investigation by James Walton, the city manager who
  followed Ray Corpuz, found that, by remaining silent about substantive matters she
  was aware of, she had broken city rules. It's
  really a moot point because she no longer
  works for the city and cannot be punished by
  Tacoma officials.

- Linda Watson. Another innocent victim of
  David Brame's desires. Made to file a sexual
  complaint against Brame after his death, Watson was put on paid leave and has not returned to work for the Tacoma police
  department. In May 2005, the city settled a

sexual harassment lawsuit she had filed by agreeing to pay her $750,000. Because the city never halted her pay, the grand total was really $910,000. She agreed to leave the force and was given a letter of recommendation.

- Sally Masters. After wrestling with her ghosts for more than fifteen years, Sally Masters finally enlisted the aid of an attorney and in the summer of 2004 filed a lawsuit against the city of Tacoma for violating her constitutional rights when the police department failed to forward her rape allegations against David Brame to an outside law enforcement agency. The case is pending.
- John Hathaway. John Hathaway still runs his Web site, "The New Takhoman," although it's doubtful that he will ever run across as big a story as the David and Crystal Brame divorce papers. Still, he does manage to scoop the Tacoma *News Tribune* from time to time. Hathaway and his wife, Carolyn, filed legal claims against the city for $99,250, alleging that the e-mail they received from Police Union official Pat Frantz caused them to fear for their safety and aggravated Carolyn's medical condition. The city rejected their claims and they too have filed a lawsuit against the city.

Author's Note

This work is the result of eighteen months reporting and at least ten visits to Tacoma and Gig
Harbor. I conducted dozens of in-person and telephone interviews and read more than ten thousand
pages of court records and investigative reports,
which included many transcribed interviews. In addition, I read hundreds of newspapers articles in
the Tacoma *News Tribune,* the *Seattle Times* and
the *Seattle Post-Intelligencer*. As always in journal-
ism, some participants spoke on the record while
some preferred to remain anonymous. Pseudonyms
were used in five cases: David Brame's first wife;
the female detective Brame harangued for sex; the
woman who accused him of rape; and three people
Brame tried to involve in theesomes or foursomes.
In some cases, conversations were re-created based
on interviews and/or transcripts. I must also credit
Puget's Sound, Murray Morgan's fine history of
Tacoma.